Future-proof Your Child

Parenting the Wired Generation

NIKKI BUSH

and

GRAEME CODRINGTON

PENGUIN BOOKS

First published by Penguin Books (South Africa) (Pty) Ltd, 2008
A Penguin Random House company
Registered Offices: Block D, Rosebank Office Park, 181 Jan Smuts Avenue, Parktown North, Johannesburg 2193, South Africa
www.penguinbooks.co.za

Reprinted 2010 (twice), 2011, 2012, 2013

ISBN 978-0-143-02580-1

Typeset by CJH Design
Cover design by Flame Design, Cape Town
Printed and bound by CTP Printers, Cape Town
Front cover photograph © Sean Justice/Corbis

Contents

Acknowledgements x
Copyright credits xiv
Introduction xvii
About the authors xix
About this book xxiii

SECTION 1: WAKE UP, THE WORLD HAS CHANGED! 1

Stop the world – I want to get off 4
Learning to surf the tsunami 8
Ages of transition 10
A new millennium, a new era 12
The end of the beginning 14
The connected world 17
Globalisation 18
Converging trends and empowered individuals 21
Chaos and disruption: The Age of Possibility 23
A generation like never before 28
Millennial generation characteristics 29
Confident and self-assured 29
Connected and wired 30
Not scared to fail 31
Screen hungry 31
Big spenders 33
Instant gratification 34
Sexuality 36

A scary world 36
Changing the world 37
We need to keep up 38
The Age of Possibility – the power to choose 44
System overload/shutdown 44
Too many options 46
Three essentials: conversations, connections and choices 46

SECTION 2: UNDERSTAND OUR CHILDREN'S DEVELOPMENT NOW 50

Some things haven't changed 51
We are multisensory beings 52
Phases of learning 53
Reaching their milestones 56
Learning through repetition 57
Children go on learning binges 60
Every child is different 62
Multiple intelligences 62
Learning styles 68
Visual learners 69
Kinaesthetic learners 69
Auditory learners 70
Dominance profiles 70
Context makes a difference 72
So, you're in the market for a school 83
School readiness 83
How to choose a preschool 88
Preschool shopping checklist 90

Commandments for the primary school shopper 93
Know your child 93
Know your values 93
Know your lifestyle 94
Know your budget 94
Follow your instincts 94
Know this is a journey 95
Be aware of shopping distractions 95
Future-proofing your children 96
Give them time 98
Make the time 101
Conversations, connections and choices 102
Conversations and dialogue 103
Connections and relationships 104
Choices and responsibility 104

SECTION 3: THE FACE OF YOUR CHILDREN'S CHANGING FUTURE 108

The world of work is changing 111
Current drivers of workplace trends 112
Major trends in the future world of work 114
Work-life integration 115
Mobile and networking technologies 119
Telecommuting and third spaces 121
An outputs-driven workplace 121
Careers as 'portfolios of jobs' 122
Self-employment, entrepreneurs and micro-sourcing 123
Lifelong learning 124

Robots, automation and artificial intelligence 125
Creativity and knowledge work 127
A global stage and a melting pot of diverse world views 127
Mobility of talent 128
The role of women 128
Ageing populations 129
Deferring retirement 130
Relationships and connections 131
The future isn't what it used to be 132
Jobs of the future 133
Growth industries 134
Healthcare and social support services 137
Medicine, genetics and pharmaceuticals 137
Financial services 138
Tourism and hospitality 139
Leisure, sport, entertainment and the arts 140
Nanotechnology and micro-engineering 141
Employment services 142
Education 142
Information technology 143
New media 144
Design 145
Alternative energy and global warming 146
Disaster relief and recovery 147
Logistics and delivery services 147
Government 148
Declining industries 152
Retail 154
Agents 155

Call centre operators 157
Manufacturing, farming and mining 157
Construction 158
Professions 158
What won't change 162
Entrepreneurs, intrapreneurs and employees 163

SECTION 4: PREPARING OUR CHILDREN FOR THEIR FUTURE 166

Will school prepare them? 167
The importance (or not) of school 168
The role of the parent 171
X-factors for success 172
Conversations, connections, choices 173
Survival of the talented 173
Talent X-factors 176
Breaking conventions (creativity by another name) 177
Imagination and play 179
Creativity 185
Experimentation 190
Initiative and proactivity 192
Resilience 195
Flexibility 199
Persistence and perseverance 201
Learning from failure 203
Self-discipline and delayed gratification 205
A sense of humour 209
Optimism 212
Self-confidence 215

Health 218
Learning 220
Curiosity 221
Hard work and focus 226
Information processing and filtering 228
Mastery of technology 232
Online security 234
Know yourself 237
Multiple intelligences 239
Know your strengths (and weaknesses) 240
Future-focused 245
Emotional intelligence 247
Relate to others 256
Communication 257
Teamwork and collaboration 259
Comfort with diversity 263
Networking 266
Marketing (Brand You) 267
Building a Talent Profile 268
Why we need a new type of CV 269
What exactly is a Talent Profile? 271
Help your child to build a Talent Profile from primary school 271
Framework for your child's Talent Profile 274
The Mirror Game© for children 275
The report card of life 285
Why you should develop a Talent Profile 286
Creating your own Talent Profile 287
The Mirror Game© for adults 287
Conversations, connections, choices 292

SECTION 5: BUILD A FAMILY BRAND – IT MAKES GOOD SENSE! 295

What is branding? 298
You are the family brand manager 298
Why create Brand Family? 300
Brand building is a process 301
Creating brand loyalty and a successful brand 302
The family brand – a personal, real-life experience 305
A framework for building Brand Family 306
Values 306
How to instil values and attitudes 308
Togetherness 312
How to promote togetherness 313
Structure 315
Natural rhythms and routines 315
Rituals and celebrations 317

SECTION 6: A CALL TO ACTION 323

The 10 steps to future-proofing your child 325

Appendix 1 Piaget's theory of cognitive development 328
Bibliography 333

Acknowledgements

From Nikki:

Writing a book is an intense and creative process. I had always envisaged a Hemingway-type scenario of writing in solitude in a beautiful place, away from the stresses of everyday life. This is not how this book was written. It was created on the move in the course of presenting talks and workshops, attending meetings, ferrying my children to and from school, watching them play sport, helping with homework and assignments, and all the other plethora of motherly duties that must be done to keep one's family moving forward. It would not have been possible without the love and support of so many close friends and family who pitched in to give me uninterrupted hours to harness my train of thought and capture it on screen – to get into 'The Zone'.

To my children, Ryan and Matthew, who not only are the light of my life and the inspiration for my work, but also my reason for striving to become a more creative and effective parent in the 21st century – thank you. Their patience during the writing process was remarkable and they understood (almost always!) when I couldn't look up from the computer screen, following it with the words: 'Not right now, darling, or I might lose this thought.' Thank you, boys, for your tolerance and for understanding that the situation was temporary.

Grateful thanks to my darling husband, Simon, for being there for the boys when I was not, and for creating activities and diversions so that I could have hours of peace and quiet in which to write. Si, thank you for the time, space and freedom you always give me to express myself.

To my wonderful family, I am blessed to have you all living close by and able to support me in so many ways. Thanks Mum, Dad, Tam and Rich, and Just and Hans for your unfailing love and support for me and my family, and for being able to read my emotional needs when I was too tired to do so myself. To Mum and Dad in particular, you need to know that all the years spent playing together (we still do!) and connecting so deeply have led to the writing of this book.

To my very special friends Margie Peel and Marylou Miller – undoubtedly the midwives who assisted in the birth not just of this book but actually the very work I do today – thank you both for your belief in me, for your constant encouragement, wisdom and love. You are my Dumbo feathers! (As long as Dumbo was holding his feather, he believed he could fly!)

To Angie Cawse and Carol Affleck for helping me to become 'unstuck' during the writing process, for listening to me and giving me very patient critiques and insight – thank you.

When things got tough, I found myself drawing on the inspiration of two special people in my life who are no longer with us: my godfather Johnny Lynch from whom I drew the courage to keep going, and my dear friend Lynn Duffus who inspired me to continue digging and asking why, and to think big.

Few books are written in a vacuum and this one is no exception. It is the distillation of years of generous sharing of information and experiences from many experts in their fields, too numerous to mention here. I would like to thank them all for my education and for the great work they are doing in the world.

I am grateful for all the inspiration that sometimes seemingly appeared out of nowhere – it was a lesson in 'Let go, let God', which was the magical part of putting this book together. I would often go to bed with many questions and became confident that I would receive the answers the next morning. (And if I didn't, it was for a good reason – sometimes waiting and patience were the answer!) It was a remarkable journey of learning to trust the universe.

Thank you to our publishers, Penguin Books, for seeing

the value of this information for 21st-century parents, and to Louise Grantham and Jane Ranger in particular for their enthusiasm for this book. And to our editor, Judith Marsden, for her thoughtful editing of our manuscript. Judith and I have worked together for many years, and it was actually her belief in my ability that gave me the confidence to even consider writing a book. Thank you, Judes.

To my friend and colleague Lynda Smith who got Graeme and I together in the first place – thank you for believing in us and for your constant care, prayers and support.

To my co-author Graeme, thank you for dancing with me. We started with one book in mind and landed up writing an entirely different one. Thanks for the interviews which turned into conversations and debates, for sharing personally and professionally, for your insights, and for helping me to find the golden thread. I know that this book is not directly linked to the core work you do, but I believe it is very much an expression of who you are. It also reflects the importance you place on your role as a parent to your three girls.

And, lastly, thank you to all my clients for their encouragement and feedback. Thank you for showing me the need. May this book inspire you on your parenting journey.

From Graeme:

This book is something of a welcome detour for me. It has a lot less of the business focus of most of my recent writing, and hones in on a phase of life in which I am currently immersed.

So, I must first thank my daughters, Amy, Hannah and Rebecca, for giving me an opportunity to learn so much as their dad. You girls have changed, challenged and enriched my life in ways I cannot describe. I thank God for the gift you are to me.

My wife Jane deserves much of the credit for the content

of this book. She is the most amazing mother, not only to our own girls, but also to many other children through her role as a parenting trainer and mentor. I am the parent I am mainly because she is the mother, wife, friend and woman that she is.

To Nikki, my co-author, thank you for extending my vision and being the bundle of energy that made everything happen. You are an inspiration, and your ability – and desire! – to get down on the floor and look children in the eye is an example to all.

To my business partners – particularly Keith, Barrie, Angela, Dean and Vicky, as well as Karin, Vicky, Aloysias, Jackie, Jude and the broader network who daily shape my thoughts, share my insights and challenge my frameworks – thanks, team. Thank you to Keith and Vicky for showing us what great parents look like, and for all the others who share the parenting journey with me.

To the team at Penguin and to our editor, thank you for – once again – having faith in what I do.

And finally, to all the people who read this book, thank you for your commitment to our shared future as members of a planet that needs a new vision. May you fulfil the desires of your heart, and raise wonderful children who change the world.

Copyright credits

The authors and publisher gratefully acknowledge the following persons for permission to quote copyright material:

The Road Less Traveled Copyright © 1978 M. Scott Peck. Reprinted with the permission of Simon & Schuster Adult Publishing Group.

Parenting the Millennial Generation Copyright © 2005 David Verhaagen. The table in Section 2 is used with kind permission of David Verhaagen.

Parenting with Panache Copyright © 2001 Derek Jackson. The rules of functional parents in Section 2 are used with kind permission of Derek Jacobson.

Bridging with a Smile Copyright © 1995 Doreen Maree and Margot Ford. The table and the list of perceptual skills in Section 2 are used with kind permission of Doreen Maree and Margot Ford and Smile Idem, a division of Nasou via Afrika.

'Children take time' Copyright © 1982 Pat King. The poem in Section 2, originally published in *The Gift of a Child* by Marion Stroud (Lion Hudson, 1982), is used with kind permission from Pat King.

The War for Talent Copyright © 2001 Ed Michaels, Helen Handfield-Jones and Beth Axelrod. The philosophy of old and new pay in Section 3 is used with kind permission from Ed Michaels, Helen Handfield-Jones and Beth Axelrod.

Happiness Copyright © 2007 Edward Monkton. The poem is used in Section 4 with kind permission from Edward Monkton.

Brandchild: Remarkable Insights into the Minds of Today's Global Kids and their Relationships with Brands Copyright © 2004 Martin Lindstrom and Patricia Seybold. The

BrandDynamics Pyramid in Section 5 is reprinted with kind permission from Kogan Page Publishers.

The quotation in Section 5 is used with kind permission from Isabel Allende.

Mind Power for Children Copyright © 2002 John Kehoe and Nancy Fischer. The quotation in Section 6 is used with kind permission from John Kehoe and Nancy Fischer.

'I kid you not' Copyright © 2005 Carol Affleck. Excerpts from this paper, including the appendix of this book, were first presented at the 26th Annual Convention of the South African Market Research Association, and are used with kind permission of Carol Affleck.

Re-Imagine! Business Excellence in a Disruptive Age Copyright © 2003 Tom Peters. The quotations throughout the book are used with kind permission from Tom Peters. See www.tompeters.com for further reading.

Every effort has been made to trace copyright holders or their assigns, and the authors and publishers apologise for any inadvertent infringement of copyright.

From Nikki:
To my gorgeous boys, Ryan and Matthew, who take me on a parenting adventure every day. I love you guys to the sun, moon and stars – and back!

From Graeme:
To my three amazing daughters, Amy, Hannah and Rebecca, who challenge me to be more than I think I can be.

Introduction

A few years ago Peter Drucker (a writer, management consultant and university professor) said: 'Every few hundred years in Western history there occurs a sharp transformation ... Fifty years later, there is a new world. And the people born then cannot even imagine the world in which their grandparents lived.' We have lived through such an age of sharp transformation. If you wish to mark its passing, consider the events in the course of just a few months at the end of the 1980s.

These events began on 21 December 1988 when the Pan Am Flight 103 airliner was blown up over Lockerbie in Scotland. Terrorism had reached the civilians of the Western world. In 1989, between 15 April and 4 June, a series of demonstrations were held in Tiananmen Square in China. Individual power had reached the East. On 9 November 1989, the Berlin Wall – a rigid dividing line between West and East – came crashing down. Capitalism and democracy had come to the communist world. On Christmas Day of 1989, Nicolae Ceauşescu, the communist dictator of Romania, was executed. Eastern Europe began to hope again, just as the 'motherland' Russia itself was experiencing perestroika. This amazing global sequence of change concluded on 11 February 1990 as Nelson Mandela walked free after 27 years of imprisonment in South Africa.

The world was changed.

We, and our children, will live the rest of our lives with the consequences of this global transformation. The last few decades have seen even more influences at work, from communications and technology innovations, to the rise of India and China. The world is shifting beneath our feet. As business people, this presents great challenges and opportunities, which can be exciting. But as parents, these shifts can frighten us because of the responsibility we carry in bringing up the next generation.

> The problems we know about and the problems we can only guess at will either destroy us or be solved within our children's lifetime.

There is an upside to living in a world of constant change. A massive shift in power has begun – from governments and corporations over to individuals like you and me. Increasingly we will have the power to create our own reality – we can be anyone, do anything, go anywhere, anytime. We have more power than any generation has ever had to influence and shape the world we live in. Today we live in an Age of Possibility. The game has changed and there are new rules. Playing the game without adopting new rules and without adapting old ones may leave you standing on the sidelines watching the game.

Parenting today is a bit like playing at being James Bond, the legendary British secret agent. Each of his missions starts with an objective and some inside intelligence from M. Then Bond is sent out into the wild and crazy world of espionage where he creates and breaks the rules along the way. His mission is always clear, but how he is going to achieve it only unveils itself in the moment. Our mission as parents and teachers is clear: to facilitate, mentor and coach our children to prepare them for the future – whatever that may hold. How we do this is unveiling itself rather like a secret mission – on the run. It involves us showing our children how to live in an Age of Possibility by role-modelling it for them now. As the Spanish poet Antonio Machado put it so eloquently: 'We make the path by walking on it.'[1]

It is increasingly obvious that the world into which our young children will enter as adults in a decade or more will be nothing like the world we grew up in. And it will even be different to the one we currently inhabit. We need a better understanding of the world of the future in order to prepare our children in a relevant way and to future-proof them.

About the authors

Nikki Bush is a creative parenting expert who qualified in the field of communications and public relations, working full-time and studying part-time through most of her three-year national diploma. Thereafter, she spent eight years in various public relations consultancies servicing the likes of Gencor, Pick 'n Pay, Wits University, Alexander Forbes and Medscheme. Designing communications strategies was always her forte as it combined her big-picture thinking acumen and scenario planning with her attention to detail and organisational ability. Nikki ran her own public relations consultancy for three years with retainer clients including the Public Accountants and Auditors Board, the US Rice Council, and Run Walk for Life. After many years of being told she was a fountain of bright ideas, Nikki renamed her business The Bright Ideas Outfit (www.brightideasoutfit.com) in 2000. She provides bright ideas for busy parents and teachers through keynote presentations, training workshops, articles in the media, newsletters, educational game designs and books.

Nikki has spent the last 13 years as a student of child development and parenting after becoming fascinated by the power of play. She was involved in direct selling and training for the well-known South African educational toy company, Smile Education, for a number of years. Thereafter she became the editor of Smile's customer newsletter, spending the next four years interviewing child development specialists, therapists and teachers, while researching her articles. Nikki's passion for play is infectious. All her workshops and presentations are designed to encourage parents to activate their natural instinct to play. She is also committed to helping parents find creative ways of staying connected to their children despite the effects of noise (technology) and clutter (consumerism), which have become the backdrop to parenting and child development today.

Nikki has the ability to take the mystery and jargon out of important technical information and to repackage it, making it interesting and accessible to parents. By adding her creative flair and personal experiences as a parent into the package, she has become known for offering real, relevant and practical parenting solutions, and as a sane voice in a world of confusing choices.

Today, Nikki is a prolific speaker who is regularly invited to speak at schools, educational conferences and corporate events nationally. She is a founder member of the Professional Speaker's Association of South Africa. At present Nikki has seven educational games on the market. *Answers to Questions You've Been Dying to Ask*, her book on sexuality education for children aged nine to 13, co-authored with educational psychologist Ilze van der Merwe, is due for release in 2009, published by Metz Press.

Nikki has been married to Simon, an electrical engineer, for 16 years. They have two sons, Ryan (born in 1995) and Matthew (born in 1999), who are a constant source of adventure, wonder and surprise. Parenting has been a huge part of Nikki's personal journey and her children are undoubtedly the inspiration for her work. She believes that every child is filled with potential and possibilities, and that the magic of parenting is in their discovery.

Nikki's dream of writing a book for parents has been simmering within her subconscious for some time. When Graeme approached her with this project, there was an immediate interest and plenty of synergy. What followed was an intense year of conversation, research, personal introspection and debate (and a lot of writing, of course!) to create this book. The labour process was not without several severe bouts of Braxton Hicks contractions!

Graeme Codrington has a varied background in terms of work experience and studies. He has five degrees in five different faculties from five different universities. His undergraduate studies comprise a degree in commerce, with majors in accounting, business economics and information systems, and an arts degree. His postgraduate studies include a Licentiate Honours in Theology, a Masters in Diacionology (a combination of theology and sociology), and a Doctorate in Business Administration, with majors in leadership and future studies. Graeme's work experience includes a stint with KPMG as an articled clerk in Chartered Accountancy, computer systems development and training, youth work, and two years as a professional musician as a conscript in the South African airforce.

Graeme now works with a company he co-founded, TomorrowToday (www.tomorrowtoday.biz), as a full-time strategy consultant, author and professional speaker. He is an internationally recognised expert on corporate talent and the future of work, and speaks to over 100 000 people in at least 10 different countries every year. In 2007 Graeme was awarded Speaker of the Year by the Academy for Chief Executives (UK) and received the Speaker of the Year Award in the same year in South Africa (voted by his fellow speakers) in the SpeakersInc awards. He is on the international faculty of three major business schools.

Graeme is probably most well known for his work on

generations, captured in his first two published books: *Mind Over Money* (co-authored with Louis Fourie, with Sue Grant-Marshall, published by Penguin Books, 2002) and *Mind the Gap* (co-authored with Sue Grant-Marshall, also Penguin, 2004). His passion is to help companies change their mindset about talented people, and to create corporate cultures and leadership structures that will attract and retain talented staff and customers.

Graeme sits on the board of St Mary's School for girls in Waverley, Johannesburg, where his daughters are learners. He is a professional member of The Institute of Directors, the World and South African Future Societies, the International Association for the Study of Youth Ministry, the International Federation for Professional Speakers, and the Businesswomen's Association of South Africa.

Graeme married Jane Booth, his childhood sweetheart, in 1991. They have three daughters: Amy (born in 1999), Hannah (born in 2001) and Rebecca (born and adopted in 2005). Graeme and Jane co-present parenting workshops based on the acclaimed programme, Growing Families International (*Babywise* and *Childwise*).

Graeme's interest in writing this book started with his work on generational value shifts. In his book *Mind the Gap*, he set out to show how today's young people are not just younger versions of today's adults. His chapter on parenting in that book instilled a desire to return to this topic and flesh it out into something more practical for parents. This book originally started as a project aimed at helping parents 'Change your Mind' about schooling, and how children need to be prepared for the future.

Graeme's work with his team at TomorrowToday has given him a clear view of what needs to be done to prepare the next generation for the future. As he worked with his own daughters, he felt that putting some of those insights and the research of his team at TomorrowToday into a book for parents would be a helpful continuation of the work he began in *Mind the Gap*. It was a simple step to connect with Nikki, who has a growing reputation as a creative parenting expert, and to collaborate on this book.

About this book

Future-proof Your Child was written precisely to give parents the knowledge required to thrive in this Age of Possibility. We cannot give you exact instructions for success, but we can provide frameworks and guidelines for the mission. Our choice to use our power or not, and how we use that power to make anything become possible as individuals, depends on our values and world view. This is why children need parental input more than ever these days. As parents, we need to acquire knowledge, insight and understanding about the world we have inherited as well as the world of the future in order to future-proof our children.

We want the contents of this book to *change the way you think* about your role as a parent of young children in the 21st century. Our focus is on the foundation phase years (birth to age 10), and the future of today's children as they enter the workplace of 2020 and beyond. The topics discussed will be revealing, some facts may be startling, and the advice will hopefully be meaningful and practical. It is a call to parents to act wisely and courageously early on in their children's lives to ensure that their children are resilient and emerge with a consistent world-view – one of the biggest challenges facing parents today.

This book is *not* a complete and comprehensive parenting manual. We do not deal with discipline issues. We do not deal with health and safety issues. We do not deal with issues of parental relationships. We think all of these issues are critical, but they are not what this book is about.

The intention of this book is threefold: First, we want to give you a glimpse of the big picture – the Age of Possibility – so that you understand the backdrop against which you are parenting today. Secondly, we want to equip you to be an effective parent of young children, today. This part of the book is the most practical as it deals with the issues parents are currently facing. Thirdly, we want to help you to understand the future and what it holds as our children grow up.

You need to be *future literate* in order to help your children to survive and thrive in the 21st century. It is our willingness to change our perspective, our resolve to learn new things and to stay connected to our children – despite the noise, clutter and chaos – that will make the greatest difference.

Through this book, we want to help you to create a framework for your parenting experience as you embark on the highly personal adventure of *raising the next generation of talent*. We trust that you will find it relevant, accessible, practical and inspirational. Come and journey with us as we take you back in time and forward into the future to help you make the best choices for your children now!

Nikki Bush and Graeme Codrington
May 2008

Endnotes

[1] Juanita Brown, David Isaacs, World Cafe Community, and Margaret Wheatley, *The World Café: Shaping Our Futures Through Conversations That Matter*, 2005.

Parents who are unwilling to risk the suffering of changing and growing and learning from their children are choosing a pathway of senility – whether they know it or not – and their children and the world will leave them far behind. Learning from their children is the best opportunity most people have to assure themselves of a meaningful old age. Sadly, most do not take this opportunity.

(M Scott Peck in *The Road Less Traveled*, 1978)

We look out, in short, on this landscape of the present and see not the [loss] of old freedoms but the rise of four new ones: to know, to go, to do, to be. And we see just ahead of us, just beyond the coming millennium, an Age of Possibility such as the world has never known.

(Watts Wacker and James Taylor in *The 500 Year Delta: What Happens After What Comes Next*, 1997)

Section 1

Wake up, the world has changed!

A hundred years ago, if a grandmother had gathered her grandchildren around her one late Saturday afternoon beneath the spreading oak tree in the back garden, the young tykes would have sat listening, spellbound, as Granny shared her wisdom and insights about the world. The children would have asked her how the world works, and would carefully have noted her answers – after all, this was the world they were soon to enter as adults themselves, and her experience of it was invaluable to them. Today, if that same scene played itself out, it is much more likely that it would be Granny, holding a mobile phone in her hand, who would ask the children, 'So, my dears, how does this thing work?'

Today's adults have lived in a world that spans not just two centuries, but the cusp of a millennium too, yet there is a real sense that our past experience is inadequate preparation for what lies ahead. If we feel only vaguely confident about our own future, those of us who have children or grandchildren can sometimes feel overwhelmed at the task of preparing a new generation for a world that does not yet exist. The difference, possibly, between today's parents and the generations of parents in the past, is that – at the start of the third millennium – we know for certain that the world our children will inhabit will not be the same as the one we live in now. It will not just be different in small, subtle ways, but in markedly, remarkably different ways. We know for certain that we *don't know* what that world will be like when our children grow up.

When your children start asking you questions which no longer have definitive answers, then you know that the world has changed irrevocably, and the place we call 'here' has never existed before. It is only with an understanding of the past and some insight into the future that you can conduct a meaningful dialogue with your children about possibilities. Parents no longer have all the answers, or at least answers that will be relevant in a few years or even a few months from now. This is how fast the world is changing. There are even times today when our children are better positioned to come up with solutions than we are, and they can be quite adamant or righteous or expressive or informed about their point of view.

Rather than attempting to give our children 'The Answers' to their questions, we need to be teaching them how to think, how to discern, and how to look at various scenarios for themselves in order to prepare them for an unknown and uncertain future. In essence, as 21st-century parents, we have been called to a new way of 'being' with our children. Parenting is (and always has been) more about 'being' than 'doing' anyway.

In the decade of dilemmas ahead we need more conversations that matter and fewer speeches that don't. We need to learn in new ways.

(Bob Johansen, as quoted in *The World Café: Shaping our futures through conversations that matter*, 2005)

We need to wake up to the fact that the world has indeed

changed. Our children are also changing. This is not *our* childhood. A shift in the way we parent our children is required. To miss this point is, quite possibly, to miss the boat and risk your children's future.

As parents of young children, we have been asking ourselves a lot of questions recently with regard to our children and their future. It is likely that some of these questions have crossed your mind too:

- What subjects should my child study at school?
- What should my child study *after* school?
- Should my child study at all?
- Is school still relevant?
- If our children are going to work on a computer most of their life, why are they still being taught to write?
- What will the world of work look like when our children enter it?
- What moral issues will our children face down the line?
- How do we, as parents, compete with the noise and excitement of the media?
- How do we engage our techno-savvy, immediate gratification-craving, low-attention span children?
- How do we connect with our wired and weird children?
- When should I buy my child a cellphone?
- How much time should my child spend doing on-screen activities each day?
- When and how should I talk to my child about sex?
- What's the point of parenting today anyway?
- What is my role as a parent today?
- What will the future look like?
- Why do I feel so overwhelmed?
- Why has everything changed?
- How the hell did all this happen?

If you have asked yourself any of these questions, then read on as we try to give you a framework to enable you to answer them for yourself. Just some words of warning: fasten your seatbelt, hold on to your hat, and read with an open mind. Let yourself entertain a world of possibilities to understand how we got 'here' and where 'here' actually is.

STOP THE WORLD, I WANT TO GET OFF!

Recently, Nikki's eldest son Ryan (12) has been asking searching questions about how a person knows what career to choose. This led to an in-depth discussion about the fact that life is a series of choices, and each choice comes with rewards and sacrifices. No longer are there hard and fast rules about how to progress through life. There is no right or wrong – just an endless menu of possibilities from which you must choose, wisely based on the knowledge of who you are and what makes up your values and world view. We cannot remember having such adult conversations at that age. Today's children really want to talk about important stuff.

Another wonderful dialogue developed with Matthew (7), Nikki's youngest son, after he had played an online computer game about how to run a successful and profitable McDonald's store. While many of these online games are part of 'under-the-radar' marketing to children by global giants, they can also be instrumental in some highly constructive conversations between parent and child. By playing the game, Matthew had developed a basic understanding that inputs and strategies are needed for a business to succeed. He explained to Nikki that if you don't farm enough beef or wheat, your supply chain will not be able to provide enough hamburger patties and bread rolls. Without stock, you will go out of business. But the teachable moment came when he stated that the way to really ensure your business does well is to remember to order enough toys to go with the kiddies' meal. 'If you forget that, then your business will go bust really quickly!' he said. Nikki and Matthew wound up having a very real and practical discussion about business principles as well as marketing to children and branding.

At age six, Ryan wanted to know whether armies were good or bad. 'Well, it depends which side you're on,' was the reply, leading to a dialogue about armies, terrorists, civilians, protection, and so forth. At age six! Graeme has had similar conversations with his children. At age seven, his daughter Amy was listening to the news on the way to school one morning. Following a report about the devastating slide into chaos taking place in Zimbabwe, she asked quite simply: 'Why doesn't someone just shoot Mr Mugabe?' You see, exposure to repetitive messaging in the media is creating a mixture of anxiety and nonchalant naivety about evil. It can be frightening to see this in your children.

A few years ago, when Amy was just three, she gave Graeme a sobering lesson in how to deal with today's generation of children. After supper, Graeme was gearing up to read a bedtime story to his girls. He instructed Amy to go and choose a story, jump into bed, and wait for him to finish what he was doing, after which he would join her. She just stood there and looked at him. He told her again – a little more insistently, with an edge in his voice – and still there was no response. Then, as he really looked at her, he saw that she was looking admonishingly at him and, at the same time, signing the word 'please' across her chest. He had omitted to say please. She was doing to him what they as parents kept trying to teach her – to say or sign 'please' when asking for something. Amy was objecting to being instructed without a 'please'. Graeme learnt a serious parenting lesson that day.

The world has certainly caught up with us. Our children seem 10 years older than we were at their age. In our regular presentations to parents, we often ask our audiences if they have experienced the feeling 'Stop the world, I want to get off!' It's no surprise really that the majority raise their hands. We have certainly felt this personally, often.

We are living with a sense that time has speeded up, yet we still have the same 24 hours each day. What has changed, however, is the rate of change and the amount of change that we are having to assimilate – on a daily basis. Just one current issue of the *New York Times* contains more information about changes than an average farmer from the early 19th century would have experienced in a lifetime. There are days when we have to learn new things – not just by the day but by the hour in order to keep up, and it exhausts us. It is becoming increasingly clear that this rapid change is not just a phase we are going through. Rather, it seems to be the new reality. In this new Age of Possibility that we are engaged in, we need to learn how to survive and thrive in a constantly shifting environment in which rules are made, changed and broken on an ongoing basis.

Alvin Toffler, futurist and author of the classic *Future Shock* (1972), was deadly accurate when he said:

The illiterate of the 21st century will not be those who cannot read and write, but those who cannot learn, unlearn, and relearn.

We are sure you would have an answer if we asked you: 'What have you learnt in the last 12 months?' It's almost impossible to live in our world without learning things on a regular basis. But what if we asked you: 'What have you unlearned in the last 12 months?' What attitudes, behaviours, habits or perspectives (world views) have you deliberately and consciously attempted to remove from your life in the last 12 months? Do you have plans to relearn attitudes and habits in the next 12 months?

Now think about preschool children – specifically those

under the age of three when the brain is at its most plastic and elastic – taking in every new experience like a sponge. They are highly able to cope with change and continuous learning. In fact, every day is an adventure of epic proportions. Admittedly, they do take an afternoon nap which helps to keep them balanced. We'd all do well to have a brief siesta each day – bring on those power naps! These young explorers are actually carrying within them an intuitive blueprint for success in the 21st century. Consider just some of the characteristics with which they are naturally imbued. Preschoolers are:

- inquisitive and curious about their world and how it works
- natural explorers
- physical learners (they create understanding and meaning by trying things out for themselves – by doing)
- original thinkers and highly creative (anything is possible)
- insatiable learners (they can't get enough of learning)
- not afraid of failure (no matter how high the couch is or how far they may tumble)
- adaptable and resilient.

'Curiosity is the best toy in the store.'[2] If we can rekindle our sense of curiosity and learn not just to ask 'Why?' but 'Why not?', then we might not want to stop the world and get off. If we are prepared to learn, unlearn and relearn, we may just find ourselves eagerly looking forward to the adventure – and actually learning to surf the tsunami of change up ahead. So let's understand a little more about what has changed and why, how it happened, and what it means.

Learning to surf the tsunami

The world of work is changing. Old ways of doing things are being replaced, improved, sometimes destroyed and cast aside as the world moves on. Products emerge and disappear; brands are promoted and eradicated; legendary names bite the corporate dust. The way we make things is being revolutionised. The way we buy and consume products is undergoing a transformation. The way we manage is being shaken like a cocktail. The list is endless and affects the fundamentals we once took for granted – the way we work, the way we play, the way we live our lives.

(White et al, quoted in *Resilience: Social Skills for Effective Learning,* Annie Greeff, 2005)

On Boxing Day in December 2005, a massive undersea earthquake triggered a catastrophic series of tidal waves that devastated Indonesia, Thailand, Sri Lanka, India and other countries in the region. Its effects were felt as far away as Africa and Australia, and over a quarter of a million people tragically lost their lives. There were many stories of loss and miracles that day. A few stories among hundreds captured global attention.

A young South African girl had studied tsunamis at school in the term before her December holiday. She knew that as a tsunami forms, it sucks the water away from the beach. As she and her parents sat on a Thai beach that morning, she noticed the sea disappearing and guessed what it might mean. Alerting her parents, they ran from the beach and were saved from certain death because of her insight.

A few hundred miles away, a young Australian surfer was out on the morning ocean swells when he saw the giant wave thundering towards him. He knew his only chance of survival was to surf the tsunami into shore. He managed to do this, eventually landing in an upper storey room of a beachfront hotel.

While so many others succumbed to the tsunami, this young man survived. His own boldness and skill had rescued him.

In some senses, we are currently facing a tsunami of change. Yet, it could be argued that the impact of the changes we're witnessing in the world is merely equivalent to the water starting to be drawn away from the beach. As much as we have experienced change in the last few decades, we 'ain't seen nothin' yet'. It will be another few decades before the tidal wave actually crashes and we experience the full implications of factors such as biotechnology and nanotechnology, space travel, globalisation, cloning, robotics, artificial intelligence, global warming and environmental damage, to name but some in the plethora of change that confronts us. The full implications of the changes we are going through will only be felt when our children are in positions of business and political leadership. Until then, the wave will continue to gather momentum while we stand on the beach wondering what has happened, and where all the water has gone. If we are smart, we'll correctly identify the signs and start learning to surf while we have the chance so that when the wave crests the part of the horizon we can clearly see, we will be ready for it.

To be able to surf the tsunami of change, you first need to understand how and why the world has changed. What is this thing called globalisation and what are its implications for us and our children? What does it mean to live through chaos and confusion, and how can we create a world of possibility through it all?

There is no doubt that parents today are going to have to arm themselves with as much knowledge, insight and understanding as possible. They need to make sense of all this change in order not only to assist their children to survive and thrive in an uncertain future, but also to help themselves through the chaos and change that will characterise life in the 21st century.

Ages of transition

In human history there have always been moments when the momentum of change builds up to a short period of extraordinary transformation. As we look back in time, we often focus on critical inventions or discoveries that became iconic of a particular era of change as well as part of a tipping point[4] from one era to the next. You may be wondering what on earth this has to do with parenting, but bear in mind that we are trying to contextualise and understand how we got to this point. We have reached 'here' largely as a result of the increasing access to, and flow of, information globally owing to these inventions and discoveries.

Consider, for example, the invention of writing and paper, the discovery of the wheel, and the domestication of animals, all of which were critical to the transition from hunter-gathering to farming. Although exact dating is shrouded in the mists of time, these inventions and discoveries appear to have occurred within a relatively short period.

More recently, in Western history, we can look at the invention of the wooden printing press and metal moveable type, completed by German printer Johannes Gutenberg by 1440. The printing press enabled the printing of books (and therefore the transmission of text) as well as of maps of the world. A decade later, Prince Henry 'The Navigator' of Portugal established a school for navigators.

In the same century, some of the greatest sea adventurers of all time undertook expeditions in the splendid Iberian tradition of exploration: Bartolomeu Dias, Portuguese discoverer of the Cape of Good Hope; Italian Amerigo Vespucci, after whom America is named; Italian Christopher Columbus, the first European in America; Vasco da Gama, Portuguese founder of a sea route to India; Portuguese Ferdinand Magellan, first to circumnavigate the world; and Spanish Hernán Cortés, vicious conqueror of the Aztec Empire.

The Renaissance, Enlightenment and Protestant Reformation followed in quick succession as knowledge increased and global connections abounded. The shift from the agrarian age to the industrial era was well under way.

The common theme in these two eras of transition was the dramatically increased ability to get more information to more people, cheaper and faster. Be it by horseback or multi-masted, heavy-hulled ships, on papyrus or printed pamphlets, information flowed around the world.

> The truth about John Henry – allegedly the strongest man ever – is obscured by time and myth. One of the most enduring legends is that he was a slave born in Alabama in the 1840s. A powerful man with enormous strength, he grew up in the era when railroads were being built. As machine power continued to supplant brute muscle power (both animal and human), the owner of the Chesapeake and Ohio Railway in Talcott, West Virginia, bought a steam-powered hammer to do the work of his mostly black driving crew. In a bid to save his job and the jobs of his men, John Henry challenged the inventor to a contest: John Henry versus the steam hammer. John Henry won the contest but, in the process, suffered a heart attack and died. John Henry symbolises people's fight against the emerging industrial age.

The flow of information began to increase again in the late 1800s with the construction of railroads and the invention – within a few decades – of the internal combustion engine, motor cars and airplanes, the telegraph, telephone, radio and television. Once again, more information became available to more people, cheaper and faster. This time there was a transition from the industrial era to the information age.

The world has generally become more efficient. We do things easier and faster. For the most part, this has been a good thing for human beings as we have evolved from hunter-gatherers to farmers, from farmers to factory workers, and then – in the information era – to service providers and office staff.

But the transitions haven't stopped there. In the past few decades, once again, we have seen more information flowing to more people – cheaper and faster – with the invention of the Internet, the proliferation of mobile phones, and global travel. When this increased flow of information takes place, we should expect to enter into a time of transition.

There are certain pivot points or watersheds in history that are greater than others because the changes they produced were so sweeping, multifaceted, and hard to predict at the time.

(David Rothkopf, a senior Department of Commerce official in the US Clinton administration)[5]

A new millennium, a new era

As we now inch our way into the new millennium, which we like to call the Age of Possibility, we are again straddling two eras. Increasingly we are living in an era of connection. The goal of the industrial age was to create extreme efficiency in production. In general, this has been achieved – little room remains for industrial improvement in the world. In fact, we live in a world of over supply. Anywhere you go, from the richest countries in the world to the poorest, consumers are inundated with choices. We can choose from among a variety of similar products, at similar prices, advertised in similar ways, from companies with similar visions and missions.

The information age has also largely delivered on its promise – the promise of an integrated world system, with information flowing freely. Embedded within this promise lay the assurance of increased customer care (because companies would know and understand their clients better), more innovation and better products (because more would be spent on research and development), and a higher quality of living (because there would be more professionals in the middle class). On the whole, these results have been realised. Unfortunately, however, globalisation has also increased the number of people in poverty; this was an unintended consequence.

> In 1996, chess grandmaster Garry Kasparov was defeated in a single game by IBM's *Deep Blue* computer. He easily recovered in the next game (by making an irrational opening move to throw off the computer's algorithms), and didn't lose again in the match. The following year, an updated version of *Deep Blue* again defeated Kasparov in a single game of a match.[6] In 2003, Kasparov played two further match series – against *Deep Junior* and *X3D Fritz*. Both ended in a draw, with machine and man each winning a game apiece in the series. These events were televised and attracted a total combined viewership of nearly one billion people. In this traditional 'man vs. machine' contest, the machines were now thinking!

And now, at the start of the 21st century, most companies know that they must do more than they have done historically to impress clients. Business is becoming less and less about *what* companies sell as they compete with similar organisations to sell similar items in similar ways to similar clients. The consumers of today are demanding that companies do more than just produce products and services at the cheapest price. Consumers are beginning to demand that companies protect the environment (or, at least, don't mess it up), that their leaders are ethical and treat their staff fairly, that they make ongoing contributions to social development, and so on.

We call this new era the Connection Economy. To be successful, you must still have the efficiencies of an industrial era mindset. You also need to utilise the market intelligence and communications of the information age. These are essential conditions for success, but they are not necessarily sufficient in today's world. Success is becoming more and more about *who* you are and *how* you sell, and not just about your products and services. Customers and clients don't just want to buy from you; they want to connect with you. They don't just want products; they also want experiences. They don't just want transactions; they are looking for relationships.

If this is not yet true in every industry, it will be soon. Certainly, this is the world our children will live in.

The end of the beginning

There never has been and there never will be a precise date on which a switch over between two eras takes place. In a way, all the hype around Y2K and its potentially disastrous consequences made us feel that this was the case – the beginning of the new millennium was the switch over. This was a misconception. The changeover of eras probably began early in 1990, as we indicated in the introduction of this book. But we need more history between us and the current world in order to see all of this more clearly.

In 2004, Hewlett Packard's CEO, Carli Fiorina, began to declare in her public speeches that the dot-com boom and bust were just 'the end of the beginning'. The last 25 years of technology have just been the 'warm-up act'. We are going into the main event now, she said, 'and by the main event, I mean an era in which technology will literally transform every aspect of business, every aspect of life and every aspect of society.'[6]

Families are not immune. Directly and indirectly, changes taking place today are touching more people on the planet simultaneously in ways that no other watershed moment in history ever did or ever could. This is the power of technology and the result of connectivity.

As we write this book, it has been said that information on the World Wide Web is doubling every two months, bandwidth is doubling every nine months, and information processing and microprocessing speed are doubling every 18 months. These figures will be out of date even before this book goes to print. In our mobile phones alone we carry around more processing power than most small nations on earth have ever possessed. In February 2007, the 'latest revolution' in mobile phones arrived – the bullet-speed '4G' service that allows mobile phone users to download from the Internet at least 10 times faster than before.[7] New technology is arriving while users are still grappling to get their heads around earlier versions.

We are connected to the digital skin of the world via computers and mobile phones which are linked to the Internet, email, and more. Our lives are becoming more digitised and automated by the day – at home, at play and at work – and our living spaces are cluttered with screens and remote controls of one sort or another. (The average home in California boasts an average of 15 remote controls!)

Three decades ago, an aspiring junior executive was required to learn perhaps one new thing a year – a new skill, a new system of calculating, a new way of conducting the affairs of whatever business was at hand. Today, under the dual impacts of the speed and mass of change, that same aspiring junior executive at the same point in his or her job trajectory might have to learn one new thing a day. Change arrives too quickly, it piles up too high to do otherwise without being entirely left behind. By 2010, it's entirely conceivable that that same person at the same career point might have to learn one new thing an hour because to survive and thrive, businesses, like ecosystems, will have to be subtly changing with their environment, subtly becoming

different day by day, hour by hour, minute by minute. There will be no other way to keep up.

(Watts Wacker and Jim Taylor in *The 500 Year Delta: What Happens After What Comes Next*, 1997)

How do you not panic when faced with change of such magnitude? And Wacker and Taylor's comment was made only in relation to change at work. Remember that just as much change will take place concurrently in the same junior executive's personal life and parenting style too.

Parents need a framework to assimilate these changes and to manage them to benefit their families. Change (both positive and negative) is always disruptive to families, whether dad gets a new job, mum has another baby, parents get divorced, there is a death in the family, or a move to a new house, school or even country. As change occurs there is always a period of chaos, then adjustment and finally assimilation. Out of chaos comes order – eventually! Life, as adults know, is changing. For our children, childhood itself is changing. This is the nature of life. We need to prepare ourselves for change, bearing in mind that we have not yet felt the full force of the convergence of technologies – it's this which is building the tsunami.

But first we need to understand the implications of the changes we're living through.

You can expect to have on your wrist tomorrow what you have on your desk today, what filled a room yesterday.

(Nicholas Negroponte in *Being Digital*, 1996)

THE CONNECTED WORLD

I am convinced that the flattening of the world, if it continues, will be seen in time as one of those fundamental shifts or inflection points, like Gutenberg's invention of the printing press, the rise of the nation-state, or the Industrial Revolution – each of which, in its day, produced changes in the role of individuals, the role and form of governments, the ways business was done and wars were fought, the role of women, the forms religion and art took, and the way science and research were conducted, not to mention the political labels that we as civilization have assigned to ourselves and to our enemies.

(David Rothkopf, quoted in *The World is Flat*,
Thomas Friedman, 2005)

One of the major themes of the modern age has been globalisation. This has to do with the internationalisation of changes in institutions (such as political structures, governments, corporations and organisations), values (what people believe and what they value), economics and other factors that affect how we live. This era of change that we live in represents a shift in the global fabric of society and a new stage of globalisation.

The issue of globalisation and the historical journey of humankind may feel out of place in a book on parenting. But we believe that it's critical for parents living in an age of transition to understand both the era that we're entering and the one that is passing. And understanding the trajectory of change will help us to gain a glimpse of what the future holds – for us, and especially for our children.

Globalisation

There have been three great eras of globalisation, each one making the world a dramatically smaller place.[8]

The first era of globalisation began in 1450 when Prince Henry of Portugal founded his school for navigators. The aim was to undertake various voyages of discovery and to map the entire world. The ancient empires such as Egypt, Babylon, Persia, China and Rome had dominated the known worlds of the time, but the thinkers, the adventurers and the power-hungry believed that a great deal still remained to be discovered. Thus, in time, the known world spread across the entire world as we know it today.

As the voyages of discovery departed from Iberia in the late 1400s, opening trade between the Old World and the New World, the globe was mapped and the first era of true globalisation began to take shape. Of course, this is a fairly Western view of globalisation. In 1421 China had also sent out its own fleet of 'treasure ships', which spent three years circumnavigating the world, only to return to discover a dynasty change in the Imperial Dragon state and a new policy of exclusion from world events.[9]

From a European and Western perspective, this first round of modern globalisation shrank the world from a size large (or even size unknown) to a size medium. For the next few centuries, the power in the world rested with the rulers of empires. Countries and governments – often inspired by religion or colonialism or a combination of both – led the way in driving global integration.

The second era of globalisation made its appearance with the emergence of the industrial age. It grew with the European mercantile stock companies as they expanded in search of new markets, cheap labour and raw materials. It continued with the subsequent great advances in sea and rail transportation. Railways began criss-crossing the rural landscape, factories sprang up, machines began replacing people, cities grew, and telegraphs and telephones allowed the world to communicate like never before. From 1800 to 1989, this era shrank the world from a size medium to a size small. In this world, power shifted from rulers of countries to the suppliers of capital and those in charge of the newly emerging corporations. Multinational companies were the driving force in integrating and connecting the world.

Well-known management innovation expert Peter Senge and his co-authors, in the book *Presence: An Exploration of Profound Change in People, Organizations, and Society* (2005), point out that the impact of the expansion of the multi-national corporation affects the life of almost all species on the planet:

Historically, no individual, tribe or even nation could possibly alter the global climate, destroy thousands of species or shift the chemical balance of the atmosphere. Yet that is exactly what is happening today, as our individual actions are mediated and magnified though the growing network of global institutions. That network determines what technologies are developed and how they are applied. It shapes political agendas as national governments respond to the priorities of global business, international trade, and economic development. It is shaping social realities as it divides the world between those who benefit from the new global economy and those who do not. And it is propagating a global culture of instant communication, individualism, and material acquisition that threatens traditional family, religious and social structures. In short, the emergence of global institutions represents a dramatic shift in the conditions for life on the planet.

(*Presence: An Exploration of Profound Change in People, Organizations, and Society* by Peter Senge, 2005)

The third era of globalisation dates from 1990 to the present.

This era has been shrinking the world from a size small to a size tiny, and flattening the playing fields at the same time. It is seeing another power shift, a shift to which Senge et al. allude – to individuals, who will have a greater ability to negotiate personally without the interface of a government or corporation. A proliferation of technologies that allow individuals to harness the power of the global digital network is driving this era. The era of the free agent has begun.

In *The World is Flat* (2005), Thomas Friedman suggests 10 'flatteners'. These are 10 major events and trends that he shows have fundamentally changed the nature of global interactions since 1989, and helped to level the global playing fields. In brief summary, the 10 flatteners are[10]:

1. **11/9/89:** 'When the walls came down and the windows went up' – the fall of the Berlin Wall, and the launch of Windows 3.0 just six months later. At this moment it was clear that capitalism and democracy had won, and the world tipped towards free markets, entrepreneurs and private capital, with an adoption of common standards. The Windows-powered personal computer (PC) brought digital power to millions of individuals.
2. **8/9/95:** This is the date that Netscape went public. In the same year, Windows 95 was launched, the World Wide Web took off, and investment began in fibre optics around the world.
3. **Work flow software:** 'Let's do lunch. Have your application talk to my application.' With more powerful, easier-to-use software, improved connectivity and email, more people could share work. This allowed more complex projects with more interdependent parts and better collaboration across larger distances.
4. **Open-sourcing:** Self-organising, collaborative communities emerged, enabling individuals and groups with common interests to produce and not just consume infor-

mation, heralding a shift from audience to participants.

5. **Outsourcing:** Any service, call centre, business support operation, or knowledge work that could be digitised could be sourced globally to the cheapest, smartest and most efficient provider.
6. **Offshoring:** Geography means nothing any more.
7. **Supply-chaining:** Delivery, sorting, packing, distribution, buying, manufacturing, reordering; delivery, sorting, packing ... could all be done electronically, creating maximum efficiencies with reduced human error.
8. **Insourcing:** The example that Friedman gives is UPS. The 'brown' company delivers packages globally, but it also repairs Toshiba computers and organises delivery routes for Papa John's pizza. Insourcing enables UPS to use its logistics expertise to help clients to create new businesses.
9. **In-forming:** Google, Yahoo!, MSN Web Search. Never before in history have so many people had the ability to find so much information about so many things and so many other people – on their own. In-forming is the ability to build and deploy your own personal supply chain of information, knowledge and entertainment, and to seek out online communities of like-minded people.
10. **The steroids:** Digital, mobile, personal and virtual, technological advances range from wireless communication to processing, resulting in extremely powerful computing capability and transmission. One new Intel chip processes some 11 billion instructions per second (MIPS), compared to 60000 MIPS in 1971.

Converging trends and empowered individuals

It was not just Friedman's '10 flatteners' on their own that made the difference. These 10 factors played powerful roles in making the world smaller, but each worked in isolation. The real power of the last two decades is also to be found in the convergence of three more potent forces: first, new software and increased public familiarity with the Internet; second, the incorporation of this knowledge into business and personal communication; and third, the market influx of billions of people from Asia and the ex-Russian Republics who wanted to become more prosperous – and who did so fast. Converging, these factors generated their own critical mass. The benefits of each event became greater as it merged with another event.

Increased global collaboration by talented people, with no necessary regard for state boundaries, language or time zones, has created opportunities for billions of people. And it is these individuals, together with the companies they work for and the countries they live in, who are currently driving global change. When a critical mass of people in the world have daily access to a PC and are connected to the Internet, as is the case today, then there is easy, instant access to information. This means that changes in one part of the world have the potential to 'go global' very quickly. As changes have become more widespread, they have wielded a globalising effect – making the world a smaller place, a 'global village'.

Bill Gates has retired from Microsoft in order to work full time in his multibillion-dollar foundation. In addition to spending money on trying to find cures for diseases that are ravaging Africa, he also has a dream of creating a personal computer that costs less than $100, and of giving Africa's children a gateway to the digital world that he was so instrumental in creating. It is estimated that 50–100 million laptops per year will be distributed to children in developing countries through this project.[10]

Bill Gates also only allows his children 45 minutes per day of computer time!

The new technologies of the second era of globalisation took time to be assimilated. For example, it took decades to widely apply the benefits of the light bulb as people replaced old technology with an electrical distribution system. But the third era of globalisation has happened far more rapidly. People have been able to apply its new technologies quickly because the combination of the PC, the Internet and fibre optics created a flat organisational structure. Businesses also built new value based on inter-departmental teams versus old top-down command and control structures.

Every now and then, a technology or an idea comes along that is so profound, so powerful, so universal that its impact changes everything. The printing press. The incandescent light. The automobile. Manned flight. The Internet. It doesn't happen often, but when it does, the world is changed forever.

(Lou Gerstner, chairman of IBM, 2000)

Chaos and disruption: The Age of Possibility

Can you see the progression? In the first era of globalisation, countries and governments controlled all aspects of life. In the second era, there was a power shift from governments to companies. We live at the height of that era now as multinational companies hold more power than governments, and – as of January 2007 – 51 of the top 100 'economies' in the world are companies rather than countries.

But we also live at the start of the transition to the third era of globalisation in which the shift of power is starting to move from companies to individuals. No longer do governments or multi-national corporations stand in the way of you and the information you seek.

As long as you can plug in, you can participate. And that is why we are saying this is the era of individual power, an **Age of Possibility** such as we have never known. Take the *Pop Idols* television show in China, for example. It gave many Chinese people their first taste of democracy when, in 2005, over eight million votes were received via SMS from cellphones belonging to individual viewers in the final show alone. They were shaping their own reality, regardless of their government's ideology.

The playing fields have been 'flattened' and everyone now has the opportunity to use his or her potential to shape the world. It is up to the individual to use this potential or not, and how the individual uses it will be dependent on his or her set of values and world view.

As in all revolutions, there is chaos and change, disruption, dislocation, relocation and reconnection. The youth are not immune from all of this; in fact, they are often the expression and embodiment of it all. Every change brings with it hidden opportunities and danger – whether it be a transition to a new era; a move to a new house, a new job or a new country; a new arrival in the family; or a change in school for your child. The symbol below is the Cantonese symbol for 'change' or 'crisis'. Like many Chinese pictograms, it encompasses multiple meanings. In this case, the symbol is made up of two parts: the top part on its own means 'danger'; the lower part on its own means 'hidden opportunity'. So change or crisis embodies two elements: either we can focus on the danger, the downside or what may go wrong, or we can direct our energies into the hidden opportunity, the upside.

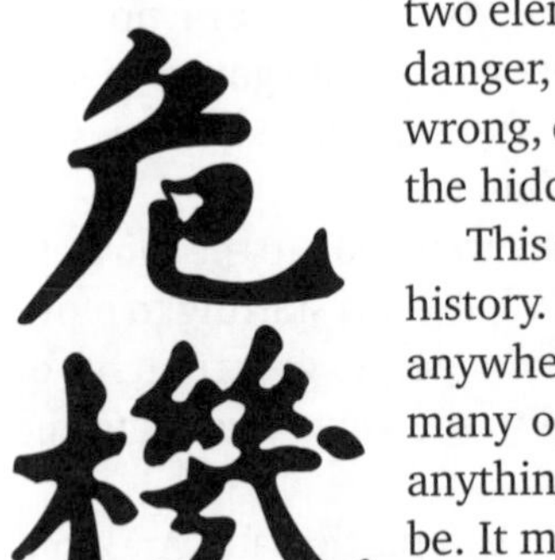

This truly is an amazing time in human history. Never before has anyone, born anywhere, in any circumstances, had as many opportunities to go anywhere, do anything, become anyone they want to be. It most surely is an Age of Possibility. *The* Age of Possibility. While this is an exciting thought, it is an equally daunting one too. Our choices will make a difference. We will not be swept along by the tide of history. But will we make the right choices? How do we know? How do we decide?

If these are powerful questions for our own lives, they become urgent and emotive when we consider our role as parents. We shape the critical formative years of our children, and set them on paths for the future. Are these the right paths? Are we doing the best for our children?

Parents are shaping the individuals of the future, which is why it is so important for them to understand what has happened in the past, what these changes have enabled, their implications for the future, and their impact on our children. For it is our belief that *parents* rather than schools (do *not* read this as parents replacing schools!) will be primarily responsible for ensuring that their children develop the critical factors that will enable them to succeed in the future.

THE POWER OF ONE – INDIVIDUALS USING TECHNOLOGY TO CONNECT

Did you know that you (yes, *you*!) were *Time* magazine's 'Person of the Year' for 2006. Every year this global news magazine selects the person it believes defined the year. Recipients have included Einstein, Gandhi, Mandela, Clinton, Gates, Stalin and Hitler. But in 2006 it was *you*! Congratulations. But what did you do to deserve such great praise and to join this esteemed gallery of eminent people?

The answer should be obvious. Among other reasons, 2006 was a breakthrough year for interactive Internet-based media, commonly labelled 'Web 2.0'. This label is generally applied to a new generation of Web-based services, such as social networking, wikis, blogs, and interactive communication tools, all of which emphasise online collaboration and sharing among users. Simply put, individuals like you and me took over as key content providers in a world afloat with information.

Just in case you haven't checked out some of these technologies, here's a quick Idiot's Guide to the Big Headline-grabbing Websites that made you the Person of the Year in 2006:

- **Skype** (www.skype.com): This enables free telephony and free video phoning as well as Skype Out, which allows you to use your computer to 'phone' any landline or mobile phone in the world at a fraction of the cost of normal telephone services. Note that at the time of writing this book, Janus Friis and Niklas Zennstrom, the co-founders of Skype and KaZaa (the file-sharing program) had just launched their latest venture – Internet-based television combining Web 2.0 functionality with traditional TV programming. It's called Joost (www.joost.com).
- **YouTube** (www.youtube.com): This is a website for sharing videos with the world. You make a video – clever or silly, serious or stupid – and then upload it. The site grabs it, converts it to a special FLV (flash) format, and makes it available for everyone to watch.
- **Flickr** (www.flickr.com): This is the same concept as YouTube, except it's for photographs. Using tags that can be added to photos, all the images are searchable in a variety of different ways. Part of what is supposed to be the genius of these sites is that nothing is copyrighted, and everything is shared for the sake of everyone. Well, sort of.
- **MySpace** (www.myspace.com): This is one of the sites that made it all happen. Reportedly the sixth most

visited website in the world, and the third most popular website in the US, MySpace is a cultural phenomenon. It's a social networking site that links people together based on common interests, although it has a bias towards people interested in music. The official byline for MySpace is an 'online community that lets you meet your friends' friends'. There's a more business-focused alternative called LinkedIn (www.linkedin.com), which connects people based on their business interests and opportunities.

- **Facebook** (www.facebook.com): This is a social networking site. Initially it was restricted to use by students, but it was made public in 2006. It has a very intuitive interface and is now being used by millions of people around the world to connect with old school friends and colleagues and to create new friends based on interests, groups and causes.
- **Second Life** (www.secondlife.com): This is downloadable software which allows you to create an avatar (an online character) that lives inside a virtual world. It interacts with other avatars being controlled by people all over the world.
- **Wikipedia** (www.wikipedia.org): For those who don't know what wiki's are, this is the best example of one. Put simply, it's a space where many different people can collaborate to create content. It sounds like chaos yet, strangely, it isn't. This is the world's largest encyclopedia. Online. For free.
- And then, of course, there's **Google** (www.google.com): This is the 200-pound gorilla sitting in the corner of the Internet cafe. Look past the search engine at Google (i.e. click the 'More' tab) and you'll find an amazing array of interactive tools – from calendars to maps of the earth – for online sharing and collaboration.

You can exercise your rights as Person of the Year 2006 by sending your news reports to basically any 24-hour news channel in the world (after all, they do have 24 hours to fill, every day). The most organised is iReport on CNN (www.cnn.com/ireport).

There are many other sites, and many more will emerge in time. Online collaboration and interaction is the way of the future.

A GENERATION LIKE NEVER BEFORE

Children themselves – their behaviour, attitudes and the ways in which they interact with the world they live in – have changed quite dramatically over the past 25 years in response to the 'flattening' of the world as discussed previously. We hope that, having contextualised the changes we have seen and are continuing to experience, you will be able to better understand how and why today's children are different. Their childhood is not our childhood.

If you are reading this book, it is most probably because you have a child or grandchild born after 1990. The generation of young people born between about 1990 and 2010 have been called *The Millennials*[12] – and they are very different to you, their parents. Born after Nelson Mandela's release, after the end of communism and the breakdown of the Berlin Wall, after the release of Windows, and growing up with laptops, mobile phones and social networking, this is a confident generation of children optimistically looking ahead into the 21st century. They are the most watched-over generation, but also the most vulnerable. Adults now subject a typical child's day to more and more structure and supervision, with a non-stop round of parents, relatives, teachers, coaches, babysitters, au pairs, surveillance cameras and curfews. Time spent on homework and housework is up and free time is down. Unsupervised time is down to unprecedented levels. Attention spans are on the decrease at the same rate that sensory input is on the increase. A major challenge to parents, teachers and marketers today is how to capture and maintain the attention of our children.

These millennial children are being forced to grow up very quickly. On the one hand, they're growing up in a world of unparalleled opportunities, with a wonderful sense of diversity in the global village. On the other hand, they're exposed to serious pressures, including terrorism, ecological collapse, open sexuality, and a working world that continually demands new skills for the jobs of the future. This is producing an entirely different set of values to the set their parents grew up with and are comfortable to impart.

Millennial generation characteristics

In a world so radically different from that of previous generations, we would be foolish to think that its children wouldn't be affected by advances in technology, the speed of life and rampant consumerism. Here are many of the typical characteristics of Millennial children around the world.

Confident and self-assured

Today's young people are confident – so confident they're almost arrogant. They know what they want and they know how they want to go about getting it! One reason for this is their role as chief technology officers in their homes. Some of their parents are not able to watch DVDs unless the kids are home – the boomer parents (born in the 1940s to 1960s – the generation that experienced a massive change in transport and the first to experience limitless travel horizons) don't know how to use the remote control. And when these parents acquire a new cellphone, they don't read the manual but prefer to enlist the help of their children to find out how it works.

The Millennial generation is growing up with a sense of destiny. They know that the world needs to be changed, and they feel that they have the ability to change it.

As adults we may shy away from technology and the sensory overload it yields, yet research reveals that today's kids appear at ease with the multitasking electronic environment. While sitting in the family room, youngsters engage in a myriad of activities simultaneously, such as watching television, doing homework, talking on their cell phones, sending text messages (SMSes), eating, drinking and talking.

(Carol Affleck, M-Net GO Channel: Project UTH Inc., 2004)

Connected and wired

Today's young people are the most technologically wired generation in history – they are literally connected to the digital skin of the world. The Millenials are confidently able to navigate technology because they have only ever known a world with cellphones, Internet connectivity and email. They use and manipulate technology intuitively, as if they were wired for it!

Millennials have access to more information than any other generation in history. They are accessing the same information that their parents and teachers can access. This is causing a shift in power in relationships of all kinds for a number of reasons: first, these children are not afraid to confront information that they feel may be incorrect; second, their parents look to them for information to assist them with purchase decisions; and third, their opinion has been taken into account from as early as the preschool years. These factors have created confident communicators with strong views which they are not afraid to share.

Children are contactable and accessible. This means that parents can keep tabs on their children and children can be in touch with their parents and friends in much more immediate ways than in the past. But it also means that children are more accessible to the likes of paedophiles and indiscriminate marketers. This is leading to a strange combination of connection and protection for this generation. In the 2004 K-TV qualitative research studies, approximately 60% of 8- to 10-year-olds owned cellphones, while over 90% of 11 to 13-year-olds had their own cellphones in the upper LSM (Living Standards Measure) groups.[13]

Not scared to fail

Failure is part of on-screen life, so this generation is less worried about failure in general. Millennial kids love the challenge of all sorts of games and reaching the next level is a driving force as they play the games over and over again. If they get shot in a computer game, they just start again. The challenge is simply to ensure that they don't get shot at the same point in the game again – because then they will have learnt something.

But this attitude to failure stretches into their 'real' lives as well. They are less scared of failure than any generation before them.

Screen hungry

Kids love on-screen activities – from TV to cellphones to iPods to Playstation, Xbox, Wii, computer games and more. They are information junkies and never have to think about how to keep themselves entertained because a wide variety of entertainment is available instantly, at the press of a button. They have been born into a 'barbed-wire culture'[14] in which it is either too dangerous to play outside, or there is no garden to play in due to high-density residential development. Children are increasingly being trapped in their homes. Fearful parents are more comfortable with the home entertainment centre playing 'babysitter and bodyguard'[15] than letting their kids out of the house.

Children are at risk of not using their imaginations and thinking skills sufficiently owing to bingeing on electronic media. It has also been said that this generation is 'information-wise but action-foolish'[16] because they are having more virtual than real-life experiences.

TELEVISION VIEWING

Average daily TV viewing by seven- to 15-year-old South Africans:

- Weekdays: 3.4 hours
- Weekends: 5.8 hours
- Holidays: 7.8 hours[17]

Toddlers are watching approximately one and a half hours of TV per day (international figure).[18]

The physical impact of this focus on the screen is that children are moving less, resulting in a rise in obesity and the childhood onset of diabetes. Additional problems which are receiving less attention include underdeveloped visual systems and listening skills, reduced concentration spans, low muscle tone and impaired coordination, to name but some.

Qualitative K-TV studies (Project Rainbow and Project Punch, (2004) revealed that three television sets per home were common, with some homes boasting as many as seven sets. In addition, approximately 90% of homes in the 2004 studies owned DVD players, and even young children appeared to have no difficulty in operating the DVD technology, namely menu

selection, extra features, and so on.

(From 'I Kid You Not', a research paper delivered to the SAMRA conference by developmental psychologist Carol Affleck, 2005)

Big spenders

Children today are the focus of media and marketers. They are the new market and part of a 'cradle to grave' marketing strategy – 'Hook 'em young and hold 'em for life'. They are constantly exposed to marketing messages; in fact, they are being bombarded by up to 5 000 messages per week[19] via various media. Millennials find satisfaction in things. Owning the latest cool gear or gadget is important for primary school children in order to feel satisfied and to belong. Kids are extremely brand conscious from a very young age. By 10 months old they can recognise brands; by 18 months old they can recognise up to 90 brands; and, by the age of 10 years, they can easily recognise 400 to 500 brands.[20]

> A few years ago, Nikki's son Matthew had been watching some kids' TV programmes. Since he was not the most verbal child at the age of five, he really caught her attention with his excitement on the way home from school one day. 'Mummy, you *have* to go to the shops. We *have* to buy some crisps. We can win some money!' Simba was running a promotion in which R1, R2 or R5 coins could be found inside random packets of crisps. This concept really lit Matthew's fire.

This is a marketer's dream, especially since what is 'cool' is being recreated all the time. Children love the excitement and hype around innovative and novel ideas so it is easy to sell them the next version of anything. In addition, technology has enabled marketers and the media to plug into children – with or without your permission – at home, at school, in the car, anywhere.

Digital inputs and the drive to consume have shifted family dynamics from parent power to child power. With access to information, children are influential in the use of the family budget. Eight- to 12-year-olds influence 60–70% of the household spend, equivalent to purchases of $700 billion a year in the US (R24 billion a year in South Africa). This is known as kidfluence.[21] Children no longer simply advise their parents what colour car to buy – they tell them which make and model too.

> If Nikki had been in the market for a high-value household gadget, she could easily have asked for advice from her eldest son from the time he was six years old. Ryan, clearly a technically minded child, loved watching the infomercials on the home shopping channel. He could wax lyrical about the features and benefits of the Big Green Machine (a vacuum cleaner) and anything else being promoted. Parents ask their children's advice from an increasingly early age.

Many children receive in excess of 70 new toys each year.[22] We believe that this figure is probably closer to 150 if you take into account all the toys obtained via cereals, crisps and takeaway meals. Toys themselves are changing, with a plethora of the electronic or computer-based variety emerging. In addition, toys are more prescriptive and less open-ended, requiring less imagination and stimulating less creative play.

Instant gratification

This generation is used to having its needs met instantly with customised solutions. You want your food hot? No problem – microwave it, and 30 seconds later it's steaming. You want to know something? No problem – log on to the Internet or the interactive TV or your cellphone, and 30 seconds later it's downloaded. Appetites of all kinds are satiated immediately.

Parents strive to keep their children happy. The result is 'I want it now, I want it like this.' This is the 'I want' or 'Gimme' generation. Many of these children are used to instant gratification and many have a low frustration tolerance – an inability to wait and high resistance to the word 'no'.

Now to answer the question about the decrease in attention spans. Simply put, the youth of today have become 'fragmented' in the sense that their attention is drawn by a myriad demands on their sensory systems. One of the fundamental reasons for this phenomenon is the infused television culture and, more specifically, the television *remote control device*. The latter enables children to change channels every few seconds and surf indiscriminately until something holds their attention. In other words, they are not forced to attend or focus on any one specific activity at a time. That which does not engage them immediately is simply 'zapped' and tuned out. Interestingly, some parents have attested to the remote control device being operated by children as young as 18 months.

With such a young introduction to the world of *self-initiated control*, it is no wonder that children demand *instant gratification* and, moreover, seek it actively. They are a hands-on generation who are technologically literate from the toddler stage – at 18 months they are able to insert a CD ROM and attempt to use a mouse. In addition, they demand *fast-paced* action on television programmes (quick cuts as introduced by M-TV and adopted by many youth channels). This same finding has been echoed in America where neuroscientists have attributed children's brief attention spans to overexposure to recurring cuts, edits, zooms, pans, and sudden noises the media provide – viewers are left craving more and constant stimulation. In addition, a similar interference in the development of attention spans emanates from the *reset button* on video games. If a child does not like the outcome of a game, he simply erases it and starts over. There is no need to attempt to rectify or improve the situation and, consequently, no time for reflection and learning as would be provided by a hobby such as building a model aeroplane or a puzzle.

(From 'I Kid You Not' by Carol Affleck, 2005)

Sexuality

Kids are growing older younger. The early onset of puberty hastens the shift to adulthood and the influence of the peer group over parents. Childhood is also being increasingly sexualised through the media, creating a striving in children to be older than they really are. This makes it easy for marketers to entice children to want new products – if an item 'up-ages' you, it's a winner.

Children are getting into relationships with the opposite sex more quickly because of SMSes, MMSes, chatrooms and other channels of interaction. It's much less inhibiting to start off a new relationship in a virtual way than by experiencing the awkwardness that comes with face-to-face communication. Kids are more sexually aware younger too. Sex and sexual innuendos are evident all over radio and TV as well as print and on-screen media. Sex is being used to sell anything – from printers to cars to jewellery and clothing.

A scary world

Despite all the advances and advantages of the new millennium, Millennial kids often feel fearful and uneasy. And why wouldn't they be when they hear and see 24-hour TV and radio news reports? Much of what is on the news is frightening to children – or, at least, it's not age-appropriate. Think, for example, of 9/11, the 2005 tsunami, and the widespread coverage of Madeleine McCann's disappearance in Portugal in 2007. TVs were left on in homes like moving wallpaper. We underestimate the post-traumatic stress of such exposure on children. It certainly tends to distort their sense of reality and they fear for their own personal safety, including rape, kidnapping and physical injury, as well as the safety of other family members.[23]

Children carry around the information-processing power of a small nation in their back pockets. This information is available instantly and wherever they are. This means that they are also at risk of exposure to inappropriate information, such as scenes of sex and violence, bad language, war and murders on movies, in the news or via information sharing from cellphone to cellphone. Children are becoming desensitised to violence and inappropriate behaviour, making them less discerning and easier prey for 'predators' of one form or another.

Changing the world

Today's millennial generation are much more health conscious than children of previous generations. Maybe it's because they have the choice to be so. Maybe it's their parents' example. Maybe they're just fussy! But the number of children on lactose-free, gluten-free, high-fibre, low-GI diets is amazing. This is just one example of how today's young people seem to have a greater understanding of the impact of their actions on their future, and of their desire to make right choices in all areas of their lives.

Millennial kids are willing to grab on to causes easily. It's not just about being personally healthy; it's also about the health of the planet. Almost instinctively, they know that the planet is in trouble and they must do something to fix it to ensure that they can have a future. They are prepared to put real emotional pressure on adults to make certain that the issues which concern them are appropriately addressed.

> Driving along the highway one day when Hannah was five, the Codrington family got stuck behind a delivery van. As the truck downshifted on a steep hill, it belched forth a cloud of acrid diesel smoke into the vents of the car. Hannah was indignant and disgusted at the pollution. As the family car overtook the truck, she waved her finger at the delivery van driver, admonishing him for 'pollutioning' the air. But then she turned to Graeme and stunned him by saying, 'Daddy, which company is that, 'cos I don't think we should buy from them any more'.[24]

We need to keep up

Parents, educators and employers will need to speed up to keep up because these Millennial kids are disengaging from us at a rapid rate. We need to understand them and relate to them in a way that is meaningful to them. Marketers and the media are constantly providing them with experiences, thrills and chills, in multicolour with fast-moving images and even faster soundtracks. This is the backdrop to our children's lives. We need both to compete with it and to find ways of balancing the noise (technology) and clutter (consumerism) in their lives to ensure that not only do they survive but also thrive in the world of the 21st century. These are the children who will have to solve the problems that are not yet problems, with technologies that don't yet exist.

We have to find creative ways of connecting and engaging with our children. Millennial kids will neither just buy into our values any more, nor will they necessarily believe what we say without good reason. They *want* to connect with us. They *want* a genuine, authentic relationship based on giving them reasons to respect us. Their mantra is: 'Give me an experience and I will give you a relationship', or 'Give me a reason and I'll give you my attention'. Parents who use 'Because I said so' are destined to widen the gap between themselves and their children rather quickly. It simply isn't a good enough answer any more.

All of this means that we have to be physically and emotionally present in the lives of our children. We must be prepared to have conversations that matter about the big questions of life which today's children, with a naturally high self-esteem, are not shy to ask.

Children are curious, natural explorers who will have far less trouble with living in this Age of Possibility than their parents. Developmentally, while they thrive on the security that a predictable, regular routine provides, they are also ready for constant and dramatic change – from crawling to walking, to talking and potty training, to starting school and losing all their teeth. Change is all in a day's work for a child.

It is us, their parents, who need to broaden our perspective and entertain the myriad choices and freedoms that come with living in this new Age of Possibility. Family life, whatever their shape, needs to be revived. It needs to provide meaning and possibility in order to restore hope to the future. For it is within families that hope lives.

Global warming, racial tension, Third World rage, rapacious epidemics, and myriad other global woes vie with less dire but no less unnerving phenomena – from information overload to media manipulation – to convince us that the apocalypse is about to pounce. Indeed, it will pounce on the unprepared, but there's no need for us to be caught unawares, if we will only learn from today's children. For those of us who grew up before computers became ubiquitous, the world is like a foreign country and we

are its immigrants. Our kids – the 'screenagers' – are like those of any immigrant, fitting themselves more naturally into this terra incognita than we can.

(Douglas Rushkoff in *Playing the Future*, 1996)

FORBES LIST OF JOBS IN 2020

(Adapted from an article published online by *Forbes* magazine, May 2006, at www.forbes.com/2006/05/20/jobs-futurework_cx_hc_06work_0523jobs.html)

See more detail about the future of work in Section 3 on page 111.

New jobs by 2020

- **Gene screener:** In the future, a genetic screen could be as common as a drug test. Employers will need technicians to collect and analyse DNA from potential hires as they attempt to screen out workers with a propensity for drug abuse or other conditions that could interfere with productivity.
- **Quarantine enforcer:** If a deadly virus starts spreading rapidly, few countries and few people will be prepared. That'll be good for certain occupations. Nurses will be in short supply. And when people really start dying, and neighbourhoods are shut down, someone will have to guard the gates.
- **Drowned city specialist:** Suppose climate change happens a lot more quickly than expected. Over half the world's population lives within five kilometres of an ocean. Belongings will need to be rescued, and houses moved to higher ground.
- **Robot mechanic:** Middle-class families worldwide will be able to buy robotic personal assistants or

companions. Sony already sells the Aibo, a robotic dog, for about $2 000. He doesn't need a vet – but he might need the occasional tune-up.

- **Animal guardian:** Should a gorilla have the same rights as a three-year-old child? Attorneys are pushing to classify some non-human animals as 'persons' under the law. As our legal definitions change, we'll need specialised lawyers to represent animal interests.
- **Dirigible pilot:** These small flying machines will revolutionise life in the developing world. They're relatively cheap to operate, don't require expensive infrastructure like runways, and can stop in midair to drop off passengers or deliver goods.
- **Hollywood holographer:** Movies aren't a Saturday night staple any more. A plethora of cheap entertainment options, including the Internet, DVDs and videogames, keep viewers in their living rooms. One solution: holography. Consumers won't be able to afford, operate or maintain the equipment at home, forcing them back into theatres for three-dimensional movies.
- **Teleport specialist:** Imagine walking to a teleport station at the end of the block, dematerialising and reappearing at work. Cars would be gone, auto mechanics would be gone, gas station attendants would be gone, and a whole new economy could develop based on the teleporter. Okay, this scenario is a little far-fetched – cars probably won't disappear in 20 years. But hey, commuters can dream.

Jobs likely to disappear by 2020

- **Union organiser:** Union organisers and leaders may soon disappear, says futurist Alvin Toffler, since they show no sign of reversing their 20-year membership decline. 'The labour movement has not come to terms with the knowledge economy at all,' Toffler says.

- **Construction worker:** Much construction work is still completed by hand. But three-dimensional printing may change that, says futurist Joel Barker. Instead of simply printing one layer of ink on paper, stereo lithographic printers could spit out multiple layers of material to make 3D structures. Eventually, Barker says, these could be used to construct houses on a mass scale.
- **Encyclopedia writer:** Britannica watch out. Wikipedia's got your number. This 21st-century encyclopedia is free, online and edited by readers.
- **Grocery store cashier:** Handling cash is oh-so-20th century. In fact, all jobs dealing with paper money, including bank tellers and toll-booth operators, could be obsolete in two decades as we rely more on credit and digital money.
- **Film processor:** If you want to stick with old-fashioned photography, better build your own darkroom. Your neighbourhood photo store will be going digital, or going out of business.
- **CD store manager:** Why browse for CDs at Tower Records when you can search for MP3s online? Music producers are going digital, and retailers must adjust as well. Compact discs don't have the artistic flair of old records, so they won't have the same vintage cachet either.
- **Miner:** Bacteria like *Thiobacillus ferooxidans* can be used to extract metal from ore. If there are further advances in the science of bio-mining, expect the guys with coal-darkened faces to take above-ground occupations.

- **Fighter pilot:** Why send a man into combat when you can send a machine? While we're still far away from using robots as front-line troops, fighter jets may soon be automated.
- **Call centre representative:** Be careful what you wish for. Many people have fantasised, while on hold, about an end to call centres. But if they do disappear, they're likely to be replaced with more automation, not more personal customer service.

Jobs that will never disappear

- **Politician:** We hate most of them. We adore a few. And we'll never get rid of them, no matter how hard we try.
- **Prostitute:** Perhaps when they make androids as realistic as humans, this job could be automated. For the next few decades, however, the 'oldest profession' shows no sign of decline.
- **Artist:** Creative writers, comedians, actors, entertainers, painters, designers. Art changes and evolves with technology, but it will never disappear.
- **Religious leader:** Many people will continue to look to religion to find meaning in their lives.
- **Criminal:** The crimes may change but the 'profession' will remain.
- **Parent:** Okay, so it doesn't pay very well. Or at all. But there will always be a demand for someone to raise our helpless human babes.
- **Soldier:** The world's population is growing, religious fervour shows no signs of abating, and precious resources are becoming increasingly scarce. Count on the military to stick around for all kinds of future conflicts, at least until 2020. Robots may be on the horizon after that.

THE AGE OF POSSIBILITY – THE POWER TO CHOOSE

Accept chaos for what it is. Slip into it. Drift with it. Have some fun. Remember: The only person in charge of you any more is you. If you've made the choices you've made based on your own internalised set of values, they'll be the right choices, whether they are right or wrong.

(Watts Wacker and Jim Taylor in *The 500 Year Delta: What Happens After What Comes Next*, 1997)

The insights that we've shared with you in these pages should've helped you understand how it is that we got 'here', and how the world is shaping our children at the start of the third millennium. We're sure you can appreciate why we are calling this the Age of Possibility. You can now choose what you want to be. You are not limited by your geography or your language. You are not even limited by your station in life – the world is a meritocracy, not an aristocracy any more. It has flattened – not just for countries and companies, but for individuals as well. The Age of Possibility is about personal choice and freedom.

System overload/shutdown

With freedom, though, comes responsibility. We have to take responsibility for the choices we make. This is something we either fear or embrace. Fear, of course, can lead to paralysis. And there is evidence of paralysis caused by fear all around. As a parent or grandparent, consider how you have responded when your young children have asked, 'What should I be when I grow up?' Our children will join the working world of 2020 or later – what will it be like? We have very little idea what the top 10 most wanted jobs will be in 2020, or even if some of today's most sought after jobs will even exist then. (As you read the list on pages 40–43, did you find yourself excited, scared or numbed?) Our minds can easily just shut down.

The question of a future career is linked, of course, to considerations about what subjects our children should study at school. We then wonder whether the schools that we've selected for our children will actually deliver on our hopes for them. As we meet their teachers, so burdened with administrative and curriculum overload, we wonder whether these people are capable of helping to shape our offspring effectively. We wonder whether the subjects on offer will lead to success in the careers we can't even conceive of in 2020. Again, our minds shut down.

But forget studies and careers. We know that it's actually key life experiences, personal skills and relationships that will be more significant in our children's development. But which ones? And how can we ensure our children have these experiences? Do they have to experience what we did to reach where we are? This gets tough. Once again, shut down!

And we haven't even considered how much pocket money to give our children, or how old they need to be before they get their own cellphone. Do we think about the pressure placed on children when a cellphone is added to their list of responsibilities? We don't know how to protect our children from what they will find on the Internet or on any number of interactive media sources. How old must they be before we talk about sex, drugs and global warming? And what do we say when we talk about these issues? And, perhaps most importantly of all, how do we help to prepare them to make their own decisions within the next few years?

Too many options

Today, when we make a decision, we have to consider so many different options. In previous eras people had no or few choices, and the factors influencing their choices were limited. Decision making was therefore relatively easy. In today's world this is no longer the case. We are faced with big and small decisions every minute of the day. Do we check the email alert on our computer in the midst of writing an important strategy, or answer our cellphone as we enter our child's classroom to pick him or her up?

We can find these decisions overwhelming and hard to make. In fact, we'd much rather know there is someone else out there to name or blame for whatever goes wrong. But this approach won't wash in this new era. We need to be knowledgeable in order to make all these necessary choices, to have conversations and dialogues with other adults and our children, and to really commit to engaging and connecting with our children in ways they understand. We have no alternative but to become comfortable with taking personal responsibility for every choice or move we make in this new Age of Possibility.

THREE ESSENTIALS: CONVERSATIONS, CONNECTIONS AND CHOICES

Now that you know 'where' we are, we hope that you'll continue reading with enthusiasm and excitement as we attempt to provide practical assistance for the parenting journey ahead. As you embark on that journey, we suggest you keep these three things in mind at all times:

- The need to have conversations and dialogues with your children, their teachers and other significant adults

- The need to maintain relationships through conscious connection and engagement with your children and other significant adults
- The need to make choices about your own future and the futures of your children, and to be prepared to take full responsibility for them.

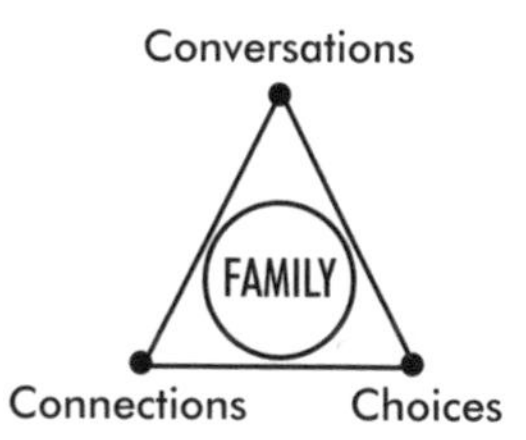

Imagine, for a moment, your family as a ball. In order for it not to roll away as a result of the disruptive constant change that you are living through, it needs to rest on a solid base. The best base is a triangle (the most stable shape known to humankind). The triangle's three corners are the three Cs – conversations, connections and choices. It's a triangle of *conscious commitment*.

As long as the three elements of conversation, connection and choice exist as underlying elements of your parenting strategy, you will achieve the stability that will be so essential for families navigating the Age of Possibility ushered in by the 21st century. If just one element is missing, it follows that one side of the triangle will become disconnected and the ball (the family) may destabilise and roll away.

We'd like to suggest that this triangle is a relevant and practical framework for parenting today. In Sections 4 and 5 you will find many tips and ideas – the 'how to', which you will be able to slot into this framework and make your own. Since every family is unique, the tips and ideas lists are just like a menu. You will choose from it what appeals to you, what resonates for you, and what is workable for *your* family. Some of the ideas will work for you, some won't. Some will be too expensive for you. Others will sound too corny or too weird. We don't expect you to do everything that we suggest. But, whatever you do, endeavour with every fibre of your being to activate the three Cs and build this framework into as much of your parenting as you can.

By reading this book you have chosen to empower yourself with knowledge and ideas. You know that things have changed irrevocably. You know that these changes are affecting your life and the lives of your children. And it's so confusing because you've never been 'here' before. But now, in addition to understanding a little more about the new world we live in (how we got here), it's time to take the next step to being an effective 21st-century parent. It's the step towards understanding *your* children and their developmental needs *now* so that you can make an educated selection from the menu of tips and ideas further on in this book.

Endnotes

[2] A statement made by veteran US educator Laurel Schmidt in *Seven Times Smarter: 50 Activities, Games, and Projects to Develop the Seven Intelligences of Your Child*, 2001.
[3] Refer to *The Tipping Point* by Malcolm Gladwell, 2002, for more information on this concept.
[4] Quoted in *The World is Flat: A Brief History of the Twenty-first Century* by Thomas L Friedman, updated and expanded edition, 2006.
[5] IBM keeps a website of the event: www.research.ibm.com/deepblue/.
[6] Quoted in *The World is Flat: A Brief History of the Twenty-first Century* by Thomas L Friedman, updated and expanded edition, 2006.
[7] *The Sunday Times*, South Africa, 18 February 2007.
[8] The concept of the three eras of globalisation is borrowed from award-winning New York Times journalist Thomas Friedman's book, *The World is Flat: A Brief History of the Twenty-first Century*, updated and expanded edition, 2006.
[9] For more details on this, see *1421: The Year China Discovered the World* by Gavin Menzies, 2003.
[10] Karl Fisher and Scott McLeod, *Shift Happens* (online video), accessed in June 2007 at www.scottmcleod.org/didyouknow.wmv. Video available in various forms at www.youtube.com, search for 'Did you know'.
[11] Thanks to Clive Simpkins, author and philosopher, for this insight from his book *Change Your Thinking, Change Your Life*, 2005.
[12] Different authors and studies use different names, and have slightly different

start and end dates for this generation. Different countries will also have slightly different difining parameters but, in general, the children and pre-teens of the 1990s and 2000s are known around the world as Generation Y or the Millennial generation. For more detailed information on generations, we recommend *Mind The Gap* by Graeme Codrington and Sue Grant-Marshall, 2004. For more on the Millennial generation, we suggest you read *Millennials Rising* by Neil Howe and William Strauss, 2000, and *Employing Generation Why* by Eric Chester, 2002. For an Australian perspective, read *Generation Y: Thriving and Surviving with Generation Y at Work* by Peter Sheahan, 2006.

[13] Carol Affleck, developmental psychologist, in her paper, 'I Kid You Not', delivered at the SAMRA (South African Market Research Association) conference, 2005.

[14] Credit goes to Youth Dynamix, BratTrax® 2005/6 for this phrase.

[15] Ibid.

[16] Ibid.

[17] Youth Dynamix, BratTrax® 2007/8.

[18] Kaiser Family Foundation research, 2006.

[19] Youth Dynamix, BratTrax® 2005/6.

[20] Ibid.

[21] Ibid.

[22] *Born to Buy: The Commercialized Child and the New Consumer Culture* by Juliet Schor, 2005.

[23] Youth Dynamix, BratTrax® 2007/8.

[24] This incident led to the creation of a boycott list by the Codrington family, which still resides on their fridge. The criteria for getting onto and off the list have now become famous in 'Hannah's Rules'. See www.hannahsrules.com for more information.

Section 2

Understand our children's development now

Fundamentally, we need to remain both current and contemporary so as to be able to engage them in their space – mental space and physical space. Therefore, we need to search for means to remain *relevant* to this generation, and this sometimes necessitates the adoption of new approaches and the tweaking of traditional methodologies. In sum, therefore, we need to go *back to basics* via an examination of *cognitive developmental ages* and, at the same time, we need to *move forward* by keeping *contemporary and innovative*.

(From 'I Kid You Not', a research paper delivered to the SAMRA conference by developmental psychologist Carol Affleck, 2005)

Living at the peak of a major shift in human history, as discussed in Section 1, we have to ask ourselves: How do we prepare our children for a world that doesn't yet exist – a world we find difficult even to imagine? We believe that it's essential for parents to take the early years of their children's lives very seriously. By laying solid foundations early, you can start preparing your children for the future, whatever it may hold.

This section focuses on what we need to understand about our children's development *now* and how, if we are not aware, 21st-century living could interfere with this miraculous developmental process. This early stage of our children's lives is called the foundation phase – and for good reason. As a parent, this is the best opportunity you'll ever have to shape, form and nurture the individuals (*who*) your children will become. Everything you do – and don't do – is part of the formation process. It is also a period of exponential learning never to be repeated, full of windows of opportunity that should be maximised in a balanced way with knowledge, insight and sensitivity.

So, before we jump into the future and try to understand the world our children will be entering in the next few years, we need to focus on what must be done now to provide a basic foundation for anything that may happen in the years ahead.

SOME THINGS HAVEN'T CHANGED

As we have said, constant change is no longer just a phase – it has become our 'new normal'. Even childhood is changing as our children become the newest market to be drawn into the fast-paced world of multitasking and time urgency. However, it may be comforting to know that children still go through the same basic developmental stages. Not everything has changed!

This is important for parents to remember when faced with young children who may seem older than their years. It is well documented that under the influence of the two factors of technology (noise) and consumerism (clutter) our children are growing up at a younger age (even the preschoolers) because they:

- are connected to the digital skin of the world
- own more stuff
- are busier and under more stress and pressure than any previous generation of children.

Developmental psychologist and specialist youth researcher Carol Affleck questions whether these children are actually able to efficiently absorb, process and integrate the infinite sensory input that bombards them, and how this will impact on them with regard to the kind of adults they will eventually become. How will they connect the dots in the future? We believe this will depend on how they connect the dots developmentally during their foundation years. This, in turn, is dependent on their parents and teachers ensuring that their development is not interrupted by the side effects of technology and consumerism, particularly in the early years.

With this in mind, it is important for parents to have a basic understanding of how children learn and develop in order to support their developmental process appropriately. We'll look at some fundamentals below and a well-known model of development is included as an appendix for your interest. If you would like to read through the model first, then fast forward to page 328.

We are multisensory beings

Children learn through their senses: hearing, sight, touch, taste, smell, movement and balance. The sensory system is the part of the nervous system that receives and processes information in the brain. Through this process, the brain will grow and develop. How your children interpret sensory information shapes their experience of their world. At the same time, their sensory system is shaped by their experiences of the world. An amazing thought![25] It is important to know this since parents are the sensory gatekeepers, especially during the first seven years of life when children do not have emotional and psychological filters to protect them. In other words, they are unable to tell the difference between what is real and what is not.

For example, it is unwise to allow children in this age bracket to watch TV unchecked. First, they cannot differentiate between programming and commercial content (this must be taught); and second, if the programmes contain inappropriate content such as violence, sex or anything that induces fear or sensory overload, they cannot protect themselves. Thus they experience everything as 'real'. Such experiences shape their reality and their world view, whether we are aware of it or not.

Phases of learning

Children are constantly moving in and out of three basic phases of learning: the concrete, the semi-concrete and the abstract. These phases are explained in Table 2.1 overleaf.

Table 2.1 *The three basic phases of learning*

PHASE	EXPLANATION	EXAMPLE
Concrete *From birth*	In the early stages: A child needs actual objects to touch, taste, see, hear and smell. A child learns through his or her senses. A child uses his or her tongue to obtain an understanding of texture and shape as well as the taste of objects. Movement is essential for learning in this phase.	**A real apple**. The way a child personally experiences an apple will give it meaning. The way a parent or teacher talks about the apple with the child as he or she holds it, and points out the properties or characteristics of the apple, will also help the child to verbalise his or her thoughts and discoveries about the apple. This is learning in the concrete – on the outside the apple is red, round and smooth with a waxy feel to it; inside, it's a different colour and texture, and it's crunchy, juicy and tastes sweet! All this information will be stored in the child's brain to be used whenever he or she next experiences something red, crunchy, round, smooth, juicy or sweet.
Semi-concrete *3+ years*	As the child gains experience, he or she is able to relate pictures, objects and models to actual objects with which he or she has had some contact at an earlier stage.	**A picture of a red apple**. Now that the child has experienced a real apple, a picture of the apple will have meaning. The child can access everything he or she has experienced about a red apple and apply it to the picture. The child is using his or her memory.

Abstract *6+ years*	At this stage, symbols, letters and numerals are able to be interpreted and understood.	**The word 'apple'**. Having had concrete and semi-concrete experiences of apples, the child will find learning to recognise the word for apple much easier because he or she can make real associations based on personal experience with apples. The child will also create categories and develop analytical skills. 'Apples' can be categorised as 'fruit', even if they are red, green or yellow, and small or big.

Source: Adapted and expanded from *Bridging with a Smile* by Doreen Maree and Margot Ford, 1995.

While this is an oversimplification of the learning process and the extraordinary brilliance of our complex brain, it does give parents a good idea of how their children learn. In fact, from birth right up to the age of 12 years, children's primary way of creating meaning and understanding of their world is through concrete, real-life learning situations. In other words, they learn through personal experience.

The three phases of learning can be clearly seen in a child who is learning to count. Initially the child should have real objects to count and be encouraged to touch each object as he or she counts, making the experience concrete and personal. In the semi-concrete phase, the child can count just by looking at the objects he or she is counting. In the abstract phase, actual numbers have meaning and the child no longer needs the visual clues of real objects or pictures to count.

The senses of touch, movement and balance are also integral to concrete, active and personal learning experiences.

Right from conception, it is actually *movement* that wires the brain for future, more sophisticated cognitive functions. There is a natural progression from one developmental milestone to the next that is driven by the connection between the brain and the body via a special substance called myelin. Parents' awareness of myelin is usually limited to ensuring that the correct fatty acids are in their infant formula. The formation of myelin – the fatty coating of the nerve fibres of the brain – starts in utero, peaking at around one to two years of age and continuing until around the age of five.

Myelination starts in the head and works its way down the body, and from the centre of the body outwards. Myelin increases the speed of nerve impulse transmission, which means that messages can be relayed more efficiently between brain cells. In highly myelinated neurons, impulses travel at 100 metres per second.[26]

This means that your child will develop in a predictable way. Physically, your child will gain control of his or her neck, then trunk, then arms and legs, and finally, fingers and toes. As the muscles develop physically, the child will also develop sensations, emotions and perceptions as myelin increases.

Reaching their milestones

Parents are usually unaware that physical developmental milestones or phases are all in line with myelination development. In fact, milestones can't be reached until sufficient myelin is laid down. Head and neck control precede rolling, for example. The quality of a baby's physical development forms the basis of all learning and academic achievement later on because it is intrinsically linked to the development of the neural pathways in the brain. For this reason, occupational therapists often say that thoughts which never possess the body, never possess the mind.

It's a myth that the sooner a baby reaches his or her milestones, the more intelligent he or she will be. In fact, research shows that there is an enormous correlation between incomplete developmental phases in babies and academic underachievement later on.[27] In other words, repetition at every phase is required in order to build a strong cognitive network in the brain.

Learning through repetition

Repetition is essential for good and comprehensive development to take place. For example, a baby should perform in the region of 50 000 crawling movements to wire the brain in preparation for the fine-motor skills of reading and writing. Effective myelination takes place through repeated body movement.

'Screen time' (TV, computers, digital games, etc.) involves passive experiences that are largely semi-concrete or abstract. These must therefore be balanced with real experiences. Remember that an elephant and a mouse can be the same size on a screen. Children will never comprehend their true size until they are able to compare themselves physically to these creatures by visiting a pet shop, zoo or game reserve. Similarly, playing a car racing game on Playstation does not provide a child with a real concept of judging speed, space and distance. The same is true, of course, for books and picture cards. Nothing can replace real-world experiences.

> Nikki picked up her six-year-old son from a play date one afternoon and found him having the time of his life. His friend's parents were doing an alteration to their home and the boys had found a plank of wood and a few bricks with which they made a see-saw ramp for their bikes. What

incredible fun they had for over two hours. The exercise was creative, challenging and very physical. It entailed thinking, planning and problem solving to set it up, and then the gross-motor skills of balance, coordination and spatial planning (how fast or slow to go, and when to accelerate so as not to fall off the ramp). This was the perfect balancing act to the hour spent playing a computer game earlier in the day.

That earlier hour of on-screen activity was also well spent playing a game called Hugo. It entailed fine-motor coordination to move the cursor all over the screen, helping worker ants to collect food for the queen. On depositing food in the anthill, the player then had to decide on his reward – select either a worker ant or a soldier ant. This introduced thinking skills and strategy to the game. The anthill was under attack from enemy ants from time to time, so there needed to be a good spread of worker ants and army ants to deal with whatever situation arose. This game involved basic thinking and planning skills in a virtual environment. It's amazing how quickly children work out how the game is played and what the rules and consequences are – and all of this without reading a rules booklet! Come to think of it, no rules book or adult supervision was necessary for the bike ramp game either. Children are so naturally resourceful!

Always bear these key points in mind:

- The American Academy of Paediatrics recommends no TV viewing for children under the age of two because it is a passive, inappropriate and abstract form of stimulation for this age group. For optimum learning and development to take place, two year olds and under need to move and be more active than this activity allows.
- A rule of thumb for *total* time spent doing on-screen

activities for children is not more than two hours a day. This includes TV, Playstation, computers, Gameboys, cellphone games, time spent in chat rooms, etc.

- Don't put a television in your child's bedroom.
- Place the computer in a public space where you can keep an eye on what your children are playing and accessing.
- Install filters on your computer to restrict inappropriate content.
- Make sure your children continue to ask for permission to switch on the TV or play a computer game or Playstation for as long as possible. It will help you to keep control of their media habits.
- Let kids get dirty.
- Encourage play dates.

Keep striving for balance between high-tech and high-touch activities. It's more important than you think!

Parents can really facilitate their children's learning – and foster a love of learning – by offering them rich life experiences, characterised by visits to interesting places and exposure to different environments. For example, how does a child understand the sea without having experienced it, or visualise the texture of grass without having crawled on it? Children also need plenty of free play, undirected by adult supervision, which enables them to access their inner world. Many 'play' experiences provided for children today are contrived, prescribed, organised and supervised to the detriment of a child's natural development.

The role of parents in the foundation phase of life is to give their children numerous varied experiences, and to provide for as much repetition within these experiences as possible.

Learning is experience. Everything else is just information.

(Albert Einstein quoted by Carla Hannaford in *Smart Moves: Why learning is not all in your head*, 1995)

Children go on learning binges

Just as children grow in fits and starts, so they absorb knowledge in the same way. They go on a learning binge and then need time to consolidate their findings. They put their ideas together and work out how the new facts modify what they thought they knew.

Your child has to process new information, make sense of it and file it somewhere in his or her brain. All this takes place by association – new information is memorised and stored in relation to existing knowledge and not as stand-alone data. For example, colour is not taught as much as caught. When you say to a child, 'Find me a red shape like this', the child's brain will be creating associations with all the other red things you have shown him or her over time – such as a red apple, a strawberry, or Daddy's red car. When shown the new red shape, the child's brain goes into a whirlwind of activity, connecting different memory knots and creating the spidery nerve nets that characterise a stimulated brain.

Every experience, whether it is a visit to the zoo or playing with an educational toy, extends the experience of children and expands their knowledge, literally exercising and growing their brain. Children need quiet and busy times, routines and challenges, sensible and serious tasks, balanced by games that are silly but fun. All of this will help to create memory and increase their attention span.

Adults have a much longer attention span than young children. They can remember about seven items, such as a seven-digit telephone number with the numbers grouped in a certain way (or, these days, a 10-digit cellphone number!), but they would have difficulty in remembering a longer credit card number. UK psychology lecturer and author of *Learning Early* (1998), Dorothy Einon, says that tiny babies have an attention span of one item, toddlers three, and a seven-year-old about five items. One of the main functions of the attention span is to hold on to a thought long enough to turn it over in your mind and relate it to other ideas. With an attention span of seven items, it is possible to use it like a scratch pad and to think things through without the assistance of props (visual clues). With a typical child's attention span of five items, these props become more important.

It's for this reason that children need concrete learning apparatus, toys, educational games and puzzles to enable them to work things out using their own experience. Bear in mind that if a child is showing little interest in a particular toy, he or she may either have mastered it and is now bored, or is not yet ready for it, which fits in with the learning binge theory. In both cases, try putting the toy away for a few weeks or even a month or two. Then take it out again and play with it differently. Children are continually growing as well as changing so fast that they may surprise you with their sudden interest or ability in a game they haven't seen for a while. This is because they have moved on and are now in a different brain-body space.

As children grow, so does their attention span. Building on familiarity is important. As they become more comfortable with repeated information, they can start storing it in chunks rather than individual bits. While repetition can be boring for adults, parents are encouraged to read the same favourite stories to their children over and over again, to sing the same nursery rhymes and lullabies, and to visit familiar places with them. Balance this with a rich variety of new and interesting experiences, which will give your young child enough food for thought without totally overwhelming him or her. As children enter primary school, especially this generation of Millennials, it will be essential to provide them with new, interesting and relevant experiences and information. As mentioned in Section 1, the mantra of this generation is 'Give me an experience and I will promise you a relationship'.

Children learn through experience, failure and practice – a learning paradigm largely absent from schools.
(Roger Schank in *Coloring Outside the Lines*, 2001)

EVERY CHILD IS DIFFERENT

While every child goes through the same developmental phases, each child turns out differently. We are all uniquely internally 'wired'. This relates to many factors, including genetics, the environment, our intelligences (we have many different ones, not just IQ), our brain dominance, personality, preferred learning style, and more. In this section we delve into just some of these areas, which you may find interesting. Some knowledge of these areas should also enable you to observe and appreciate your child's reactions and interaction with the world.

Multiple intelligences

Harvard professor Howard Gardner is famous for identifying seven different types of intelligences present in human beings, which are outlined on page 67. These intelligences are:[28]

- **Verbal-linguistic:** The ability to communicate, use language and articulate thoughts. Lawyers and politicians would use this intelligence.
- **Musical-rhythmic:** An artistic ability, specifically linked to appreciation and expertise in making music. Entertainers would need this intelligence.
- **Logical-mathematical:** The analytical intelligence. Accountants and actuaries rely on this intelligence.
- **Visual-spatial:** An ability to understand dimensions and environment. Architects and engineers would need this intelligence.

- **Body-kinaesthetic:** Often linked with sports, this is the ability to control the body and push it to its limits. Professional sportspeople need this intelligence.
- ***Inter*personal:** This has to do with the ability to connect easily with others, to network and form relationships. People in the hospitality industry would use this intelligence.
- ***Intra*personal:** This is the ability to be self-aware and to see oneself in context. This has become well known in recent years as 'emotional intelligence'. It could be argued that spiritual leaders should exhibit this intelligence.

According to Gardner, intelligence is not the single IQ number we were raised with, but a mosaic of abilities located in many different parts of the brain. These intelligences are interconnected but they also work independently. Perhaps, most importantly, they are not static or predetermined at birth. Like muscles, they can grow through an individual's life if they are nurtured and strengthened. This means that, in the right environment, people can get smarter.[29]

Gardner has since added a further two intelligences to his original list: **naturalistic intelligence** and **spiritual intelligence**. The former refers to the ability to recognise flora and fauna, to make other consequential distinctions in the natural world and to use this ability productively. The latter is the ability to appreciate and accommodate views and opinions from people of other spiritual persuasions.

The mental abilities most valued in the Western world are linguistic and logical-mathematical intelligences. The importance of these nine intelligences has shifted over time, and varies from culture to culture. In a hunting society, for example, it is a lot more important to have extremely good control over your body (body-kinaesthetic intelligence) and to know your way around (spatial intelligence) than to add and subtract quickly. In Japanese society, the ability to work cooperatively in groups and to arrive at joint decisions (interpersonal intelligence) is highly valued. While schools in the last century have focused on linguistic and interpersonal skills, Gardner speculates that linguistic abilities will become less important in schools in the near future as logical-mathematical abilities take on more significance in relation to developments in the areas of technology and IT (information technology).

The point is, while both logical-mathematic and linguistic intelligences are important today, it won't always be that way. Hence, Gardner's argument is that we need to be sensitive to the fact that what is valued in terms of 'intelligences' is changeable. This is something we need to keep in mind as we plan curriculums, teach students and raise our children.

Some researchers and authors have identified as many as 23 different categories of intelligence. South African researcher and edu-profilogist Dr Annette Lotter disputes the traditional assumption that 'smart is fast' which underlies the overwhelming majority of time-controlled IQ and other aptitude tests. For Lotter, the critical aspect of what constitutes 'intelligence' is not necessarily the speed with which you arrive at a solution, but the *processes* you use to get there. She suggests that there are four more highly important intelligences. We include them here because they are so relevant to learning and information processing in the 21st century:

- **Componential intelligence:** This is the facet of a person's mental ability that enables him or her to reason logically, to think analytically, to identify connections among ideas, and to see various aspects or 'components' of a problem.
- **Experiential intelligence:** Associated with a person's capacity to combine disparate experiences in insightful ways, this is the ability to see new combinations and possibilities in the world around you. It is the capacity

not only to make sense of your own experiences, but to reorder, recombine, and reinterpret your experiences in new and possibly creative ways. (We like to call this 'connecting the dots differently', which will be an X-factor for success in the world of work in 2020.)

- **Contextual intelligence:** This is used in the context of a person's external world. It is practical intelligence or common sense, which might loosely be defined as all of the really important things that you never get taught at school.
- **Moral intelligence:** This measures our motives and methods by their results. Since humans accept feedback, we can learn to close the gap between the good we intend and the good we achieve. Morally, we need to learn to act intelligently and to attain the best achievable level of good practice, as in every other part of our life. Moral intelligence in action means we have to access the best available information, minimise the risks, and optimise the benefits for all involved.

Intelligences do not exist or operate in isolation. We are all born with potential for certain intelligences and combinations of intelligences. While we need to develop all of them, each of our life experiences will determine how much and how many we develop.

CATEGORIES OF INTELLIGENCES

The many different types of intelligences listed may seem overwhelming. But it is possible to categorise and summarise the different types as follows:

- **Emotional intelligence**, which includes interpersonal (social) intelligence, intrapersonal intelligence and spiritual intelligence.

- **Intellectual ability**, which is made up of linguistic, logical-mathematical, visual-spatial, musical, body-kinaesthetic and naturalistic intelligence.
- **Common sense**, which is made up of componential, experiential and contextual intelligence.

In Dr Daniel Acuff's highly acclaimed book *What Kids Buy and Why?* (1997), he explains that while all seven intelligences are being developed or otherwise impacted upon to some degree throughout a person's life, there are critical periods or 'windows of opportunity' during which the development of particular intelligences/skills is most focused. Many of the most essential and foundational learnings, in fact, occur before the age of approximately 11. He cites research which finds that, at approximately the age of 10, a major 'cleanse' occurs within the brain. All unmyelinated neurons (those neurons and neuronal structures that have not been protected by myelinating sheaths) are 'swept out' – ideally leaving behind a much more efficient brain.

Acuff then explains the problem that lies within these critical periods. If key neuronal structures related to different kinds of learnings, learning capacities and abilities – such as first and second language learning, or emotional awareness and expression – have not been firmly established by this time, then this 'foundational' period is over and the window of opportunity is closed. This leaves the individual 'disabled' or at least not fully developed in one or more areas.

Furthermore, since the window of opportunity for maximum neuronal 'structuring in' of certain capabilities is closed, the opportunity for maximum learning of these capabilities is also closed. This, of course, makes the learning of these particular capabilities more difficult, but not impossible. The period from the pre-natal months up to the age of three is perhaps the most critical period of all for learning. The child's need for love and emotional safety is especially intense at this time. Foundational learnings are also occurring in motor skills, early language, and mathematics.

The critical periods of development for Acuff (1997) can be summarised as follows:

- Prenatal to age six – Motor
- Birth to age three – Emotional
- Birth to age two – Vision
- Birth to age two and a half – Social attachment
- Birth to age three – Vocabulary
- Birth to age ten – Second language
- Birth to age four – Maths/logic
- Age three to ten years – Music

Understanding your children's intelligences is vitally important to ensure that their learning button is turned on and not off. This is essential if we are to encourage a love of learning that will last them a lifetime.

In *Seven Times Smarter* (2001), creative educator Laurel Schmidt comments:

> **I think kids know the ways that they're smart and they struggle to give us clues, seeking our validation and guidance. Yet day after day we damage them by failing to notice and respond ... Remember, you're the most powerful force in shaping your child's self-image. If you delight in your children, they feel loved. When you're fascinated by their projects, you confirm their value. Praise their intelligence and you bolster against the negative reviews of the world.**

Schmidt advises us to be exceptionally supportive of our children as they explore their intelligences. She has various simple rules for responding to their development:

- Be a good listener

- Ask good questions
- Avoid criticism
- Be patient
- Do nothing for kids that they can do for themselves
- Be a good watcher
- Be a good cheerleader.

Learning styles

By the time your child is ready for primary school, you may have a good idea of his or her natural intelligences and preferred learning style. Do you have a visual, auditory or kinaesthetic learner on your hands? Is your child dominantly left- or right-brained? Is your child logical and orderly, or creative and imaginative, or a daydreamer? What's your child's concentration like? Is he or she outgoing or reserved? For more detailed and helpful information in this regard, you can have your child's dominance profile tested. It's a quick process that does not require your child to draw or write anything, but it will give you valuable information about how he or she takes in information, processes it and uses it. It can give you excellent guidance about the type of education or school system that may best suit your child, as well as the most effective study methods for your child – and much more.

Children are born with a predisposition to receive information in a certain way. They take in information through their senses and, in every child, some senses will be stronger than others. A child's preferred sensory modality will determine his or her natural learning style – whether the child is a visual, auditory or kinaesthetic learner. The benefit of understanding your child's learning style is that it will help you, the parent, to present information to him or her in a suitable way. It will assist you both to motivate and discipline your child appropriately. This understanding will also enable you to protect and nurture the relationship you have with your child instead of becoming frustrated, exasperated or angry.

How a child *receives* information about his or her environment and the workings of the world is actually more important than how his or her brain *processes* it because the reception determines the quality of information that the child's brain works with. Here are some guidelines to help you to determine your child's natural learning style. Some of these clues will be obvious from babyhood, while others will only reveal themselves as your child moves into toddlerhood and early childhood. Some children are clearly strongly dominant in one sensory modality, while others may utilise a combination of modalities.

Visual learners

- As babies, visual children enjoy looking around and often make noises when they see things of interest. They may also be quick to notice things that are out of place.
- Visual children need to see to learn. Simply telling them about something doesn't help as much as by showing them. As long as visual input is given, such as a picture, the information is likely to be absorbed.
- Visual children tend to look upwards towards the ceiling in a learning situation, which indicates that they are accessing the visual part of the brain.
- Visual learners benefit from sitting in front in class so that the chalkboard and teacher can be clearly seen.
- They also need to summarise their work.

Kinaesthetic learners

- As babies, these children like contact – to be touched and carried around. They also enjoy movement (being rocked, going for a walk in a stroller, etc).
- In a learning situation, the eye movements of kinaesthetic children tend to travel downwards, towards the heart and

hands.

- Kinaesthetic children need to touch, feel and experience. Learning is hampered if there is no physical involvement, or no opportunity for movement, or no triggering of their emotions.

Auditory learners

- As babies, auditory children love making sounds and start 'talking' earlier. They also like musical mobiles.
- Auditory children's eye movements tend to travel towards the ears in a learning situation.
- When auditory learners are told about something, they listen and learn well. They love being asked questions about the tasks they are busy with.
- Auditory learners like to listen first and then to discuss the issue afterwards.

A good teacher presents the same information in all three ways in a single lesson in order to capture the attention of every different learning style represented in the class. When executed effectively, this is one of the benefits of true outcomes-based education.

If information is attractive to your child's learning style, learning becomes fun and your child will have a better chance of grasping new information, understanding it, storing it, and being able to retrieve it for later use. In other words, if you present information to children in their preferred way of learning, it is more meaningful to them. When information has meaning, it is easier to store it in the long-term memory.

Dominance profiles

Information-processing theorists focus on the input of information, how information is stored in the brain, and how it is retrieved when it is needed to solve problems. They are also concerned with attention, concentration and memory. Certainly they all agree that every child thinks differently and solves problems differently, depending on his or her age, maturity and unique wiring.

Most people think of brain dominance as a person being right- or left-brained, and dominance per se as being left- or right-handed. But there is a great deal more to the subject of dominance than is first evident. In fact, the genetic brain dominance profile of a child has a definite impact on his or her personality and behaviour. It also determines how the child will take in, process and act on information for the rest of his or her life.

Your brain dominance profile is determined by many variables, such as eyes, ears, hands, feet and brain parts. A qualified profilogist can perform quick, simple kinesiology tests and put together a detailed report that makes this information accessible and easy to understand and use. This is a very helpful tool for parents and teachers. Understanding your child's profile can help you to unlock his or her potential in a most meaningful way.

A host of other profiling techniques exist, which can be useful in understanding and guiding your child. These are beyond the scope of this book, but information on these techniques is easily available. It's always a good idea – and very interesting too – to test them out on yourself as well!

A USEFUL LIST OF PROFILING TOOLS

- The Seven Intelligences Profile and the Metacognitive Mapping Approach® in *Switch On Your Brain* by Dr Caroline Leaf (Cape Town: Tafelberg, 2005) and www.switchonyourbrain.co.za.
- Genetic Brain Organisation Profiling by Dr Annette Lotter & Associates at www.eduprofile.co.za.

- Brain Dominance Profiling by Dr Melodie de Jager at www.theconnexion.co.za, as well as her books *Brain Gym® for All* (Cape Town: Human & Rousseau, 2001) and *Mind Moves®* (Johannesburg: The BG ConneXion, 2006).
- The Neethling Brain Instrument® by Dr Kobus Neethling at www.solutionsfinding.com.
- The Enneagram at www.enneagram.net; *The Enneagram: Understanding Yourself and the Others in your Life* by Helen Palmer (New York: Harper Collins, 1988) and *The Wisdom of the Enneagram: The Complete Guide to Psychological and Spiritual Growth for the Nine Personality Types* by Don Richard Riso and Russ Hudson (New York: Bantam, 1999).
- *The Five Love Languages of Children* by Dr Gary Chapman (Chicago: Northfield Publishing, 1992, 1995) and www.fivelovelanguages.com.
- Marcus Buckingham's *StrengthsFinder Profile* at *www.strengthsfinder.com* and *Now Discover Your Strengths* by Marcus Buckingham and Donald O'Clifton (UK: Simon & Schuster, 2005).
- *Personality Plus for Parents* by Florence Littauer, (US: Baker Publishing, 2000) – essential reading for personality profiling.

CONTEXT MAKES A DIFFERENCE

Parents must understand the context in which their child is growing up so that they can create the space to enable their child's intelligence and talents to flourish. In their early years we need to make the best decisions and choices for our children. Later we need to help and guide them in making those decisions for themselves to prepare them for their future.

Every context has the potential to enhance or interfere with our children's learning. So let's take a look at early learning in the context of the 21st century:

Qualitative researchers and teachers alike have noticed a marked decline in the length of time that children are able to concentrate attentively during class or a focus group discussion. In a qualitative M-Net study that has been conducted annually for the past ten years (Project Rainbow), findings indicate that peak concentration levels and active attention have declined from 1.5 hours in 1995 to approximately 1 hour amongst primary school children in 2004. This occurs despite the fact that the stimulus material in the particular study is enhanced every year in order to engage the young respondents.

(Carol Affleck, 'I Kid You Not', 2005)

While experts are saying that childhood is changing and that we are even witnessing the disappearance of childhood as we know it[30], the basic developmental needs of children have not changed. Yes, they are a new generation with a new set of challenges, but they are still children. As such, they have predictable needs. For whole and healthy development to take place, these needs must be respected and fulfilled.

In particular, the first seven years of life are highly miraculous and form the foundation for the rest of a child's life. These years are sacred and should be celebrated and supported in every way possible. Preschoolers carry within them the blueprint for success in the 21st century. By having their basic developmental needs fulfilled, this blueprint can be energised and activated, better preparing them for the future.

I need to be seen
I need to be heard
I need to be respected
I need to be safe
I need to belong
When all of my basic needs are met … then …
I am ready to learn.

(Anonymous)[31]

The basic needs of children for development in the foundation phase are listed below. We also need to understand how the new world in which we live could interfere with these developmental needs if parents and teachers are caught unawares.

Table 2.2 *The basic needs of children for optimum development in the foundation phase and potential threats*

A child's developmental needs	How the world is interfering
Children need freedom to explore, to find out how the world works, and to discover how they fit into the world.	Children live in a 'barbed-wire culture'[32] with limited access to the outdoors, playgrounds and nature. Technology is encouraging them to be sedentary screen slaves. Lack of parental presence or role-modelling is also affecting this need.
Children need plenty of physical movement to develop the neurological pathways that wire the brain for more sophisticated functions later on. Physical exercise also develops resilience, perseverance and social skills.	The body is in fact the architect of the brain. Too much sedentary activity fails to stimulate the visual, vestibular and proprioceptive systems, which are the foundations for reading, writing and maths later on in a child's life.

	Childhood obesity and diabetes are the most common problems which relate to lack of exercise and physical movement in children as a result of an increase in on-screen activities.
Children need to eat a healthy diet since their development and mental and physical performance are influenced by their intake of water and nutrients.	Much of our food today is depleted of nutrients for a variety of reasons – from over-processing to sterile soil, among many others. The side effects of added growth hormones are also cause for concern. Most food advertisements on TV promote junk food rather than broccoli – the opposite to a healthy eating plan.[33] They encourage snacking on convenience foods, which are high in salt, sugar, trans-fatty acids, colourants and flavourants, while watching television.[34] Such foods, as well as fast foods, are also convenient for busy parents who are generally in a hurry. But all of them contribute to obesity, diabetes, food allergies and intolerances, as well as concentration and behavioural issues, and even disorders.[35]
Children need plenty of rest. Sleep is essential and important: • for physical growth and a	Children have so much packed into their day that it is often difficult for parents to keep a regular routine,

strong immune system • to balance intense periods of physical activity, which should characterise a healthy childhood • to enable the body to balance sensory overload and prevent stimulation from overwhelming the child • to enable the child to process and consolidate what he or she has learnt and experienced each day.	including bedtime. Sometimes a child's routine is governed by a parent's diary, and parents today are very busy. Children can battle to fall asleep after spending time watching TV or playing on-screen games The fast-moving light rays in these games affect the melatonin levels in the body, which are necessary for good sleep. Stress, anxiety and fear can also affect a child's sleeping patterns.
Children need to develop their imagination and creativity in order to have original thoughts that will help them to solve the problems of the future that are not yet problems. A strong imagination and creativity are highly useful in subjects such as English, art, maths and DT (design and technology).	Excessive TV viewing and on-screen activities are limiting this development in an alarming way.[36] On-screen activities are replacing much of playtime, which is affecting social and emotional development, in addition to limiting creative and imaginative play. The same can be said of children who are over-scheduled from a very young age with extra-curricular activities from lunch time until dinner time with little opportunity for rest, free play, alone time and reflection.

	Even creative art programmes are often so outcomes-based that there is little room for imagination, creativity and originality. In many instances, stances, these programmes are being replaced by creative craft programmes, which is far from ideal because of their prescriptive nature.
Children need to play. Play is the language of childhood. It's a child's work – it's how they learn about the world and find meaning. Children also need play dates in home environments. Remember that they learn the most important things in the sandpit, or swinging from the jungle gym, and not in the classroom. Most of what children really need to learn is caught, not taught, from you, their parents.	Many preschools today are falling into the trap of teaching via semi-concrete or abstract worksheets rather than providing a play-based curriculum through which children discover and learn for themselves through their own physical experience with their world.[37] Some parents push their children into competitive sports and fast-tracked learning experiences at the expense of play. Many children are enrolled in too many extramural activities from a young age, or spend their afternoons in aftercare, which means that play dates are impossible to arrange. Qualitative research conducted among the upper LSM sector in the primary school

	market in studies for K-TV (Project Rainbow and Project Punch, 2004) and for other youth brands reveals that children as young as seven engage in four extramurals on average per week, with some children participating in as many as nine over a seven-day period. This includes sports coaching and matches on a Saturday morning – the latter no longer being regarded as traditional leisure time for primary school children. As adults we question whether children as young as seven or eight still enjoy childhood pursuits and freedom in the traditional sense of the word. The majority of children report that friends do not visit or play at one another's houses during the week, and that socialising is limited to certain weekend timeslots in and among family activities and shopping.[38]
Children need real-life, real-time experiences, especially in the first seven years of life. It is only around the 12th year that the brain is able to handle abstract learning with ease.[39]	On-screen activities are transporting children into a virtual world that is not real. This is fine in moderation and when balanced with plenty of concrete play experiences. On-screen activities should not be a young child's default setting.

Children need to develop social and emotional skills in order to build solid relationships with themselves and others. They learn this best by copying their parents and caregivers. They also need conversation, face-to-face contact and human touch. Emotional intelligence is a better indicator of how well a child will do in life than his or her IQ. (See the marshmallow experiment page 206.)	Children are being bombarded by thousands of messages from advertisers and marketers telling them that satisfaction is based on the consumption of 'things' rather than on relationships. On-screen activities are replacing conversation and affecting relationships, even among siblings.[40] Many families spend family time watching one screen or another instead of engaging in face-to-face conversation. As a result of more working parents and fewer parents at home with their children, there is less conversation taking place between the parent and child on a one-on one basis, as well as less spontaneous interaction. Much day-to-day living is scheduled to fit in with the demands of work.
Children have a driving need to feel that they belong. This is natural for all human beings. If children don't feel this sense of belonging within the family, they will look elsewhere.	This fundamental human need is being exploited by marketers and brands selling the latest in 'cool'. If you don't have it, you can't or won't belong! Owning or wearing the right 'things' now defines who you are and whether or not you fit in. Of course, what's considered cool changes daily, forcing children into a cycle of conspicuous consumption.[41]

	This also forces children into wanting to be 'the same' as everyone else instead of being unique individuals.[42] Our jam-packed schedules are threatening time spent together as a family and can impact on a child's sense of belonging.
Children need to develop and own a healthy set of values. In a world of chaos and change, these will be their anchor and guide. Sound values help us to feel more secure in the world. They assist us when we have to make decisions or take action, even in the sandpit. Values are caught and not taught. They are demonstrated through our words and actions and it is essential that we be consistent in this regard.	Will children get their values from their parents or peers, as in the 'old days'? Or will the brash, noisy marketers, brands and media win their hearts and minds first? Some values being conveyed to our kids through various media include: • Adults suck, kids rule • Don't worry about anyone else's feelings, just look after yourself. • Win at all costs Yet children are also hearing the opposite – and sometimes from the same channels such as: • Because every minute of every day you are a part of everybody. They must find this rather confusing – and who should they believe?

Children need to feel safe and secure in order to access their learning potential. They need to be calm and have a steady heartbeat for optimum learning to take place.	Constant exposure to inappropriate content via news programmes, reality TV and frenetic kids' programmes does not lead to feelings of safety and security.[43]
Children need information to be presented to them in many different ways to appeal to their different intelligences and learning the workings of the brain. styles in order to encourage and activate learning rather than inhibit or stifle it.	When a child is stressed for any reason, his or her heartbeat goes up, which can affect the workings of the brain. Even fast music or computer game soundtracks that play above the heart tempo of 80 beats per minute will affect a child's brain. At this point, the thinking brain shuts down and all input goes into the emotional brain (limbic system) where the child's values, culture and beliefs sit. The child is now totally open to suggestion without protection.
Children need boundaries. Of course, this does not mean living in a straitjacket. But it does mean that establishing a regular routine (boundaries or rules by which we live) provides a certain amount of predictability, which can bring sanity into your household.	With so much on offer today, parents need to be consistent in the boundaries that they set for their children. Where possible, choices for goods and services should be based on children's developmental needs and the family's values. Parents must learn to overcome pester power.
Routine provides a feeling of safety and security for children, which is an optimum environment for learning. Routine does not mean inflexibility. Within	Children thrive on routine from the earliest of days. This does not mean inflexibility. In fact it means quite the oppo-. site. With parents being so

routine there is plenty of flexibility and room for creativity. (Read educational psychologist Dereck Jackson's list of basic rules below, which comprise a good, common sense guideline for parents.)	busy and overscheduled themselves, routine is often overlooked or broken for convenience.
Children need parents and they need time. The importance of parental input cannot be overemphasised. Children need as much time and attention as we can give them, and preferably in a way that they recognise as loving and supportive. It's not about quality time or quantity time – it's about both! (See below for more detail.)	Due to economic factors and changing family structures, we are not giving children the time or attention that they need. Yet parents are the facilitators of their children's lives and play a pivotal role. As far as possible, therefore, they need to be present and accessible. Parents fill the leadership role. When they are absent, children will step into the gap and take control.

Source: This table was developed as part of the presentation by Nikki Bush entitled 'Connecting with Children through the Noise and Clutter', which deals with technology, consumerism and a changing childhood.

The rules that functional families all over the world have in common are few, and they are very simple. Here they are:

1. **We, the parents, are in charge.**
2. **There is a time to go to bed at night and a time to get up in the morning.**
3. **There is a time to eat.**
4. **There is a time to tidy up after you have untidied.**

5. **There is a time to do your homework (once the child is at school).**
6. **There is a time to bath or shower.**
7. **You speak to your parents with respect.**

(Reprinted by kind courtesy of Dereck Jackson, from his book *Parenting with Panache,* 2001)

SO, YOU'RE IN THE MARKET FOR A SCHOOL

Before we know it, the small children who entered our worlds, made us parents and changed us so much, are ready to step into the world of formal education. We enter into partnerships with other people who get to shape our children's lives over a period of 12 years or more. Education is one of the most important things we will do for – and with – our children.

School readiness

We wait with great anticipation for the day our children are able to read and write. But we don't often appreciate the really important stuff – that the foundations for all these sophisticated tasks, including reading, writing, maths and spelling, are laid down long before your child even goes to primary school! This happens in ways that are seemingly unrelated, such as playing shape- or colour-matching games, building puzzles, threading beads, stacking blocks, catching balls, playing imaginary games and climbing trees.

In fact, play is one of the most effective vehicles for early learning. Play is the language of childhood – it is how children learn in a fun, incidental and stress-free way, as opposed to abstract, worksheet-based systems which are more appropriate from primary school onwards. (From 2008,

Grade R will be incorporated into all government primary schools.) Young children need plenty of exposure to concrete learning apparatus (toys and games), movement and outdoor equipment (such as jungle gyms, scooters and sandpits), and creative opportunities (drawing and painting on large sheets of paper). In addition, they need to socialise with other children and adults while also spending time alone.

Believing that childhood is a special time of life brings with it a commitment to honour what children do during this time. Play is extremely important to children, but this importance is not widely understood.

(Ann Miles Gordon and Kathryn Williams Browne in *Beginnings & Beyond: Foundations in Early Childhood Education*, 2003)

School readiness is a journey that starts from birth and takes seven years. It is a process that cannot be completed the year before a child enters formal education. A school-ready child should be able to cope socially, emotionally, physically and perceptually in a formal learning situation. To be 'school ready' implies that a child has reached a certain stage in his or her development where it is felt that benefit will be gained from formal education. However, a child does not become school-ready alone. The child needs to be prepared for the first day at school – a highly memorable day in his or her life. The child needs to build a bridge to enable him or her to move from the known life world to the greater environment of the 'outside world' with its emotional, social, normative, physical and intellectual demands.[44]

A child's ability to learn easily and efficiently is influenced by early childhood experiences such as the degree of bonding with a primary caregiver, physical or emotional traumas (such experiences in utero will also have an effect), overall physical health, nutrition, overall socio-economic factors, the achievement of developmental milestones, sleeping patterns, and much more. A child's maturity will also impact on his or her school readiness.

The foundation for academic success is laid during the preschool years. From birth to the age of six, the brain is at its most plastic and elastic.

- By the age of three, 70% of the brain is physically developed.
- By the age of four, 50% of adult intelligence is already employed.
- By the age of five, your child will have a speaking vocabulary of around 10 000 words – adults only commonly use about 20 000 words!

Veteran preschool educator Martie Pieterse says that unique demands are placed on children when they start big school for the first time.[45] For example, they will have to:

- get used to being away from their family and home
- communicate with and relate to strangers
- hold their own in a group (often large) and be able to assert themselves
- be capable of handling conflict and criticism
- be capable of switching from spontaneous and informal play to a more formal way of learning and working
- be able to work without being continuously praised
- be able to work on their own
- be capable of working quietly and calmly
- be capable of expressing their needs in words
- be able to use basic language and writing skills in order to learn to read, write and draw
- be able to concentrate and complete tasks.

This list makes it obvious that the role of parents and teachers in a child's development should not be underestimated.

> **Remember, even if your child has all the necessary physical skills in all the areas of development, but still does not have the inner skills such as independence, perseverance, resilience, the ability to concentrate on a set task, endurance, self-discipline and daring, she is like a brand-new car without an engine.**
> (Martie Pieterse in *School Readiness Through Play*, 2001)

During the foundation phase, children will acquire and develop a large array of perceptual skills through their interaction with people and the world, their play experiences, and their early childhood education programmes. Perception is about becoming aware through the senses. It's the way the brain interprets the messages it receives through the senses, which is how babies and young children learn.

Perceptual skills should be acquired through a child's experimentation and personal experience – by learning through play as opposed to being taught. Each child will acquire these skills in his or her own time, but he or she will follow a general, age-appropriate developmental timetable.

For your interest, here is a comprehensive list of perceptual skills:

- **Auditory (hearing) perception:** The way in which the brain gives meaning to what the ears hear; vital for all forms of auditory learning.
- **Auditory discrimination:** The ability to hear and discriminate between differences in sound; vital for speech development and spelling.
- **Auditory memory:** The ability to remember what the ears have heard.
- **Body image:** The way in which a person perceives his or her body.
- **Body awareness:** The awareness of the body, its parts and how they function.

- **Classification:** The ability to group objects according to kind or class.
- **Discrimination:** The ability to recognise similarities and differences.
- **Eye-hand coordination:** The way in which the eyes work together (coordinate) with the hands and fingers; vital for sewing, threading, drawing, writing, etc.
- **Figure-ground perception:** The ability to isolate and focus on an object/figure which may be in the foreground or background of a composite picture; vital for reading, writing, spelling and mathematical ability.
- **Fine-motor coordination:** The ability to coordinate the movements of the small muscles of the body, namely eyes, hands, fingers, toes and tongue; vital for writing, speech, sewing, etc.
- **Form perception:** The ability to recognise and name shapes and forms.
- **Form constancy:** The ability to recognise a form or shape, regardless of size, angle, position or colour.
- **Gross-motor activities:** Activities involving large muscles of the body, such as the neck, back, buttocks, arms and legs.
- **Gross-motor coordination:** The coordinated movement of the large muscles of the body.
- **Gustatory (taste) perception:** The way in which the brain interprets messages received through the tongue.
- **Olfactory (smell) perception:** The way in which the brain interprets messages received through the nose.
- **One-to-one correspondence:** The ability to match similar objects or groups to one another.
- **Phonics:** The sounds of the letters of the alphabet.
- **Spatial relationships:** The ability to recognise the position of two or more objects in relation to each other and the observer, e.g. above, below, next to, left and right; closely related to laterality (awareness of left and right),

directionality and language.

- **Tactile (touch) perception:** The way in which the brain gives meaning to the messages received through the sense of touch.
- **Visual (sight) perception:** The way in which the brain gives meaning to what the eyes observe; vital for all forms of visual learning.
- **Visual discrimination:** The ability to recognise similarities and differences by sight; vital for reading, writing, spelling and mathematics.
- **Visual memory:** The ability to remember what the eyes have seen.
- **Visual sequencing:** The ability to arrange objects, symbols, words or numbers in a logical order.
- **Visual seriation:** The ability to place objects or thoughts in an orderly series, e.g. from most to least, small to large, lightest to heaviest, darkest to lightest; essential for mathematics.

(Adapted from *Bridging with a Smile* by Doreen Maree and Margot Ford, 1995)

How to choose a preschool

Few areas of parenthood create more anxiety than the selection of the right school for our children. In our parents' day we were either sent to the government school for which we were zoned or, if our parents could afford it, we attended a private school of which there were only a handful to choose from. Today's parents are faced with an entirely different scenario. We are not necessarily limited to the government school in our area, and a plethora of private schools now exist to choose from, all offering a variety of teaching approaches, value systems and facilities.

While we revel in the wide selection, the responsibility for parents to really investigate their options accompanies this choice. It can be a time-consuming and confusing exercise, but it is one that will really make you think about your own beliefs and values. What is important to you? Where are you going as a family? What do you want for your children? What preparation do your children need to survive and thrive in the future world of work?

Parents usually look for a preschool for their child when they are still fairly green and know very little about the educational development of young children. With this in mind, it would be wise to know what to look for – and why – because this phase of a child's development is hugely important and sensitive. Preschool teachers have a very different academic background and training to primary school teachers because the developmental needs of a preschool child are so different to those of a primary school child. This is also the time when the foundations for academic learning are laid down through the process of play. Teachers without the correct training do not understand this. They may push preschoolers into abstract learning too quickly, which puts undue pressure on them and could possibly interfere with their developmental process.

Uneducated parents often put pressure on preschools to 'show evidence of learning' by way of worksheets and crafts, etc. This can lead schools without strong early childhood development foundations to fulfil these wishes to the detriment of the young learners themselves. Learning through play is a process and not an outcome; it is an experience and not a result. It takes a specialised teacher to facilitate this process and to develop the whole child in partnership with the parents.

Remember that life success is not necessarily determined by academic success. Today there is more focus than ever before on the importance of developing your child's social and emotional skills. Emotional intelligence and the ability to relate to – and handle – people effectively are greater indicators of success than any other factors. Your child is a whole being and you need to find an education system that takes this into account. It's more than evident that the world is changing at a rapid rate, so what kind of future does the school you are considering think it is preparing its learners for? It is essential to consider such important questions.

Preschool shopping checklist

If you are in the fortunate position of being able to choose a preschool for your child, here are some aspects to check:

- The professionalism of the staff: Is the person in charge of the nursery school a qualified educator in early childhood development?
- Are the staff specifically qualified for preschool? Do not be afraid to ask about staff qualifications. At the pre-primary stage, teaching is not only about what your child learns but about how he or she is taught. Your task in the early years is to teach your child that learning is fun and this task must be continued by the pre-primary school.
- What is the teacher-to-child ratio? The younger the children, the lower the ratio should be. In some schools in which there are larger numbers of children, the teacher may have one or two assistants.
- Is the programme geared towards the development of the whole child? Activities should be developmentally appropriate for the age and stage of the child. This varies vastly in the preschool years. It is important to look for a balanced programme that is child-centred and play-directed. The programme should stimulate your child's social, emotional, motor, perceptual, mental and physical development.
- Ask to see a checklist of the daily activities. The daily programme should consist of routines (toilet time, snack time, rest time, etc), creative artwork, free play, gross-

motor development work, manipulative play (problem solving e.g. construction toys and puzzles and fine-motor work such as threading and pegging). Preschool children require a structured day with short 'activity rings' with ample time for free play. Through the routine of the programme, children become familiar with what is going to happen next. This makes them more secure in their preschool experience which is part of their journey to independence.

- Look around the playground and check out the equipment. Is there sufficient equipment and is it well maintained and safe? Check for grassed areas. Ensure there is no concrete under jungle gyms etc. Is the sandpit covered at night to keep pets out and is it covered to provide shade for children during the day?
- Are swimming pools, ponds and water features fenced or netted? Ensure there are swings, jungle gyms or other climbing apparatus. A sandpit and bike track for scooters are also necessary.
- Check if teachers have playground duties. The playground must be supervised at all times.
- Pay attention to the artwork on the walls. Look for large pieces of paper using many different mediums and varied subject matter. Every child's work should be different, which shows that individuality and creativity are encouraged.
- Be wary if you see lots of photocopied, coloured-in pictures on the walls.
- Check the layout of the classroom. This is important in the preschool environment as it is part of providing structure for the children. Are there areas demarcated for different activities, such as fantasy play, a construction corner, a book corner and interest tables?
- Check the cleanliness of the grounds, classrooms and toilet facilities. This shows that the staff care and are careful.

- What security exists to keep children inside the school and to keep strangers out? This is an important fact of life today that must be considered.
- Enquire about the disciplinary measures carried out in the school. Bear in mind that smacking is prohibited by law and humiliating children in front of their peers is unacceptable. What about the concept of a thinking chair, etc?
- Check equipment inside the classroom such as toys, dolls, etc.
- Is there enough equipment for all the children and is there a large variety? Because children need to repeat tasks and movements over and over again, they need a wide variety of games and toys in order to keep their attention and interest.
- How will your child's development be monitored and assessed? Are there formal assessments? What feedback will you receive and when? Regular formal evaluation is essential to identify possible problems at an early stage and to address these. This is one of the important reasons for having qualified staff in a preschool.
- Does the programme and approach make provision for the fact that all children develop and progress at a different pace? Is each child able to participate according to his or her ability? Yet is each child learning to function in a group context?
- Check the aftercare facilities. Who runs the programme and what does it consist of? You do *not* want your child watching TV all afternoon or being left alone unsupervised in the playground.
- Is the school registered? Check for registration with the health department or the Department of Education. Schools with less than 20 children must be registered with the Department of Health, while those with more than 20 children must be registered with the Department of Education.

- Does the school have an Aids policy? What education and guidance are given to the children in this regard? It is vital that children learn and understand not to touch another child's blood and to call for help if a child is injured or bleeding.
- What is the religious or educational approach at the school? Make sure it is in line with your thinking or the way in which you aim to bring up your child. The school might be affiliated to a particular faith, or it may follow a traditional, Montessori or Waldorf approach.

Remember that preschool is not just preparing your children for primary school, but for life. A strong grounding should enable them to take their rightful place as well-balanced adults in society one day.

Commandments for the primary school shopper

Know your child

Every child is unique and has his or her own strengths and weaknesses and unique combination of characteristics. Use the preschool years to track these traits. When shopping for a primary school, you need to bear these factors in mind. The school you select for your child should be one in which he or she will thrive and blossom. Your child's preschool teacher may be a source of good advice.

Know your values

Is it important for you that the school you choose strives to develop the individuality in your child, or that it produces children in a particular mould? This is a significant question because the answer will be different, depending on your outlook. Some people really value the type of child turned out by particular schools. Ask schools what values they stand for and see if they match those that you are trying to instil in your child. The number and sex of your children might also have a strong bearing on whether you choose a single-sex or co-educational option.

Know your lifestyle

Do you work full time, part time or not at all? Are you a single or two-parent family? Where do you live or work? How far away is school from your home or place of work? Choosing a school that is perfect for your child but far out of your way can make life difficult. School needs to fit as comfortably into your routine as possible so that you can arrive on time every day and manage to participate fully in your child's school activities. Is the school family-friendly or totally school-focused? Does it consider the requirements of working parents? Is it emotionally supportive within the classroom of children who come from difficult family circumstances?

Know your budget

It is pointless to send your children to an expensive private school if this demands that both parents work themselves to a standstill to afford it and then have no quality time to spend with their children. Remember that a good education is no substitute for spending quality time together as a family. School fees should not be such a drain on the family budget that you are unable to afford to go out for the odd treat, or give your children other rich life experiences outside of the school environment.

Follow your instinct

When you have looked into all measurable aspects of a school, such as facilities, fees, and so on, it is important to take a bit of quiet time to assess what your gut feel is telling you about the school. Ask yourself about your first impression of the school. Look at the intangibles. Was the human touch evident? How did the teachers speak to the children? You are probably going to look at many schools, which can become quite confusing when they all have similar facilities and profess to have similar values. Talk to other parents who you trust and who know your child. It is always valuable to listen to other points of view. Remember that school selection can be a highly charged issue and everyone has a very personal and even emotional view. Think carefully about the people you choose to speak to.

Know this is a journey

Getting your child school-ready is a journey – that starts from birth – and the next stage of your child's education is no different. It's a constantly evolving process that will need to be fine-tuned from time to time with a visit to the teacher, perhaps some extra lessons, a pair of glasses, extension activities, or even a change in school if necessary. There is a kind of evolution that takes place within your child as he or she grows and develops. Today we are not faced with a one-school-fits-all scenario. If you feel that corrections to the course you are pursuing are required at times (by you or your child), then these are perfectly acceptable and necessary. Children are more resilient than you think. As long as they feel loved and secure, they do adjust to new situations.

Be aware of shopping distractions

- Where are most of your friends sending their children?
- Where are most of the children in the preschool going?
- Where did you and your spouse or partner and the

children's grandparents go to school?
- What is the distance from home to school, or from school to your place of work?

These distractions can heavily influence your choice of school instead of allowing the child's needs and family values to drive the school selection process. Obviously you should not ignore the practical implications of choosing a school that is convenient for you, but you need to find the best balance possible.

FUTURE-PROOFING YOUR CHILDREN

Growing up in the 21st century has its own risks, as we have made clear in the previous section. Indeed, it is parents themselves who are becoming the guardians of their children's hearts and minds and their very development. As a result of globalisation and our exposure to diversity, we can no longer rely on society, our community, our friends or even our religious group to support the upbringing of our children in the same way as we do. Today, even your child's Sunday school teacher may have a radically different world view and set of values to you. This is the way of the world.

In his book *Parenting the Millennial Generation* (2005), psychologist Dave Verhaagen discusses a number of risk factors facing this generation. He then lists 21 'protective factors' associated with good outcomes for children, which fall into six broad categories: emotional, cognitive, academic, personality, social and family. Verhaagen's outlook fits in well with our belief that parents have a greater role to play in their children's development today than at any other time in history, and that there is a great deal parents can do to help future-proof their children, thereby enabling them to shape a more satisfying and successful life.

Verhaagen (2005) explains that the exciting thing about these protective factors is that the majority of them can be enhanced in some way. 'In fact, only two of the 21 – early temperament and high intelligence – are locked in. With the rest the door is open ... if you increase the number of protective factors your child has, you will improve his chances of having a good life.' He takes a common-sense view that there is no point in even trying to be Supermom or Wonderdad who does it all. 'It simply can't be done. However, you might be able to focus on three to five protective factors that have the best chance of improving in your child'.

To help you decide, Verhaagen provides a list of the protective factors and the general chance of improving each of them. This is a useful tool for parents to enable them to make choices and take responsibility for their children's development.

Table 2.3 *Protective factors and their chance of improving*

Protective factor	Chance of improving			
	None	Low	Medium	High
Easy temperament (easy, outgoing, curious)	X			
An average or better intelligence	X			
A likeable personality		X		
Positive and supportive friends			X	
Talks about feelings openly and honestly			X	
Cares about the feelings of others			X	
Feels bad after doing something wrong			X	

A good sense of humour			X	
Believes good choices lead to good results			X	
A good overall student			X	
A strong interest in school			X	
Attends an excellent school			X	
Reads at or above grade level			X	
Feels a strong connection to family				X
A warm and positive relationship with parents				X
Good social skills				X
Enjoys support from members of the same religious faith				X
Involved in at least one positive group activity				X
A strong ability to cope with stress				X
Comes up with solutions to problems in life				X
Positive and realistic goals for the future				X

Source: Adapted with kind permission from *Parenting the Millennial Generation* by David Verhaagen, 2005.

Give them time

All children have a natural and miraculous developmental timetable, as we have already discussed. However, often this timetable does not match the hectic pace of their parents' lives! Do you ever feel that your child operates at a totally different pace to you, or that your child has absolutely no concept of time? How often do you find yourself using the words 'Hurry up' or 'Quickly now!' when talking to your children?

With technological advancements and constantly improving connectivity, it is a fact that we are doing more in less time. Productivity is up and we are busier than ever before. While technology has saved us time, it can also be said that it has stolen our time. Few of us are using our 'extra time' to meditate on a mountain top, or to play an extra game with our child, or to read an additional bedtime story. No, no. The action list beckons. The more ticks on that list at the end of the day, the better we feel about ourselves. *The list o*ften carries more weight for us today than precious moments of quality connection with our loved ones.

Children need time to learn, and they learn a great deal by doing things by themselves and for themselves. As parents we need to be aware of adding in an extra five or 10 minutes here and there to allow for the development of our young child's independence, such as mastering how to do up a seatbelt in the car or to unlock a door with a key. Our children need to know that we believe they are capable.

> What about creating time and space for special moments of quality connection to happen? Nikki distinctly remembers being in such a rush to get to playgroup and not be late for a meeting one morning that she nearly missed such a moment. Ryan, then three, had wandered away from the car while she was packing the boot and had picked a spring flower from the garden to give to her. She was about to tell him to hurry up when she saw the joy radiating from his face as he ran towards her with his gift. It was one of those 'magical Mummy moments' that will always be with her.

Older children love talking in the dark. Just as you have tucked them in and kissed them goodnight, and are heading purposefully through the doorway to finish up some chores or extra work that you haven't handled during the day, you hear 'Muuuum ...' It is likely that many parents have wound up enjoying some of the deepest and most extraordinary conversations with their children in the dark at bedtime. The warmth of bed and the comforting veil of darkness seem to encourage children to talk and share – if you only make yourself available to listen.

Don't forget that we must not deprive our children of time alone when they are not being rushed from one organised activity to the next – time when they can simply potter around at home in a quiet space, contemplating life. They need down time too to allow them to assimilate all that they have learnt during the day. Like any adult, they need to just 'be' – to take a break from the constant state of 'doing'. And, for our children to enjoy this luxury from time to time, we need to role-model it for them – a key healthy habit to cultivate.

American psychiatrist Robert Shaw, a veteran with 40 years of experience in treating children and their families, states that parents are so caught up in the time-pressure 'epidemic' that they think they are doing their children a favour by filling their days with numerous extramurals to ensure they don't 'miss out'. The values of down time and relaxation have been negated in the pursuit of 'smarter, more socially adept and superior children'. An even more serious consequence of pressure on children is highlighted by Shaw's fellow psychiatrists: 'The pressures placed on many children, while undoubtedly inculcating a constricting discipline in a child's life, probably have the unintended effect of delaying a child's finding herself and succeeding on her own terms.'
(Robert Shaw in *The Epidemic: The Rot of American Culture, Absentee Parents and Permissive Parenting, and the Resultant Plague of Joyless, Selfish Children*, 2003)

Make the time

Whether you work full time, half day, are self-employed, or have chosen to be a full-time, stay-at-home parent, there is no doubt that all parents are busy and time stands still for no one. The gap between our pace of life and that of our children seems to be continually widening. This means that we all need to be more conscious of making time to really focus on our children and to leave the outside world behind for a short while so that they don't feel caught up in our generally rushed and harried lives. It is so easy to become impatient if you cannot see and appreciate the miracle of a child's development, or how the presence of your children is so much a part of your own personal development.

Ellen Galinsky, the author of the 'Ask the Children Study' (2000) about working and parenting, found that 40% of children say that the time spent with their mothers and fathers is rushed. When children have less rushed time at home, they usually see their parents in a more positive light. They equate parent effectiveness with the amount of time they spend with their parents. Research by Lewis and Galinsky shows that children say they want more time with their parents in which they can interact informally with them through play and shared tasks.[46]

A recent study by Dr Virginia Lewis of the Australian Institute of Family Studies shows that approximately two-thirds of children think that their parents work about the right amount of time, despite the fact that two-thirds of parents in the same study want to spend more time with their children. The children in this study would like their parents to be available to them but were more concerned with the *nature* rather than the frequency of their interactions with their parents. Children would certainly like their parents to spend more time with them but they want them to be less stressed and tired by work.

We need to find creative ways to connect with our children, no matter what our working scenario is, so that we touch them emotionally and stimulate them developmentally, even when we are on the run. In this way we can banish the guilt that so often plagues us as well as robs us of the joys of parenting.

CHILDREN TAKE TIME

Children take time. Therein lies the problem ... children take so much time.

It takes half an hour to feed a toddler breakfast.
Half an hour to bathe and dress him.
Half an hour to clean up what he shouldn't have gotten into.
It takes half an hour to sit with a four year old working a puzzle for the first time.
It takes half an hour to listen to a six year old's reading lesson.
It takes half an hour to coach a teenager in history.
It takes twenty minutes to share a cup of camomile tea with a young daughter.
It takes fifteen minutes, six times a day, to discipline a child who has decided to test you.
It takes fifteen minutes each night to listen to each child's prayer.
It's easy to see why we may have a problem. All these things that must be done with our children are at war with all that society tells us or that we tell ourselves we must do elsewhere ...

Pat King

(Reproduced from *The Gift of a Child* by Marion Stroud, 1982)

CONVERSATIONS, CONNECTIONS AND CHOICES

We finish this section by reminding you of the triangle of conscious commitment that will provide your family with a framework for stability as you move into the future. The three cornerstones which should receive priority attention are:

- conversations and dialogue
- connection and engagement
- choices and responsibility.

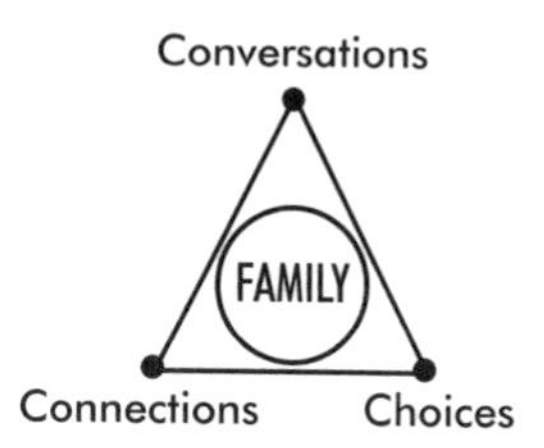

Let's look at what this means in terms of your child's developmental needs *now*:

Conversations and dialogue

- What conversations should you be having with your spouse/partner about your child's developmental needs?
- What conversations should you be having with your child's teachers and caregivers during the important early learning phase?
- Stimulate conversation with your children by playing word and observation games. Convert 'wasted time' into quality time by having fun and connecting with them during everyday routines and while doing mundane chores.
- Let your children help around the house from an early age and talk to them as you are doing things. This is how they improve their vocabulary and learn to care for possessions and property. Teach them how to be kind and helpful.
- Use teachable moments to have conversations about things that matter. For example, your child's questions about mating doves in spring could lead to an age-appropriate conversation about how babies are made.
- Make time to talk. Literally talk your child clever.

Connections and relationships

- How are you going to stay connected to your children and create an environment in which they want to engage with you?
- What do you need to change in order to really connect with your children in a meaningful and relevant way?
- Spend time together doing things or play games *with* your child. Sometimes you may need to do different activities with each of your children because they are unique.
- From time to time, spend one-on-one time with each child.
- Look forward to spending time with your children, in the same space and at the same pace. They know when you *want* to be with them or when you are just being with them because you *have* to be.
- Learn how to be more than physically present with your children but emotionally accessible too. This can be quite a challenge for the multitasking, stressed parent who is over-stretched.
- Leave behind or switch off your cellphone for a few minutes when you collect your child from school so that your moment of face-to-face connection is not disrupted.
- Cook and eat together. These are quality moments which can be inclusive and celebratory.
- Create special family celebrations and rituals – these are the stuff of warm memories.

Choices and responsibility

- What choices do you need to make now for your child's future? Discuss these choices with your spouse/partner, your child's teachers and other relevant adults in your child's life.

- These choices need to be made in the best interests of your child's developmental needs now, with a view to the future for which you are preparing them.
- The choices you make may not be the same as those being made by other families you know. Many people do things differently. This is the 21st century.
- Instead of compartmentalising your time into personal time, work time, leisure time and parenting time, choose to see all of these things as *your time,* integrating them into who you are and where you choose to be at any given moment.
- Children spend only 14% of their time in school from birth to the age of 18, so you are responsible for *what* they do with the rest of their time, *where* they do it, and *who* they do it with. Choose wisely, based on the knowledge you have acquired from their list of inherent needs on pages 74-82.
- Don't panic. Always be flexible. Forgive yourself for any choices that don't work out and make the next best choice you can. Everyone makes mistakes and no one can be perfect. Remember that you are inventing the journey as you go along. What you choose for your child or family and how you put the choices together will be unique to you. There is no 'one size fits all' solution here but just some basic principles to follow.
- Remember that much of what children learn, or need to learn, is caught – and not taught – from you. You are the role-model
- Choose to be fun to be with and your children will want to engage with you.

By connecting effectively with your children – sharing the same time, space and pace, you are building emotional collateral[47] that you can draw on in the years to come. We can be effective parents, even if we are on the run.[48] A highly important aspect of parenting today is integrating our needs and those of our children with the demands and opportunities presented by this Age of Possibility as we battle to adapt to a world that is operating at top speed and changing as we speak. Sections 4 and 5 give numerous practical suggestions on developing the parenting framework for the three Cs (conversations, connections and choices).

Bear in mind that your children's childhood is not *your* childhood. You cannot re-live your glory years through your children or, even worse, try to fulfil your unresolved dreams through their lives. They may be genetically related to you, but they are unique human beings, different from you in many ways. They are on a journey to independence from the day that they are born. As parents, it is your responsibility to prepare them for the world they will enter as adults around 2020.

You should now understand a little more about the new world that we live in (how we got here) and about your child and his or her developmental needs. It's time to turn our attention to the future – to the world for which we need to prepare our children. And now you really need to clutch your hat tightly!

Endnotes

[25] *Toddlersense* by Ann Richardson, 2005.
[26] Dr Gillian de Vos, neurodevelopmental paediatrician, in an interview with Nikki Bush.
[27] Melodie de Jager, educator and Brain Gym expert in 'What is your child's learning style?' by Nikki Bush, 2003.
[28] Articulated in most detail in *Frames of Mind: The Theory of Multiple Intelliogences* by Howard Gardner, 1999.
[29] *Seven Times Smarter* by Laurel Schmidt, 2001.
[30] *Born to Buy: The Commercialized Child and the New Consumer Culture* by Juliet B Schor, 2005; *Consuming Kids: Protecting Our Children from the Onslaught of Marketing & Advertising* by Susan Linn, 2005; Campaign for a Commercial-free Childhood.

[31] Quoted in *Resilience: Social Skills for Effective Learning* by Annie Greeff, 2005.
[32] Youth Dynamix BratTrax®, 2005/6.
[33] *Born to Buy: The Commercialized Child and the New Consumer Culture* by Juliet B Schor, 2005
[34] Ibid; Organisation for a Commercial-free Childhood.
[35] Organisation for a Commercial-free Childhood.
[36] *Brandchild: Remarkable Insights into the Minds of Today's Global Kids and their Relationships with Brands* by Martin Lindstrom and Patricia B Seybold, 2004.
[37] Glynis Courtney, chairperson, ISASA Preschool Committee.
[38] 'I Kid You Not', paper presented at SAMRA Conference by Carol Affleck, 2005.
[39] *Evolution's End* by Joseph Chilton Pearce, 1993.
[40] *Born to Buy: The Commercialized Child and the New Consumer Culture* by Juliet B Schor, 2005.
[41] Ibid.
[42] Ibid.
[43] Campaign for a Commercial-free Childhood, www.commercialfreechild hood.org.
[44] *Bridging with a Smile* by Doreen Maree and Margot Ford, 1995.
[45] *School Readiness through Play* by Martie Pieterse, 2001.
[46] *Working Parents* by Michael Grose, 1996.
[47] This phrase is attributed to Stephen Covey.
[48] Nikki runs an interactive workshop called 'Parenting on the Run'. She educates busy parents on how to cheat time and convert 'wasted time' into quality time with their children. Nikki also has a product called the 'Fun on the Run Box' to help over-stretched parents to connect with, and teach, their children in moments which they would usually consider wasted time.

Section 3

The face of your children's changing future

If each future is unique, if every reality is different, then predictions aren't the point of futuring in any event. Predictions, after all, are answers to questions about the future. It's the questions that count, and each of us has to answer them separately, according to our separate journey through the world. And according to the separate choices we make ... The role of the visionary [isn't] to be a seer but to be a provocateur: to present a series of visions of the future against which those who want to prepare for the future can react. Nobody, after all, knows what the future holds; or who can really know what frames of mind, what receptivities, what structures you need to have in place to meet whatever does eventually come down the pike? And no one is less ready for tomorrow than the person who holds the most rigid beliefs about what tomorrow will contain.

(Watts Wacker and Jim Taylor in *Visionary's Handbook: Nine Paradoxes that will Shape the Future of Your Business*, 2001)

In this next section of the book we take a look at what the world might look like in 2020 to get a feel of what kind of future we need to prepare our children for. It's just a glimpse of what we see coming down the line. Some of it is so radically different from our world today that it should convince you of how essential it is to help your children to build solid foundations in their early years.

Just as our world has gone through radical shifts to reach this point in history, we are going to continue to see *shift happen at an increasingly exponential rate.*[49] In 2007 alone, it was expected that 1.5 exabytes[50] of new information would be generated in the world. This is more information than has been generated in the last 5 000 years put together! We're not saying that all the information is good or valuable – in fact, a great deal of it is junk on the Net! But it really does illustrate the term 'drowning in information'! Information and access to information changes the landscape completely. Remember that whoever has access to information has the potential to shape his or her world, thereby impacting on the rest of the world too. These individuals also carry the responsibility for using that information for good or bad purposes.

Here are some alarming statistics that should make you take this section very seriously:

- Students today are being prepared for jobs that don't yet exist, using technologies that haven't yet been invented, to solve problems that aren't yet problems.
- In 2007, all the computers combined together in the world had about the processing capability (but not speed) of a human brain. It is predicted that, by 2023, when today's first graders are in their first job, a single $1 000 computer will exceed the computational ability of the human brain. By 2049, a $1 000 computer will exceed the computation capabilities of the entire human race!
- The amount of technical information in the world is

doubling every six months. This means that for students studying a technical four-year degree, half of what they learn will be outdated by their third year.

- Right now, there is a one in four chance that you have been in your current job for less than one year.
- At least half of the top 10 job opportunities for 2020 do not yet exist.
- It is expected that today's learners will have 10 to 14 jobs by the age of 40.
- Today's learners will not retire.
- And they will probably live to be over 100 years old. (Consider that in Graeme's 94-year-old grandmother's lifetime, life expectancy in most wealthy countries has almost doubled. Even now, medical science has the means to replace almost every part of the body, and especially those parts that tend to wear out. Why should life expectancy not double again in our children's lifetime? Can you imagine a world in which the leading causes of death are accidents and choice?)
- We have reached a point in human history where the problems we know about – from global warming to nuclear threats, from superbugs and Aids to diminishing oil supplies – will either be solved in our children's lifetimes or will destroy our current way of life forever.

If you are sitting up, wide-eyed, in your seat, then bear in mind that you can – and need to – take two important steps now:

- **Step 1:** Understand the future (read this section).
- **Step 2:** Take action today (read Sections 4 and 5).

THE WORLD OF WORK IS CHANGING

The corporation as we know it, which is now 120 years old, is not likely to survive the next 25 years. Legally and financially, yes, but not structurally and economically.

(Peter Drucker, quoted in *Business 2.0*, 2005)

Graeme's grandmother lives in England. She will receive a letter from Queen Elizabeth II (if Her Majesty continues to hold on to the throne!) on 16 February 2014, which is the day she will turn 100 if her incredible health keeps up. If anyone had sat her down as a teenager in the 1920s and told her what the world would be like in the 21st century (and that she would be around to see it), she would have been incredulous. Not only would the technologies have sounded fanciful, but the very nature of our lives and work would have been unbelievable to her. Could she have imagined the nature and extent of international interactions, open-plan offices filled with diversity of every kind, the casual approach to dress and talk, 24/7 operations, working mothers, mobile phones, laptops, 24-hour news channels, online shopping (online *anything*, in fact), cheap airfares from anywhere to anywhere else, and a global mindset among her own grandchildren? And the list could go on. All of these characteristics are new in her lifetime. In fact, most are new in *our* lifetimes too.

The amount of change Graeme's grandmother has experienced in her nine decades to date is almost nothing compared to what Graeme's children will experience in just the first two decades of their lives. By 2014, when their great-grandmother turns 100, they will be selecting the subjects they will study for their secondary school years. By 2020, they will be deciding on tertiary studies and their first full-time jobs. But what will the world be like? What can we tell them today that, although it might seem fanciful and leave them (and us) incredulous, would nevertheless be helpful in preparing them for that yet unseen world?

Before looking at any specific predictions, it might be helpful just to step back and analyse some key drivers of change in the world at present.

Current drivers of workplace trends

Trends are about change. Every trend is the visible expression of a 'driver' of change. To predict or spot new trends, the easiest place to start is to look at the basic forms of drivers. For example, in a capitalist economy, business is driven primarily by a need to maximise profit. There are only two ways to increase profits: increase revenue (money coming in) and decrease costs (money going out). At one level, all business behaviour can largely be seen as aiming to achieve one or both of these goals.

Society as a whole, and people in general, are also driven by basic needs. We saw some of these in the previous section as we looked at how children develop. Maslow's hierarchy of needs is probably the simplest and most widely quoted summary of the most basic drivers of human needs. These needs include – in this order – physiological needs, safety needs, the need for love and belonging, the need for esteem, and the need for self-actualisation. In addition to these needs, we believe that the following needs will be significant drivers of behaviour and change in the workplace over the next few decades (in no order of importance):

- The need to use time more effectively (it is one of the only resources over which we have absolutely no control)
- The need to do things faster
- The need to make things easier to use
- The need to improve safety and reliability
- The need to lessen our impact on the environment

- The need to connect with others
- The need to filter information and choose who and what to trust
- The need to take responsibility for our own lives.

Probably the single biggest workplace driver of change is the shift in power from the employer to the employee, in line with the effects of globalisation and the emergence of the Age of Possibility, as discussed in Section 1. In the old contract, employees traded loyalty for security. But, in the 1980s and 1990s especially, companies broke that contract with multiple rounds of retrenchments, restructuring, outsourcing, rightsizing and re-engineering. Clever consulting-speak could not hide the fact that security was no longer on offer.

So, employees stopped being loyal. It's about as simple as that. Job-hopping for money became the norm, but even that is changing once again as today's young 'employees' increasingly trade money for the lifestyle they desire. The employer, in many instances, is no longer 'The Boss'. And this has huge implications for individuals living in the Age of Possibility.

The new organization of society implied by the triumph of individual autonomy and the true equalization of opportunity based on merit will lead to very great rewards for merit and great individual autonomy. This will leave individuals far more responsible for themselves than they have been accustomed to being during the industrial period. It will also reduce the unearned advantage in living standards that has been enjoyed by residents of advanced industrial societies throughout the 20th century.

(James Davidson and William Rees-Mogg in *The Sovereign Individual: Mastering the Transition to the Information Age*, 1999)

Major trends in the future world of work

We wish we knew for certain what will happen in the future. We wish we could be completely confident about some of the predictions we will make below. The Hollywood producer and studio owner Samuel Goldwyn once said: 'Never make forecasts, especially about the future.' He was probably right. Predictions are almost always wrong – either in their content or their timing. For that reason, we are not planning on predicting specific events or activities. Our focus will be on major trends and themes – some of which are already evident, and others which we believe will emerge within the next decade. At the risk of being laughed at by our own grandchildren if they should ever read this book, we therefore present an incomplete vision of what the world of work might look like in 2020, and beyond. Our intention is not to predict the future, but to assist this generation of parents *now* to help our children prepare for the possible futures that lie ahead for all of us.

We will also specifically not make predictions about technologies of the future – these will most certainly be wrong, either in their scope or their timing. Although changing technologies are certainly key drivers of change, our interest is in how these technologies will drive change in the workplace. Later in this section we'll speculate on some of the jobs that will be in hot demand by 2020. But our focus is not on the 'wow' effect of newly released technologies or conjectures about an unseen future. Rather, it's on what we need to know about the future to help our children today.

For those readers who might be interested in the basis of our predictions, we have relied on doctoral research done by Graeme in the areas of leadership and future studies. This research was conducted by a team in Graeme's company, TomorrowToday.biz, which includes people studying at the University of Stellenbosch's Institute for Future Studies in the

Western Cape, university professors specialising in sociology and trend analysis, and a global network of researchers who scan and scour media and books from around the world, looking for workplace trends. We also know that the youngest employees and customers of 2020 are already nearly ten years old. As such, their value systems are largely in place and we can analyse them to see what they may be looking for when they arrive at a company's door in 2020. (More details on generational predictions can be found in Graeme's book *Mind the Gap*, 2004, co-authored with Sue Grant-Marshall.)

We're not trying to impress you with amazing facts and information about the future. We're actually just trying to point out the implications of some of the most powerful and obvious current trends. By doing so, we hope that we'll get you thinking. And we hope that you'll understand why it's so important to start as soon as possible to future-proof your children.

Most people overestimate the effects of change in the short term, underestimate them in the long term, and fail to spot where change will be the greatest ... There will be evolution rather than revolution, and it will take years to work through.
(Frances Cairncross in *The Company of the Future*, 2003)

Whether you agree with our predictions or not, we hope that they will motivate you. You need to create some scenarios for the future, and to work out what these scenarios mean for you and your children *today*. Of one thing we are absolutely certain: the world of work that our children enter will be different from the world of work that we inhabit today! Let's take a look.

Work-life integration

The issue of work-life balance is already an increasing workplace trend. People are less and less willing to work

18 hours, seven days a week. They want to be able to work hard, but also to play hard and to have time off as well. They are looking for a better quality of life which entails work-life integration. We prefer this term for two reasons. First, we do not like the implication that work and life are opposites. Work is part of life, and our lives include work. Trying to create a separate box for our work experience is part of the problem that today's young people want to move away from. Second, we do not believe that work-life balance is possible. On the one hand, balance means different things to different people. On the other hand, many people who think about work-life balance tend to think of it as an excuse for lazy staff members to be even lazier. This is *not* what the concept is about.

To this end, we are witnessing the falling away of traditional office hours and an increase in weekends that don't necessarily take place over a Saturday and Sunday. There is also the rise of the corporate concierge service which offers employee support for personal issues, including assisting people to get their cars to and from services, delivering and collecting everything from dry cleaning to pets at vets, making reservations for restaurants, movies or anything else, and much more. The focus is on companies or employers accepting that the 'personal lives' of staff should be something in which they are involved. A plethora of support services are emerging for busy, working parents, from child care and children's taxis to meals-on-demand services. These are just a few of many examples related to time savings.

There is also a shortage of talent and therefore a war for the talent that exists or will exist in the future. This has led to a proliferation of perks to attract and retain the most talented staff members. As part of the new deal that comes with the shift in power in the workplace mentioned earlier in this section, valued employees will be wanting and expecting travel, international work, cultural experiences, mobile technologies, sabbaticals and more. They will want increased control over remuneration package structuring, and constant adjustments thereof. This new generation of talent will increasingly choose more time over more money, and will constantly tinker with the ratios. Time will become the new currency. In recent surveys, as many as a third of workers in the United States said they would prefer more time off rather than more hours of paid employment.

A century ago, futurists were predicting the 'end of work'. A few decades ago, countries were experimenting with the 'three-day week'. We certainly do not predict this for the future. People will be working harder and for longer hours. But we believe they will demand more flexibility and more integration of their 'personal' issues into the work they need to do. So, we need to begin thinking of integrating all the various aspects of our lives.

An illustration might be helpful here. Most people, whether using digital or paper-based diary systems, have a single diary that covers work and personal engagements. The technologies used to manage our diaries – including emails and text messages to confirm meetings, and the Internet to look up details and directions – were all designed to improve efficiency and productivity in the workplace. Yet we have integrated these technologies into our personal lives. So much so, for example, that husbands and wives will often schedule a date with each other by using emails and Outlook meeting requests.

Meeting request from Graeme to Jane: Movies, Tuesday night, 7pm?
Reply: Accept? Reject? Alternative arrangements?

Most people make good use of workplace technologies to enhance interactions in their personal lives. The reverse situation must now also become more of a reality.

- If I answer emails on a Saturday night, can I go to movies on a Tuesday morning?

- If I allow my Blackberry to interrupt my family dinner time, will you allow me to let my family interrupt your executive committee meeting time?

If not, why not?

The arrival of children brings all kinds of chaos into the equation that could never be anticipated, and which will also need to be integrated. Children often present their parents with opportunities to make decisions about work-life integration that require a lot of soul-searching and introspection. They also give us reasons to break out of 'the system' to make changes to our work-life integration that are more workable for us as families. For each family, this will be different.

When Nikki's eldest son Ryan was just three years old, she had been going through a particularly busy few months with her direct selling team. They were doing very well, breaking sales targets each month, and Nikki was working towards earning an incentive trip to the Comores, an idyllic tropical island. To put you in the picture, the team was selling educational toys to parents by educating them on the importance of playing with their children. Needless to say, Nikki was so busy working towards her goal that quality playtime with her own son diminished rapidly.

She will never forget one afternoon when she was deep in multitasking – throwing a meal together in the kitchen, answering endless phone calls, and completing countless orders, all at the same time. Her three-year-old son looked her straight in the eye and pronounced: 'Mummy, you so boring (pronounced borwing)!' It was as if Ryan had actually slapped her across the face. The truth cut her to the core and, in that moment, she knew she was being called to make a very important decision, as much for Ryan's good as her own.

Nikki spent the next four months considering her options. A threatened miscarriage of her second child finalised Nikki's decision to quit. This decision opened up a whole new avenue for expressing her talents and abilities. Building on everything that she had done over the years, but in a more creative and flexible way, Nikki was able to remain true to her values as a parent and to her vision of herself in her various roles of wife, mother and businesswoman.

Such moments cause us to take a breather and to look deep inside ourselves. What do we want out of life? What kind of life do we want for our children? What kind of old age do we want? All these questions deserve serious thought, but they must also be framed in a relevant context. Today, looking back doesn't give us much guidance. We need to be forward-looking and to take our cues from what we know of the future – and not just our future, but the one our children will inherit too.

We can create our own reality if we are prepared to take full responsibility for every move we make in this Age of Possibility. The choice is ours.

Mobile and networking technologies

The Internet and mobile phones have dominated communications since the early 1990s. Their power to change the way we work is obvious. But the immense power of the planet's digital skin will only be truly realised as the implications of Web 2.0 are felt.

At present, in the early 2000s, it is evident that digital social networks are used mainly by teenagers and young people to connect with others who have similar interests. For teenagers it's mainly about common likes and dislikes – music, movies, fashion and other fairly inane commonalities. But social networks are starting to get serious. All of the top candidates for the 2008 US presidential elections used digital networks to connect with potential voters. This is true in other countries too. It was estimated that one in eight Americans who got married in 2006 met through an online dating service. This number will only increase – for two reasons: first, as more and more people use these digital techniques successfully, others will lose their fear and use them too; and second, as young people grow older, they will naturally convert their usage from teenage chats to young adult connections, and then to adult interactions.

We looked at some of the current software and tools for social networks earlier (page 25). This type of software will proliferate, and new applications will be found. The convergence of technologies will fuel increasing digital connections – any content, any software, on any device, anywhere, all the time. Already we are expecting the roll-out of TV shows on our mobile phones and can imagine a time in the near future when every device in our home is connected to the Internet. You'll be able to download recipes directly to your fridge door screen or oven top. You'll watch the news on the mirror while shaving in the morning. None of this is science fiction, yet imagine the impact when everything can speak to everything else, and you have access to it all from anywhere at any time?

For example, a person arrives at the gate of your house and presses the intercom system. You will be alerted, can see the person and talk to him or her through the intercom system, open the gate and the house, watch the person deliver the parcel and leave – all without being there. It's done through your mobile phone's screen and interactive system with your home security. This is what convergence of technology is all about (see page 14) and what Hewlett Packard's Carli Fiorina alluded to when she talked about 'the main event'.

As an increasing number of today's young people enter

the workplace, they will use these types of technologies to collaborate more effectively; to interact with teams, customers and suppliers; to create virtual communities across multiple countries and time zones; and much more. This will mean more mobility and more connections. Conversations and dialogue are important to this generation, and undoubtedly they'll use technology to help them achieve it.

Telecommuting and third spaces

One of the most important implications of the first two trends that we've looked at is the expected increase in telecommuting. This concept refers to people who do not go into an office on a regular basis, but rather contribute from a remote location. This could be their home, a suburban company hub, or even a coffee shop.

We will see a proliferation of so-called 'third spaces'. Not home, not the office, but somewhere in between – both home and office at the same time. The provision of such spaces will become a huge industry. It requires digital connectivity, good food, an ambience that combines both a social vibe and a mix of public and private spaces, and a range of ancillary services.

An outputs-driven workplace

The days of nine-to-five jobs are almost over. Today's talented young generation want their outputs measured and not their inputs. Their approach to their managers is to know *what* is needed and by *when* it is required. Then they expect to be left alone to do it – whenever, wherever, however. It is not about being in at 9am and clocking out at 5pm, irrespective of just how productive you are in this time. Being measured on inputs provides little incentive for this young generation to work harder or be more productive. After all, if they do work harder and are more productive, more tasks will simply be poured into their spare time for the same returns. This is a tough logic to fault!

Perhaps this logic can best be summarised in a table[51]:

Table 3.1 *The philosophy of old and new pay*

Old pay philosophy	New pay philosophy
Pay for the job	Pay for the person and for performance
Job scope and seniority drive pay	Value creation drives pay
Pay what others in the company get (internal equity)	Pay what the individual could get elsewhere (market equity)
Set a range and hire within it	Break the compensation rules to hire the right candidate

This concept is not only applicable in office environments or among professionals. It can also be applied in manufacturing and primary industries. Probably the most famous example is Semco, a Brazilian manufacturer.[52] Simply put, the concept can work like this: a 10-*hour* mining shift can rather become a 10-*ton* shift. The output of tons is measured against an agreed target. The workers have a set time in which to complete the task. When the task is complete, the remainder of the time becomes discretionary – workers can knock off early or continue to work and earn more money for additional output.

Careers as 'portfolios of jobs'

Charles Handy, the British management guru, coined the phrase 'a portfolio of jobs' to replace the outdated concept of a 'career'.[53] When he started work at Shell in the 1950s, there was an expectation of cradle-to-grave employment with a single company. That is now a fantasy in which very few people live.

In 2007, the average 30-year-old had already had five or more jobs, and nearly half of 30-something professionals were not using their original qualification.[54] This trend will simply increase over the next few decades, with young people abandoning all thoughts of a traditional career in favour of a series of jobs, often spanning multiple industries and focus areas.

Self-employment, entrepreneurs and microsourcing

> **Lifetime employment is over. Stable employment at large corporations is gone. The average career will likely encompass two or three 'occupations' and a half-dozen or more employers. Most of us will spend sustained periods of our career in some form of self-employment. Bottom line: we're on our own folks.**
>
> (Tom Peters in *Re-Imagine!*, 2003)

If we are moving more and more, then – for at least a portion of our working lives – it is highly likely that each of us, at some stage or another, will be self-unemployed. This is not a euphemism for unemployed – it is the new reality. People know that their skills can be used on a temporary basis at almost any company. Being an entrepreneur in the 21st century is not just about starting a company and growing it into a listed entity. It's about micro-enterprises that start up, offer a service for a period of time, and then perhaps shut down again as the owner-managers move on in a new direction.

Companies have been outsourcing for many years. They have been using temps for even longer. In the future, they will 'microsource'. They'll employ the services of a small company to fulfil a specific function – usually with a limited time frame – and pay handsomely if the skills and inputs they require are rare and essential.

Daniel Pink tracked the current implications of this trend in his 2001 bestseller.[55] Here are various facts which indicate a shift in this direction (current in April 2001):

- Fewer than one in 10 Americans now work for a Fortune 500 company.
- The top private employer in the US by headcount is no longer GM or AT&T, but rather Manpower Inc., the temporary work mega-agency.
- Between 16 and 25 million Americans are freelancers or independent contractors (the figures are vague because governments don't even know how to measure them yet). There are now three million temps, including temporary lawyers, engineers, project managers, accountants, and CEOs.
- More than half of America's workforce work for companies with less than 100 people.
- As many as 27 million Americans work for a micro-business – a company with four or fewer employees.

Lifelong learning

The two previous trends will require this trend: that people continue to do formal learning and on-the-job training throughout their careers. More universities and colleges will offer short courses and multiple-learning channels for 'mature age' students. It will become commonplace for people to take time out from their careers to do extensive study, often as a prelude to a major direction change in career and industry. This is not about the accumulation of certificates and academic qualifications, but rather about the continual need to keep up to date and relevant.

Robots, automation and artificial intelligence

This is one of the most significant trends of which professionals need to be aware. All routine jobs and tasks that require no creativity will soon be automated. Unfortunately for many professionals, as much as they feel that their work is complex, it is actually not creative. It may take a complex system to replace them, but they are replaceable nonetheless.

> Doctors who work as general practitioners (GPs) are possibly a good example of this trend. They respond completely reactively to patients who walk in to their consultation rooms. Their task is to apply a standard and fairly basic process of diagnosis. If they cannot do a simple diagnosis, they resort to blood tests. But they don't perform these blood tests – they send you to a separate company where a different individual extracts a sample of your blood and sends it to a laboratory. There a machine processes your sample and (if you're lucky) sends an electronic set of results to your doctor, who phones you and reads the diagnosis to you. Once a diagnosis is attained, the treatment is predetermined and not creative. (Who wants to be a doctor's guinea pig?) As soon as the technology becomes cheap enough to do home self-diagnosis, the GP will basically be redundant. Like accountants at present, GPs will probably hold on to their jobs for a decade or more owing to legislation around the scheduling of prescribed medicines. But that will be an artificial environment which cannot be sustained forever.

The 20th century was marked by the automation of physical labour in factories. This trend will continue, and even more labour-intensive work will be automated. But, even more importantly, the 21st century will be marked by the automation of knowledge work – utilising computerisation, thinking systems, artificial intelligence, webbots, and more.

Jobs that depend on routines, jobs that basically follow a set of rules, and jobs that can be reduced to an algorithm or 'recipe' will be replaced first. These will start with basic bookkeeping, basic research, computer programming and similar tasks, but will quickly reach higher up the food chain to accountants, quantity surveyors, registering attorneys, pilots, and any other task that does not require creativity. (Remember, a creative accountant is one who should be behind bars!) These jobs used to be the pathway to the middle class, but soon they will either be outsourced or automated.

The best current example is the voice-activated call centre. These centres may cause frustration for users now, but their sophistication will increase exponentially, and similar systems will be used throughout organisations and industries. An intelligent robotic workforce will change how companies value employees as businesses employ whatever type of mind can do the work: robotic or human. Future human workers may collaborate with robotic minds on projects for a variety of enterprises, rather than work for a single employer.[56]

It's not just repetitive physical activities (such as shelf-packing or mining) and specialised, non-creative activities (such as surgery or manufacturing) that will be automated by robots of varying levels of complexity. Many experts envisage artificial intelligence advancing sufficiently within the next three decades to produce robotic managers, capable of identifying unfolding problems or opportunities, and responding to them automatically. As Freedman (2006) states:

'Right now, the systems depend on managers to provide the 'business logic' – that is, you have to 'teach' the systems how to react to different data ... The next step will be enabling the systems to teach themselves the logic they need to make key business decisions ... None of this means that companies won't need smart managers. It just means that managers will be relieved of much of the monitoring and troubleshooting that

make up their days now. With this new technology in place, their emphasis will shift toward more strategic and creative decision-making efforts.'

(David H Freedman in 'Meet your new executive',2006)

Creativity and knowledge work

It goes without saying that automation will continue to destroy manual labour jobs. Computerisation will also have a huge impact on the new world of work as more and more office jobs become automated. In order to ensure that jobs in the service sector as well as those of 'knowledge workers' are secure, these people will have to infuse their work with creativity and imagination, qualities that are not characteristic of computers (for the foreseeable future anyway).

As Florida (2006) confirms: 'Creative-sector occupations – in science and technology, art and design, culture and entertainment – have grown since 1980 from 12% of the workforce to between 30% and 40% in most advanced countries today. This makes talent the fundamental factor of production, and attracting such talent the central battle in global competition.'[57]

A global stage and a melting pot of diverse world views

The company of tomorrow will extend across traditional boundaries. It will be more diverse than ever before, and connect to an increasing diversity of suppliers and customers. This relates to different countries, as globalisation continues. But it also refers to different languages, cultures, religions and world views. We don't believe that an inevitable 'clash of civilisations'[58] will occur in the future. We are actually optimistic that the next generation of young people will find ways to integrate diversity into their world views.

We believe that today's young people will learn to see

themselves as global citizens with a rooted cultural heritage. It is likely that a period of deep soul-searching on the issue of identity will take place. People will come to identify themselves as much with the companies they work for as they do with the nations they live in, the languages they speak, and the gods they worship.

Mobility of talent

The demand for skilled workers will continue to outstrip the supply on a global basis. The mobility of skilled labour around the world means that competition for talent now stretches across the globe. As a result, there will be an increase in creativity in recruiting, benefits, perks, retention strategies and 'employee value propositions' (EVPs) in all industries. This mobility will only add to the previous trend, multiplying the diversity factor in workplaces.

In addition, today's generation of American young people will migrate heavily overseas. 'For the first time in its history, the United States will see a significant proportion of its population emigrate due to overseas opportunities. According to futurists Arnold Brown and Edie Weiner, Generation Y, the population segment born between 1978 and 1995, may be the first US generation to have many of its members leave the country to pursue large portions of their lives, if not their entire adult lives, overseas.'[59] The US has experienced a century of being the land of immigrants. It will certainly be a different world: for Americans at home, and for everyone else with more Americans abroad.

The role of women

The connection economy requires leaders to show increased proficiency in relationships, emotional intelligence, co-operation, and networking. The leadership characteristics required to make a success in this new world of work are classically 'feminine' characteristics.

Masculinity in the workplace ensures focus, but femininity gives everyone permission to connect on an emotional level. Without emotion, the workplace is like a machine without oil! For too long the focus in the business environment has been on gender issues and on emphasising the differences between men and women. The futurist view is more inclusive. When an organisation adopts more 'feminine' values, such as teamwork, recognition, less hierarchy and more flexibility, an Ernst & Young Work/Life Balance study done in the USA in 2003 found that the organisation became a better place for both men and women to work. Feminine values increasingly make business sense, across genders.

(Grant Driver and Helen Nicholson of the 'He Says–She Says' presentations, 2008)

At present, many women try to succeed in the workplace by adopting what are generally seen as male characteristics. They too play the power-based, competitive, testosterone-filled, dog-eat-dog, workaholic game. It's not that women *can't* compete – they can if that is what they wish. But rather, women need to recognise that there is no necessity to compete. In the near future, we believe that more and more women will see their function as changing the workplace to exhibit more feminine characteristics. Men must learn these competencies too – if they wish to survive.

Ageing populations

While the world's population will continue to grow (it's likely to reach nine billion people by 2050), the average annual growth rate will continue to decline. Most developed nations will soon have declining populations, with fertility rates below the replacement level. The countries most immediately affected by ageing populations include Japan, Germany, Italy and the Scandinavian countries. Other countries, especially in Western Europe and North America, will find a need to import young workers within the next few decades.

A key implication of this probable trend is that companies will see the age range of their workers span four generations. In the US, 'workers over the age of 55 are expected to grow from 14% of the labor force to 19% by 2012'.[60] This will have huge implications for management and team interactions as well as the customer base of companies.

Deferring retirement

As the baby boomers (born in the period after World War II in 1945 into the 1960s) head for their mid-sixties, they are the youngest, healthiest and richest old people the world has ever seen. And they realise that they are nowhere near ready to retire. This is partly because they don't have the nest egg they thought they would have (their consumption levels, lack of savings and bad investments are coming home to roost), and partly because they have longer to live than they thought they would have. Additionally, they don't *want* to walk off silently into the night. They have a lot left to contribute, and nothing is going to stop them.

There is an additional reason why boomers are not going to retire – their companies don't want them to. As we saw in the previous section, the developed world is experiencing a collapse in birth rates. This means that as older workers prepare to leave for retirement to 'make space at the top', their companies are finding that there are insufficient young people willing to join at the bottom and make up the numbers. The 'war for talent' will not only be at the young end of the workplace, but also among mature workers as companies become increasingly desperate to hold on to the staff complement they need to get their work done.

A major possible implication of this trend is a looming generational war. In most developed nations, wealth is disproportionately held by the older generations. For the first time in history, it seems unlikely that the wealth will be handed down to younger generations in significant amounts. The baby boomers are unlikely to retire or give up their positions of power, making it increasingly crowded at the top of the pyramid. In countries with large retirement costs looming (such as the United States) in which younger generations are expected to pay for the retirements of older generations rather than each person paying his or her own way, difficult and painful changes will be required in the near future. This is likely to divide voters along generational lines as never before. This has already started in some countries. In Israel, for example, a political party was voted into office (in 2005) with a mandate based solely on entrenching generational privilege.[61]

Relationships and connections

From everything that we've said so far, it might seem probable that people will retreat into separate and isolated worlds, only connecting with others through digital screens and voicemails. While it is true that we expect a massive increase in digital communications, this does not imply that we believe people will become disconnected. In fact, we believe the opposite.

As a result of the choices and options available, people will default to what they have always defaulted to – doing business and connecting with people they trust. Trust is the new currency. Within the next few years, 'trust passports' will be common on the Internet. Like Amazon.com or eBay's current systems for evaluating people within an online e-commerce community, we will all have trust ratings that will help us to interact with each other with more confidence. Consumer watchdog bodies and advocacy groups will continue to proliferate.

The future isn't what it used to be

Experience isn't what it used to be. In fact, by its very definition, experience is something you get just after you need it (think about that!). Experience is most valuable in an environment in which what happened yesterday happens again tomorrow – an environment with little change or, at worst, in which change is predictable and the future is little more than an extrapolation of the past.

But in an environment of discontinuous change, such as the world of the 21st century, the easiest way to fail is to attempt to repeat or even simply improve on past successes. Just as 'good is the enemy of great'[62], so experience is the enemy of innovation and adaptability in tempestuous times. When 'tomorrow' is hardly ever a repeat of 'yesterday', the danger is to think that we understand what is going on because 'we've seen this before'. In fact, experience is actually what you get when you don't get what you want.

The trends that we have looked at in this section are not the most mind-blowing trends. Nor do we begin to claim that we've given a comprehensive list of trends. Our goal was to encourage you to leave yesterday behind and focus on tomorrow. For those with young children, tomorrow seems a long way away. Yet it will be here sooner than you think. You can't plan for it. But you have to prepare for it, starting now.

One of our key themes – choices and responsibility – will best be taught as it is caught from you. Our view of the future is not a prophecy, it is a possibility. It is your responsibility to do what we have tried to do – to look into the mist of the decade that lies ahead in order to discern the shape of things to come. You then have to choose how to respond to it. Are you simply going to hope it stays predictable and similar to what you know now, or are you going to realise that we live in a time when monumental changes are taking place? If you do believe this, then it is your responsibility to stop doing what you have always done, and to stop thinking the way you always have thought, and to start making changes to your attitudes, mindsets, behaviours and activities.

The discussion that follows will help you to change your mind about what jobs your children should be considering, and give you an idea of what qualifications might be useful.

JOBS OF THE FUTURE

The sun is setting on the Information Society – even before we have fully adjusted to its demands as individuals and as companies. We have lived as hunters and as farmers, we have worked in factories and now we live in an information-based society whose icon is the computer. We stand facing the fifth kind of society: the Dream Society ... [It] is emerging this very instant – the shape of the future is visible today ... Future products will have to appeal to our hearts, not to our heads. Now is the time to add emotional value to products and services.

(Rolf Jensen in *The Dream Society: How the Coming Shift from Information to Imagination will Transform your Business*, 2001)

Lawyer, doctor, engineer, accountant, actuary, architect, vet or various other of the fairly limited range of 'professional' qualifications is what parents of the past few decades have desired for their children. While some of these are safe bets for the next few decades, we're not convinced that all of them are great choices for the children of the 21st century.

As we saw in Section 1, the professions were the first winners in the shift from the industrial era to the information age. But now we're heading into the Age of Possibility where it's not just about head knowledge but also about connection. Some universities are working this out. The University of the Witwatersrand's Medical School in Johannesburg, for example, has started to set entrance exams that do not simply test academic ability. The ability to obtain distinctions in subjects such as science, biology, and maths does not predict whether a teenager will make a good doctor. Doctors require emotional intelligence, empathy, resilience and other characteristics not measured by final-year school examinations (Matric, A-levels and the like). So, some very clever kids are being turned away from medical school – much to their disgust and dismay. But, these universities have a point. The world of work is changing, and some of the old established norms and rules for success are being altered.

In this section we continue our predictions and become more specific about which types of jobs we think will be in demand in the future, and which jobs will not. Our focus is not on specific job descriptions, but rather on categories and industries. Once again, we are not aiming to impress you with almost unbelievable, wild and breathtaking predictions of super-sexy job titles and careers based on technologies that don't yet exist. That sort of fantasy thinking is exciting and we encourage you to indulge in it at some stage – just to stretch your mind. The task we have set ourselves is different: we want to help you to prepare yourselves and your children for some of the possible futures that are likely to emerge if the trends we identified in the previous section are realised.

Again, we don't expect you to agree with our analysis completely (especially if, as a parent, you have made your money as a lawyer, accountant, engineer or actuary!). But, once again, we hope that we will provoke your thinking, and that you will act today to secure your children's future.

Remember, your children are still likely to be working in 2070! Now, there's a thought ...

Growth industries

The following is a summary of some of the industries that

are likely to experience significant growth over the next two decades. These industries will offer important career options for our children as they enter the world of work around 2020.

We start with a graph from the US Department of Labor, based on research it completed in 2003. Few other countries undertake this sort of research at government level in quite the way that the US does. This list is a good indicator of what could happen across many developed countries, as well as in the developed sectors of developing economies.

Of course, in large and important developing economies such as India and China, as well as in countries with large disparities between upper and lower class such as South Africa, Brazil and Russia, there may be slightly different opportunities and dangers for jobs and careers in the near future.[63]

Figure 3.1 *Occupations with the largest numerical increases in employment, projected 2004–2014*

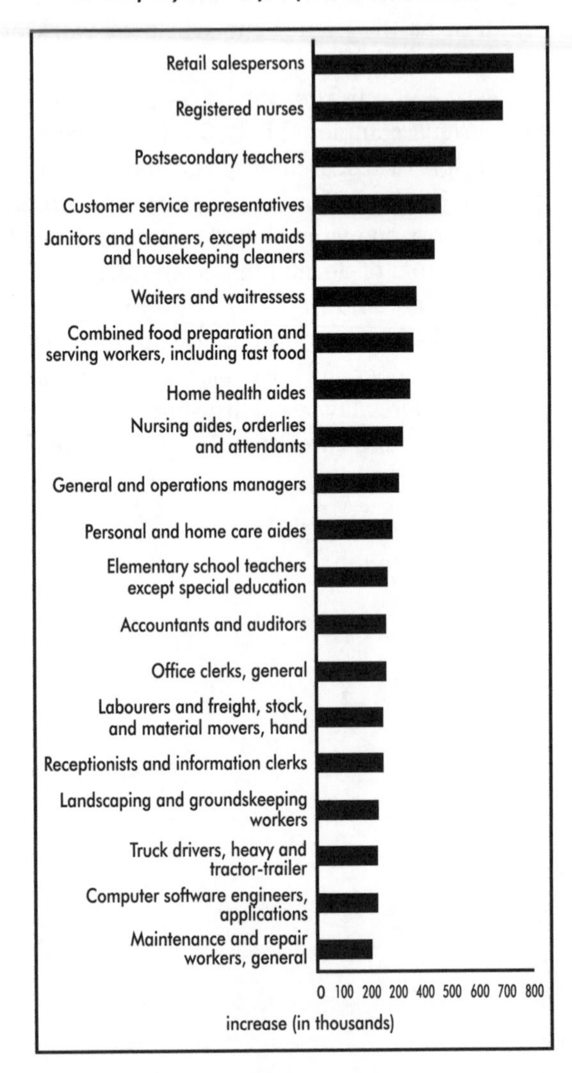

Source: US Department of Labor, Bureau of Labor Statistics. 'Tomorrow's jobs' (time horizon: 2004–2014); www.bls.gov/oco/oco2003.htm

Healthcare and social support services

Worldwide, no industry will grow faster than healthcare and social assistance, including private hospitals, nursing and residential care facilities, and individual and family services. It is estimated that this industry will grow by more than 30% in the next decade alone in the USA, adding nearly 4.5 million new jobs to the US economy. Around the world, increasing levels of income will bring an increased demand for quality of life and healthcare. Governments will also be placed under increasing pressure to provide minimum levels of healthcare for all people in all layers of society.

Employment growth will be driven by increasing demand for healthcare and social assistance because of an ageing population and longer life expectancies. Also, as more women continue to enter the labour force, demand for childcare services is expected to grow.[64] Advances in medical science will bring new cures and treatments. This is happening at the same time as some diseases appear to be mutating, with the spectre of a global superbug emerging. Whichever way it goes – good or bad, or both – the requirement for medical and social services will increase exponentially over the next few decades.

Medicine, genetics and pharmaceuticals

Linked to the previous section is the role of medical research and drug development. Obviously there will be continued efforts to cure some of the diseases that afflict humanity – from the killers such as malaria, TB and Aids, to the diseases associated with an ageing population such as Alzheimer's, cancer and dementia. There will also be continued research into 'lifestyle cures', including sexual dysfunction, hair loss and weight control.

In addition to current trends, however, there will be a

marked increase in work in the arenas of biotechnology and genetics. As we write this book, debates rage about stem cell research and cloning. We are convinced that more and more countries will not only allow, but also actively promote, research in these areas. And medical talent will flow to these countries very quickly when it happens.

Research into genetics will also focus on the two areas of disease and lifestyle. For example, in addition to a cure for Aids or a vaccine for malaria, there may be a huge demand for genetic dieticians – people who create diets and weight-control medicines tailored to people's individual genetic make-up. This new field of pharmacogenomics will account for an explosion in medical training and employment opportunities.

In addition to research, there will be an increased demand for medical sales representatives. But owing to the increasing complexity of medicines and the proliferation of options, these reps will need a high degree of medical training. There may also be a marked increase in information and technology that allows home medical care and self-diagnosis, supported by travelling pharmacists and medical practitioners.

Another growth area will be in genetic research on plants and animals. For example, to feed everyone on the planet for just the next 40 years, we will need to produce as much food as we have done in the whole of human history up to this point, combined! In order to do this, genetically modified plants that can grow in less than ideal conditions will become widely utilised. Research, new-style farmers, support staff, geneticists and advocates will all be in high demand.

Financial services

Individuals will increasingly take control of their own savings, financial management, and especially retirement planning, with a proliferation of technology options for day trading, asset management and flexibility to move investments between funds, investment options and countries. The need to create additional investment options, and to provide less risk and greater reward in an increasingly complex and interconnected world, will see a huge increase in the 'back office' part of the financial services industry. As employers shift more of the responsibility for health decisions and financing onto employees, both groups will require assistance in navigating the evolution. There should also be an increase in the need for financial advice and brokerage to assist people to understand and manage the complex options being developed around the world. Of course, technology may do much of this, but then, someone has to build and maintain the systems.

Other major reasons for the expected increase in this category of employment is the increased number of baby boomers in their peak savings years, the growth of tax-favourable retirement plans around the world as governments attempt to encourage people to save more and the globalisation of the securities markets. An interesting possibility is the coming together of the healthcare and financial services industries to deal with issues of retirement healthcare planning, with offerings that incorporate the sophistication of financial planning into consumer healthcare.

This is just one example of a trend that is likely to affect many industries: cross-discipline or multi-disciplinary professionals. Doctor-actuaries, engineer-doctors (to create and implant bionic body parts in people and animals), legal-accountants (this combination has been around for some time already, created mainly by the big auditing firms becoming involved in consulting services), architect-occupational therapists (to design ergonomic and therapeutic living spaces), and so on.

Tourism and hospitality

The rise of nearly two billion middle-class Indian and Chinese citizens with increasing levels of disposable income will lead to a global surge of tourists. This has only just started – a flood is expected in the next few decades. In addition to new countries entering the tourist market, the baby boomers will become a generation of 'denture venturers'.[65] These are people taking a gap year in their senior years to globetrot. The difference between them and young adult backpackers is the amount of money that will accompany them and the luxury in which they can afford to travel.

In addition to all the obvious services – from the booking and arrangement services of the travel agency, insurers and financial services, to the airlines, cruise ships, rental agencies, food and accommodation providers, tour guides and extreme sport coaches, there will be additional requirements in the future for services such as technology support, the shipping of purchases, security, translation and the provision of trusted information.

Travel will extend itself to parts of the world that are currently untapped, from remote deserts and ice floes to the ocean floor and space. This will impact on construction, transportation, engineering and the many more jobs required to design, create, maintain and utilise new areas of our world.

In addition to changes in tourism, the hospitality industry – including MICE[66] travellers, and local restaurants and pubs – will continue to grow. Job growth will be concentrated in food services and drinking places, reflecting worldwide increases in the adult population and in dual-income families (often with fewer children and less discretionary time) as well as greater dining sophistication.

Leisure, sport, entertainment and the arts

Closely related to the previous section is the issue of how people choose to use their leisure time and discretionary income. There will be an increased demand for all forms of entertainment, both passive and active, as well as for content in all manner of media that deliver entertainment. Job growth will also stem from public participation in the arts, entertainment, and recreation activities – reflecting increasing incomes, leisure time, and especially an awareness of the health benefits of physical activity and fitness.

We will always need artists and entertainers. There will be continued work for those who write books, who screen movies, plays and TV shows, for music, and for the artists and sportspeople who perform and entertain. Positions requiring a high level of creativity and originality will still be highly valued for decades to come since these are the most difficult jobs to automate and computerise.

Nanotechnology and micro-engineering

'The next big thing is very, very small.'[67] Nanotechnology is engineering at an atomic scale – creating tiny machines that will do everything from mining gold to keeping your clothes wrinkle-free without ironing. These miniscule machines are sometimes called MEMS: microelectromechanical systems. There will be an increasing requirement for micro-engineers to build these machines, but designers will be required to conceptualise them, 'mechanics' to service them, and salespeople and advocates to introduce them to the market. They will generate an entire industry.

As an aside, this is the first of our categories of jobs of the future that will create a wholly new industry, with wholly new jobs and infrastructure. Can you imagine what skills will be required to make this industry successful? What subjects do you think your child should study today to be best prepared to join this industry? Do you know who to ask to find these answers?

For a different perspective on these questions, ask yourself what *you* should have studied and what *you* should have done back in the 1970s in order to be prepared for the IT revolution that took our world by storm during the eighties and nineties? That revolution changed the world, creating millions of millionaires, and it will continue to shape our future for years to come. Were you ready for it? What would you tell yourself if you could go back to 1976[68] now? How can you help your children prepare for this nano-world that doesn't exist yet?

Employment services

As a result of the increasing outsourcing of non-core functions and the need for more high-level temporary and project-related staff, the provision of employment services, placement agencies, head-hunters and staffing solutions providers will increase. As we noted in the previous section, the need to develop micro-enterprises to outsource even more non-core issues will increase. One example of how this might work is the current growing demand for e-lancers. These are freelance workers who use the Internet to bid on doing work for anyone, anywhere.[69] This will allow individuals around the world to make money from any and all of the skills they have available, and to be completely flexible in the provision of these services to the highest bidder.

Education

The US Department of Labor expects private educational services to grow by 32.5% and to add 898 000 new jobs to this field by 2014.[70] Rising student enrolments at all levels of education, together with the increasing demand generated by 'mature age' students, will create high demand for educational services. In view of all the other changes taking place in the world, workplace training and skills retraining will continue to be a growth industry.

In addition to traditional educational solutions, there will be an increase in the use of multimedia, training via videos and video games, online learning solutions and intelligent learning systems. Designers and programmers for these systems will be required, as well as content specialists and educational experts. We have begun to feel the implications of the overwhelming flood of data into our lives. We will need to spend several decades adapting new ways of learning, filtering, analysing, processing and transmitting data, information and wisdom (while working out the difference between these things). The Internet allows us to access information faster than ever. But most of us still require guides to help us use what we find there. This means huge job potential for people who can organise, filter and streamline information, or train us to do it ourselves.

Information technology

In addition to traditional IT functions, there will be increasing demand for some of the fast-growing, computer-related industries such as software publishers, online publishing and broadcasting, online collaboration ('social networking'), Internet service providers, search portals and data-processing services. The US Department of Labor expects employment in computer systems design and related services to grow by 40%, adding almost one-quarter of all new jobs in professional, scientific, and technical services by 2014. Employment growth will be driven by the increasing reliance of businesses on information technology and the continuing importance of maintaining system and network security.[71] This issue of security – at national, corporate and personal levels – will continue to grow in importance and presents significant career opportunities for the foreseeable future.

As we already know, there is a need for people to work in IT companies, and an ever increasing need for IT professionals of all kinds to work in companies – large and small. Most countries around the world are currently experiencing a shortage of skills in this industry, and will continue to do so for years to come. For example, The Canadian Advanced Technology Alliance, an industry association representing 1 000 high-tech Canadian companies, estimated a current need for more than 52 000 technology workers in Ontario alone in 2007. Adding weight to our previous suggestion about cross-functional professionals, the president of the Alliance, Paul Swinwood, suggested: 'There is huge potential for people who have strong work experience or a degree in another field to re-educate themselves in this rapidly expanding sector.'

New media

Often called multimedia, the new media refers to the convergence of television, radio, video, graphics and text – delivered digitally to you through a multitude of global networks. Examples of new media jobs already available in 2007 include video game scriptwriters, web page designers, animators and compositors, bloggers, journalists and vloggers (video bloggers, who mainly use YouTube and other similar video-sharing sites to upload TV-like content and make it globally available for free). The overlap with IT jobs in providing the technology platforms and infrastructure is obvious.

WHO DO YOU TRUST FOR YOUR NEWS?

John Stewart's *The Daily Show*, a feature of Comedy Central and CNN, was ranked in late 2006 as one of the top three most reliable news programmes on US television, even though it is clearly a satirical comedic look at the news. Traditional news media will continue to lose public trust.

The new media reflects the artistic side of information technology. And, as we stated earlier, there will always be work for people who can write or draw.

Kathryn Saunders trained as an architect and then studied computer animation before she was hired by the Royal Ontario Museum in Toronto as a creative director. One of her team's recent projects combines live-action video with computer graphics and realistic sound effects to simulate the experience of being inside an erupting volcano.[72]

Design

If you agree with what has been said in the previous few sections then this set of career opportunities should come as no surprise. Almost every product, every service and every industry needs to be packaged and delivered to the market in new and exciting ways that capture attention. In a world of oversupply and proliferation of goods and services, only those items that compete successfully for attention and connect emotionally will be sold. People who can design packaging, develop advertisements and create connections through visual, auditory and other sensory design will become increasingly important. Tom Peters reckons that they'll be more in demand than MBAs. In fact, they already are – mainly because of under supply, but still, he makes an interesting point.

The MFA [Master of Fine Arts] is the new MBA [Master of Business Administration].
(Daniel Pink in *A Whole New Mind*, 2006)

For every ten MBAs graduating in the USA in 2005, there was one job available. For every one Fine Arts graduate, there were ten job offers.
(Tom Peters in *Re-Imagine!*, 2006)

Companies that already understand this design issue include Apple computers, BMW, Nike, Manchester United, Virgin and many others. They will require more and more people to fill design positions across different functions and line areas within their businesses.

If we are slightly more futuristic, we suggest that employment will grow for those people who design experiences for others. This includes those involved in hospitality, tourism and adventures. Success will go to those who are able to put these services into exciting packages and market them effectively using enticing design.

Alternative energy and global warming

There is massive debate about the world's oil and gas supplies – at worst we have supply left for a few decades, and at best about a century or so. Either way, it's a problem our children will increasingly need to deal with. One of the major future energy sources will be nuclear power. The British government unveiled plans in 2006 to train thousands of young people to work in the industry at a special Nuclear Skills Academy.

Of course, there are major untapped oil reserves that would require concessions from governments, the public and environmental groups to mine, but the necessity to keep us fuelled would probably overrule the desire to protect areas such as the US Arctic National Wildlife Refuge in Alaska. Or perhaps not!

In addition to the dwindling supplies of fossil fuels, there is the related issue of environmental destruction being caused by the way we are living on the planet. The media hype is currently around 'global warming' – a concept that encompasses concerns ranging from rising sea levels to droughts, and the lack of recycling to the depletion of the ozone layer. Environmental issues will become increasingly sensitive, with the consequences of neglect, indifference, ignorance and arrogance becoming ever more evident, and the demands of the general public ever more insistent.

Employment opportunities will abound in this arena. Research is required into alternative energy supplies and sustainable usage of resources. More and more companies will emerge to assist individuals and organisations to become more 'green'. And, inside corporations, do not be surprised to find job titles such as 'Director of Energy Efficiency' or 'Environmental Manager' as companies become increasingly aware of these issues and realise that they require conscious management and supervision.

Disaster relief and recovery

The ravages of global warming and extreme weather, potentially resulting in natural disasters including tsunamis, monsoons, droughts, floods and rising sea levels, will see an increased demand for specialists in weather forecasting (and control, if that becomes possible), disaster management and emergency relief. Of course, there will also be room for creative solutions to prepare for devastating natural or human-made disasters, including opportunities for structural and civil engineers, surveyors, architects, politicians and town planners.

Logistics and delivery services

As online retail sales continue to climb, the world's postal services and overnight delivery services will have to deliver more and more packages. This industry is likely to remain outsourced, as it is today. All of this is great news for drivers, pilots, mechanics, packers and other jobs associated with this labour-intensive industry, which requires large warehouses and massive haulage assets, and is restricted by – and reliant on – geography.

Of course, home delivery of purchased items, from groceries to high-end electronics, has already been on the rise and will continue to be driven by the need to save time and increase convenience. This trend should continue until someone invents a sci-fi-like teleportation or replicator system. But that's probably just fantasy, so don't hold your breath. The delivery industry will be here for a long time yet.

> Logistics is already a lot more than simply delivering goods. For example, as early as 2004, UPS had signed a deal with Toshiba laptops. When customers contacted Toshiba and required repairs to their laptops, UPS would not just collect the laptops but would also fix them. Toshiba's entire PC and laptop support system was outsourced to UPS, the 'brown' delivery company.
>
> Not only will there be new employment opportunities, but you might also have to look in different places for those opportunities. An IT repair technician as a delivery company![73]

Government

The power and influence of governments may be decreasing as the influence of international organisations, multinational companies and online communities increases. But the requirements for government to attract and retain top-quality talented people at all levels will increase as citizens of countries demand higher quality service delivery and more infrastructure over the next decades.

The role of government will continue to include the provision of basic essentials such as water, electricity, gas, etc, through utility companies, as there is an increasing demand from business and residential customers alike. There will be growing demand for planning and development functions too. This will include urban planners who will need to have expertise in areas as wide-ranging as architecture, horticulture, ecology and technology.

Recent experiments in privatising utilities have been overshadowed by massive fraud, especially in the Enron scandal when California attempted to privatise energy supply. The market has been spooked by this, and for many years will continue to rely on government for a fair proportion of basic services in communities. If there is another major global economic depression, it is highly likely that governments would step in with massive job creation programmes. This means that there will always be jobs in the public service.

FAST COMPANY'S TOP 10 JOBS FOR 2007

Let's step back from the future, and look just at the year in which most of this book was written. In their January 2007 edition, this is what *Fast Company* magazine predicted for the year ahead.

- **Experienced designer:** These talented individuals work in the retail industry, creating the essence and aura of a store. Experience designers go beyond the look of a place, creating a unique experience in which shoppers can immerse themselves. The shops created by an experience designer are often considered works of art – mini universes unto themselves.
- **Medical researcher:** Researchers in cancer and Alzheimer's and the developers of prosthetics are the most coveted titles in the healthcare industry. Major developments are taking place, not only in medicine but also in the way that doctors file medical records. Individuals with the know-how and creative juice to mix tech with medicine can expect seven-figure salaries.
- **Web designer:** Trendsresearch.com reports that the

profession is still in its adolescent phase and 2007 would herald a new era of web design. Monster.com[74] charted a 26% growth rate in this field for 2006, which would continue to grow. And it certainly is doing just that ...

- **Security systems engineer:** Monster.com reports that individuals in the protective services industry can expect a rise in demand and salary. Advances in Vegas casino-like security systems and satellite maps are helping to wire the world for defence. Individuals with a head for engineering and computers can easily expect a seven-figure salary in this industry. From sonar imaging to keystroke identification, keeping our country and our world safer has never been easier or more profitable.
- **Urban planners:** From the Hong Kong International Airport residential tower to suburban 'McMansion' sprawl, individuals in residential planning and development can expect a lot of work in the near future. Urban planners must meet the demand for real estate that is both decadent and practical. Prefab one-level homes engineered for the ageing baby boomer population are changing the face of suburban America, and boosting the demand for urban planners.
- **Viral marketers and media promoters:** Not to be confused with people in advertising or public relations, a viral marketer knows how to build an audience from nothing – with little more than rumour and excitement. Known for such coups as MySpace's *Lonelygirl15* and *The Blair Witch Project*, viral marketers begin 'contagious' campaigns that spread largely through word of mouth and social networking websites.
- **Talent agents:** As Clint Eastwood would say, 'These days, everyone is famous.' And as fame and fortune grows for performers and athletes, a new arena opens

for their managers, promoters, and general go-to guys. Although these titles may speak for themselves, duties for those fortunate enough to get close to the stars often include things such as latte retrieval and limo reservations. Yet, next to the celebrities themselves, these positions are some of the most competitive in the entertainment industry.

- **Buyers and purchasing agents:** Trend forecasters predict that the retail industry, specifically the department store, need major rethinking and restrategising. Much of the fate of department stores lies in the hands of the buyers and purchasing agents. These individuals are in charge of store inventory and make decisions on the colour, size, quantity and country of origin of items. The recent vicissitudes of the retail industry have made these jobs often hard to come by. They can be very lucrative if store profitability increases.
- **Art directors:** From Broadway to movie sets, any job that involves paint, lights, cameras and action is in demand. Now perceived as the ultimate career for inspired artists with an affinity for pop culture, art directors, set directors, and stage production directors clamour for the top positions, which call for hands-on creative genius with a couture designer's eye.
- **News analysts, reporters and bloggers:** The Internet has created a new realm for reporters and writers, who previously only saw their names and ideas in print. At present, publications with an online division often hire three levels of correspondents: print news writers, online news writers, and bloggers. Although most personal blogs are not sufficiently profitable to stand alone as businesses, writers can use their increasing popularity as another gateway for their voices to be heard.

Declining industries

As part of our tour of the future, it is also helpful to see the flipside of the picture, and to identify various current industries and jobs that are likely to decline or disappear in the next two decades. We will also make some suggestions about where opportunities exist within these industries. We start again with a graph from the US Department of Labor.

Figure 3.2 *Graph of declining industries and jobs*

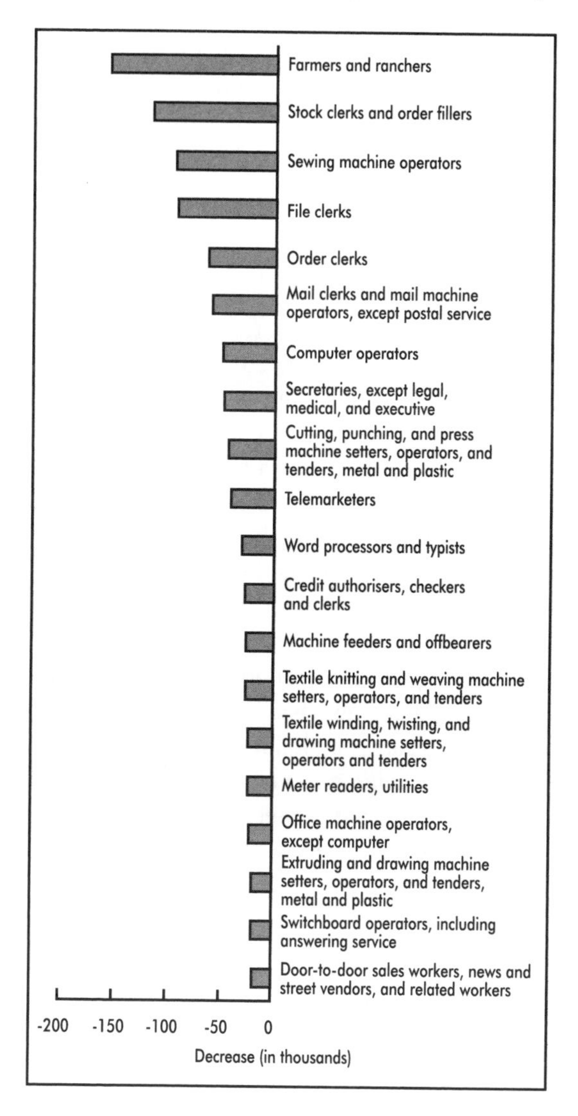

Source: US Department of Labor, Bureau of Labor Statistics. 'Tomorrow's jobs' (time horizon: 2004–2014); *www.bls.gov/oco/oco2003.htm*

As customers become increasingly comfortable with online purchasing, the need for massive malls and shops that carry large amounts of stock will decrease. Customers who need to see, touch, taste and smell goods before they purchase will still need to go to shops, so they won't disappear completely. However, we can envisage large department stores that carry just one of each item that they are selling. Customers will stroll through with handheld scanners selecting the items they wish to purchase. Having created their 'wish list', they will download it to a website, edit it, and then pay for it. Their 'shopping trolley' will then be delivered from a central warehouse a few hours later.

The need for store shelf packers, cashiers, floor staff and managers, security and all the other people who make big stores functional will gradually be reduced. Only shops that cater for experiences and provide entertainment in various forms will survive, but they will not look like they do today.

There is nothing new about shopping but the methods of shopping are changing. The virtual world is redefining economies of scale, as digital information can be reused infinitely. The Net allows a company to make information available that is simply too expensive to deliver in the physical world. Information can represent interactive, value-added services that will save you time and put you first.

(Ronnie Apteker and Jeremy Ord in *Do You Love it in the Mornings?*, 1999)

There is an interesting upside potential for small, local stores. We can easily imagine that people will do all their pre-packaged grocery shopping online, but would want to pop down to the local greengrocer for fresh fruit and veggies. Employment in IT and information-related services will increase as customers search for assistance in making purchasing decisions. Another way to ensure continued retail employment will be to create experiences, rather than just opportunities to purchase. Although the Internet has changed the way consumers buy almost everything – from books and DVDs to holidays, flights and hotel bookings, many consumers still want to get out and visit the shops for social opportunities that cannot easily be replaced by online interaction.

> In New South Wales, Australia, there is an experiment in providing information using text messages. While shopping, you can SMS the bar code of a product and your current location. Within a moment, you will receive a return text message giving you comparative prices and alternate store locations within five kilometres of your current location for the product you're looking at. Customers can already use their web-enabled cellphones to compare global prices with the price a local store is offering on various products. They have to factor in delivery costs, import duties, insurance and the delay they will experience in getting the goods – but at least they have all the information required to make an informed decision. People who provide this type of information can be paid by the users or, more likely, by advertisers.

Agents

The middle person in many business transactions will gradually disappear, largely as a result of technology and competition. This is called disintermediation, which is happening in every industry, from supply chain management to estate agents. The loss of agency jobs will not only affect car salespeople, but all agents at all levels of sophistication, such as stockbrokers and investment bankers (who are agents between investors and users of capital).

Technology and increased consumer awareness are removing the need for intermediation from agents – sellers and buyers are connecting with each other directly. And, with increased competition, neither the supplier nor the customer will be willing to pay for the added cost of a middle person unless he or she adds substantial value to the transaction.

TACTICS FOR A 21ST-CENTURY ESTATE AGENT

The real value an estate agent can add is not only to assist you in setting a fair price for your house, but also to tell you how you could get a better price. Tell the clients what to spend money on to improve their chances of a favourable sale – anything from planting flowers to putting up mirrors in small rooms. It may not take a lot of effort, but there must be a hundred little things that can make all the difference to a potential buyer. In other words, the agent should actually bring some expertise to the task of sprucing up a house for sale.

Why not go even further? Agents could put their own money into a property in order to raise its value. This changes the agency relationship – the seller and agent agree on a set price. Anything over that price is given to the agent. In this case, if the agent feels a coat of paint would be a good thing, the agent pays for that paint because he or she knows how much extra value that coat of paint would add.

The only agents likely to survive are those who are the agents of a new breed of talented people. Among a multitude of voices, Tom Peters[75] and Daniel Pink[76] have best articulated the trend of free agents. Just as talented sports and entertainment stars need agents to represent them, we predict that talented 'stars' of the future world of work will have agents too. We see no reason why not.

Call centre operators

The continual theme of this section is that those careers based on scripts, which do not require (or do not *allow*) creativity, will decline. Automated systems, artificial intelligence, voice recognition and voice-activated technologies will continue to replace human beings in contact and call centres and on help desks.

Note that we're not saying that call centres will decline. In fact, quite the contrary – they will proliferate. But they will become increasingly automated. The best paying jobs are likely to be the technicians, programmers, scriptwriters and possibly even the voice-over artists.

Manufacturing, farming and mining

Primary and secondary industries are all likely to see technology and automation continue to destroy jobs. Farm labour has declined by nearly 90% over the last century as combined harvesters, computer-controlled irrigation and nutrition systems have changed farm work forever. Factories have been automated over the past 50 years. Mining is still quite labour-intensive, but it is also increasingly becoming automated. Some futurists even predict that mining could take place using smart bacteria that eat away at rock and minerals, and are then harvested. However it happens, the reality is that there will be fewer and fewer labourers, which means fewer and fewer supervisors, which means fewer and fewer managers will be required.

There will be some job creation but again, these jobs will be for creative thinkers and technology experts. Precision farming will provide some opportunities, especially the computerised management of crops to suit variations in land characteristics. Automated tractors will drive across fields, constantly mapped according to pinpoint GPS coordinates. As they progress, precise data about soil composition, water levels, required nutrition, and other crucial factors will influence and control how much seed, fertiliser, water, and pesticides are delivered in order to ensure optimum production. Farm equipment manufacturers will need high-level technical skills and creative experts in farming on their teams. Farmers will need computer programmers and system designers on their farms.

Similar requirements for top-end architects and engineers will emerge in factories and mines. But these will not be engineers as we know them today – they will need a broad range of skills, especially design (as in aesthetic design, rather than structural design), computer programming and system design, as well as creative flair.

Construction

The experts are heavily divided about this sector. On the one hand, employment in construction is expected to increase, driven by a demand for new housing and an increase in road, bridge, and tunnel construction. On the other hand, similar to the previous section, advances in technology and the use of robots may reduce the requirement for physical labour, supervision and engineering oversight on these projects.

Professions

This is probably the most contentious category on this list of declining jobs, but we agree with Tom Peters, world-renowned management guru, that white-collar jobs will decrease in the next few decades in the same way that farming jobs disappeared over the past century. All those people who sell their knowledge by the hour are in danger, and especially those who do not bring creativity to their jobs.

Here are some examples of professions that are in danger of

being replaced:

- **Airline pilots:** We may feel unsafe thinking about planes flown by computers, but early evidence indicates that they may be safer. Most fatal plane crashes are due to human error anyway, aren't they? Pilots are not there to be creative – they respond quickly in predictable ways to specific and predetermined circumstances.
- **Quantity surveyors:** A design plan entered into a CAD (computer-assisted design) program can calculate precisely what materials are required. Linked to the Internet, it can even get spot and future prices and give an instantaneous quotation for the job. Of course there is more to quantity surveying work than this, but it can be automated when it is just responding to prescribed work.
- **Accountants:** Bookkeepers can obviously be replaced by technology, but even chartered accountants who act only as historical auditors are in danger. They follow specific rules and ensure that you follow them too. They are not allowed to be creative.
- **Lawyers:** In 2006, certain legal practices in England began to provide free legal advice for the general public. You go to their website, type in your concern or issue, and you will receive a free response regarding the legalities of your situation. In many routine issues, lawyers do not use creativity – they are simply the custodians of knowledge that the rest of us don't have. But if we can put all case law on to a DVD, make it intelligently and intuitively searchable, a lot of work for lawyers will fall away.

That being said, there will probably always be a need for attorneys. However, we think that as the public begins to understand how the cost of doing business has risen due to the influence of trial attorneys, there should be some reduction in demand for that sort of lawyer. We can only hope. There is likely to be an increased demand for patent and intellectual property lawyers, as well as estate and tax-planning lawyers. But these will most likely be specialist experts in specific fields such as bio-tech, tax law, copyright law, etc. They will be experts first and lawyers second.

- **General practitioners:** As mentioned previously, even doctors are in danger. For most common diseases, the general practitioner does nothing more than diagnose. This is done through a set series of observations (about swollen glands, bloodshot eyes, high blood pressure or pain). If you know what to look for, anyone can make these observations. Doctors don't even do blood tests – a nurse usually takes a blood sample from our bodies and sends it to a laboratory. We could either utilise home blood-test kits, or go directly to the lab ourselves (and there won't be any human beings at the lab either). Only doctors who go beyond diagnosis to real empathy and care will survive.

Other professions are in danger too. Many professionals are simply in danger of being offshored. For example, when surgeons use micro-tools for keyhole and specialised surgery, they do not actually touch their patients. As long as we can trust the computer connections and networks, the surgeon could be thousands of kilometres away and it would make no difference. This is already happening where patients located in the US are being operated on by Indian doctors located somewhere in India. If that can happen with *surgery*, consider how easily we could offshore lawyers, accountants, engineers, architects and any other profession.

If you think it can't happen to you, then cast your mind back 100 years and think of all the people who thought that machines could never replace them. And yet it happened. To think it couldn't happen to you is a delusion.

So, how then do we prepare our children for such an

uncertain future? What should they study? What aptitudes, knowledge and skills will they need to secure their employment, no matter what happens to the labour landscape? The answers to these questions are the focus of the next section.

LOOK BACK TO LOOK AHEAD

If you don't think that these jobs could disappear, then take a quick look back over the past few decades at various examples of jobs that were once in great demand but are now almost extinct in most developed countries:

- **Typesetting (the 'typing pool'):** Typesetting began in the 1400s with the first printing presses. The trend away from typesetting to desktop publishing started in the early 1980s and was completed by the mid-1990s. The golfball typewriter made way for the personal computer, and thousands of typists lost their jobs.
- **Secretarial dictation:** Individuals now do their own word processing, with no need for secretaries.
- **Punch card operators:** Prior to 1985, punch card data entry employed tens of thousands of people. They were made obsolete almost overnight as punch cards were replaced by other forms of digital input.
- **Telex operators:** They became obsolete with the advent of the fax machine in the early 1980s.
- **Fax machine operators:** As the cost of fax machines decreased and they were no longer considered prized technology assets, most people handled their own faxes. Of course, most fax machines gave way to email in the mid-1990s.
- **Telephone and switchboard operators:** Once a premier job, demand was reduced significantly by touch-tone systems and then later by voice recognition technology.

- **Film splicers and editors:** Digital formats for filming replaced the old cut-and-paste approach to editing film, both for home video and Hollywood.
- **Draftspeople:** Manual drafting using a pencil and ruler was replaced by computer-aided drafting/design (CAD) in the 1980s.
- **Dockyard loaders:** Unloading a timber ship in 1970 took 108 men five days. By 2000, it took eight men only one day. That's a 98.5% reduction in man-days (540 to 8), owing to containerisation.[77]
- **Farm labourers:** The formal agricultural sector employed about 80% of the workforce in 1820. By 1900, this had fallen to 40%. By 2000, this number had fallen to 2% as a result of combined harvesters and similar technologies.[78] While not 'extinct', the reduction in these last two labour sectors is simply sensational.

What won't change

Now, at both ends, there are jobs that are going to be fixed. At one end are people who are really special and specialized: Michael Jordan, JK Rowling, your brain surgeon – no problem, they're safe. They're not going to be outsourced or digitized. At the other end are people who are localized and anchored: your butcher, your baker, your candlestick maker, this camera-man here until they get a robotic camera, so they're all fine.

(Thomas Friedman, 2006)[79]

People's fundamental needs will remain unchanged for many decades. We all need to live somewhere, to eat, interact, connect, be entertained and so forth. Jobs that are related to servicing basic and local needs are unlikely to be relocated, although the technology used to complete the jobs may change over time. These very local jobs – including artisans such as auto-repair technicians, plumbers and electricians; product and service providers such as restaurants, supermarkets, retail shops and shopping malls; and local amenities, such as petrol stations, utilities and Internet service providers – are all likely to remain in business for decades to come. Our children must be equipped to keep up with technology changes, but these basic products and services will still be required to help local communities to function.

Equally, as the quote from Thomas Friedman points out, the most highly specialised jobs of today, especially those that require high levels of skill and/or high levels of creativity, are likely to remain in demand for many decades to come.

It is the non-creative, intermediary, middle-management type of jobs that will disappear before our children reach adulthood.

Entrepreneurs, intrapreneurs and employees

In everything we have said in this section and the previous one, we have made little distinction between three major categories of employment. *Entrepreneurs* are those who work for themselves and start their own companies. *Employees* are the individuals who work in those companies, sometimes with access to share options and partial ownership, but mainly working for a salary. *Intrapreneurs* are a hybrid of the two – creative and innovative employees who, with or without prior management approval, attempt to bring the rigours of an entrepreneurial mindset to bear on their workplace. The benefits that may arise often become the property of the employer. But then, the risks of it not working are probably also held by the employer.

We believe that more and more people will prefer to work for themselves, and small companies and entrepreneurs will abound. But of course, being an entrepreneur is not for everyone. Some people flourish in more structured and predictable environments. Others simply don't want the stress of starting their own companies.

It is not within the scope of this book to guide you or your children in deciding what form your future employment should take. Understanding who you are and how you can be your best, however, is a critical factor for future success. The traits that will assist in making this decision will begin to emerge during the teen years. Thus, some form of assessment should be taken as early as possible so that decisions and plans can be formulated during the middle-school years.

Whether as an employee, intrapreneur or entrepreneur, there is a set of skills, attitudes and characteristics that will help our children to be successful at whatever they attempt, wherever they find themselves. It is to this list of success factors that we now turn our attention.

Endnotes

[49] Karl Fisher and Scott McLeod, 'Shift happens' (online video), ibid.
[50] An exabyte is one million gigabytes or 10^8 bytes.
[51] Reprinted from *The War for Talent* by Ed Michaels, Helen Handfield-Jones and Beth Axelrod, Harvard Business School Press, 2001.
[52] Read about this concept in the writings of Semco's CEO, Ricardo Semler. His books include *Maverick!*, 2001, and *The Seven-Day Weekend*, 2004.
[53] Handy has used the phrase a few times, but perhaps most impressively in *Beyond Certainty: The Changing World of Organisations*, 1996.
[54] Research done by The Association of Graduate Recruiters in the UK and South Africa.
[55] *Free Agent Nation* by Daniel Pink, 2001.
[56] The World Future Society, 'Forecast 2007', accessed on 10 July 2007 at www.wfs.org/forecasts.htm.
[57] 'Minds on the move' by Richard Florida, *Newsweek*, 2006.
[58] For more on this, read Samuel Huntington's book and essay of the same name, 1998.
[59] 'Forecast 2007', ibid.
[60] Ibid.
[61] The Pensioners Party gained a number of seats in the 2006 election in Israel by promising elderly voters free medicine, free public transport and a variety

of other privileges for retirees.
[62] *From Good to Great: Why Some Companies Make the Leap ... and Others Don't* by Jim Collins, 2001.
[63] For some insights into how companies can change to connect with poor communities, we recommend *The Fortune at the Bottom of the Pyramid: Eradicating Poverty through Profits* by CK Prahalad, 2006.
[64] US Department of Labor, Bureau of Labor Statistics. 'Tomorrow's jobs' (time horizon: 2004– 2014), www.bls.gov/oco/oco2003.htm.
[65] Credit for this label goes to Sophie Campbell in an article by the same name in *The Spectator*, 2006.
[66] Meetings, Incentives, Conferences and Exhibitions – this category of global traveller is one of the fastest-growing travel demographics in the world.
[67] *10 Lessons From the Future: Tomorrow Is a Matter of Choice, Make It Yours* by Wolfgang Grulke, 2000.
[68] 1976 is the year in which Steve Jobs and Steve Wozniak of Apple computers unveiled their 'portable computer', which became the PC as we now know it.
[69] Many websites have been set up to put your job request out to 'auction'. The label 'elancer' comes from one of the most well used of these sites, www.elance.com.
[70] Tomorrow's jobs, ibid.
[71] Ibid.
[72] 'Jobs for the Future' by Elinor Florence, 2006.
[73] 'The Next Delivery?' in *Business 2.0*, July 2004.
[74] Monster.com is the world's largest online recruitment and placement service.
[75] Probably best seen in *The Brand You 50 Or: Fifty Ways to Transform Yourself from an 'Employee' into a Brand that shouts Distinction, Commitment, and Passion!*, 1990.
[76] *Free Agent Nation* by Daniel Pink, 2002.
[77] 'What will we do for work', *Time* magazine, 22 May 2000.
[78] *The Economist*, Millennial special edition, December 1999.
[79] Thomas Friedman, author of *The World is Flat*, in an interview for the updated edition of his book, 2006.

Section 4

Preparing our children for their future

So, whose job is it to prepare our children for their future, and what needs to be done? These are the questions we will attempt to answer in this section.

We believe that keeping an eye on the future, and doing what needs to be done to prepare our children for that future, is a primary responsibility of parents today. As individuals, parents can adapt to changes more quickly and more easily than educational institutions can. Family units are smaller, more nimble and flexible, and therefore more able to respond to the world and prepare for change. Schools can only build on family foundations.

What is the best preparation for our children? We need to be honest in our assessment of what helps – and what does not. Whatever the answers to this question, it is clear that the role of parents has become more significant in the preparation equation than for any previous generation. As parents, we are largely responsible for the development of our children's talent as well as how they will use their access to information to respond to the opportunities and challenges on offer globally.

WILL SCHOOL PREPARE THEM?

The simple answer is no, schools alone cannot prepare our children for the future. Let's explain why.

For many centuries, societies have relied on a formal education system to develop their children. In ages past, this entailed private tutors for the very rich and on-the-job artisan training for labourers. Over the past few centuries, however, a system of public education has made schooling accessible to everyone. Of course, a significant divide in the quality of education that money can buy still exists but today, almost every child in the world has access to at least a decade's worth of formal education.

Yes, most certainly, we need to send our children to school for numerous good reasons, including the opportunity to socialise, to experience human nature at work and to learn from each other. But as many experts today agree, the system is rather outmoded, with its roots going back to the industrial era in the 1800s when children were educated to join the production lines of the world. In those jobs, they did what they were told and they didn't ask questions.

The problem is that many schools have not changed their teaching techniques to meet the advances of the Information Age. If we are correct in stating that we are now at the zenith of that age, and a new era of connection and possibility is currently emerging, then schools have to undertake a massive catch-up job. Yet most of them are mired in politics (the education and health portfolios tend to be the most controversial in any democratic government), and endless debates over the curriculum and timetabling.

Add to this the fact that teachers' wages have steadily decreased in real terms over the past century, and you end up with an industry staffed partly by overworked, underpaid saints who feel a calling to their task, and partly by grumpy, outdated civil servants who can't wait to retire. Of course, there are some great schools and some superb teachers, who do their best under extremely trying conditions, but the reality is that teaching and schools are currently in crisis. And that's not great news if you are the parent of a young child at the start of the 21st century.

The importance (or not) of school

School *seems* to dominate the lives of our children. Although they spend most days there, in reality they only spend 14% of their time in the classroom from birth to the age of 18! It seems much more than that, we know, but it really isn't. Of course, it's a critical 14% because of the content and focus on teaching, yet it's only a sliver of our children's time.

School will help, but it is not grades that will prepare your children for the world of the future. Bearing in mind that schools 'teach to the test'[80], the X-factors for success are not that easily tested. They are competencies that need to be role-modelled by parents to their children, which are more likely to be caught and not taught (see page 176). Children learn a great deal on the run by interacting with real life and conversing with their parents and other significant adults.

Thomas Stanley has not only found no correlation between success in school and an ability to accumulate wealth, he's actually found a negative correlation. 'It seems that school-related evaluations are poor predictors of economic success,' Stanley concluded. What did predict success was a willingness to take risks. Yet the success-failure standards of most schools penalized risk takers. Most educational systems reward those who play it safe. As a result, those who do well in school find it hard to take risks later on.

(Richard Farson and Ralph Keyes in *Whoever Makes the Most Mistakes Wins*, 2002)

So, why do we place so much emphasis on getting good results at school? It's because we don't know what else to do! The herd mentality is strong. We know that, even if we are wrong, and even if school results are no predictor of success, at least our children will be ahead of the pack if they get good results. The fact that the herd may be hurtling towards a precipice is a thought we block from our minds!

This is a tough thing for us to face as parents. We really don't want to experiment with our children's futures. We know the whole system is set up in a certain way and so we feel compelled to ensure our children fit into the system's mould. Universities look at school-leaving results to determine entrants. School results are determined by being less creative and learning how to memorise and regurgitate information. New curriculums and new approaches (such as outcomes-based education or OBE) attempt to address these concerns, but very few parents (and many teachers!) trust or even understand the system.

The best schools in the world, and the countries that rank the highest in educational achievement, do not follow a national curriculum – they have designed their own.[81] The imposition of a national curriculum in many countries presents serious threats to excellence, especially for exceptional students and individuals.

Societies build schools that achieve much less than they promise, tend to frustrate students, and generally fail to assist children to become adults who can think for themselves. The development of flexible, enquiring minds has rarely been the primary consideration in the design of educational systems. Of much greater concern has been moulding students into proper members of society than developing students who are creative thinkers.[82]

A QUICK EXERCISE

We are presenting a fairly negative view of the education system in this section. Here's a quick exercise to prove that, for most of us, this is how it has been for many years.

1. Think back on your own school experience and list the top 10 lessons that you learnt. Do it now, quickly.
2. Now list your best three teachers/mentors from your school days. What made them great? What were the things they taught you?
3. Finally, try to work out – as a percentage of the total amount you learnt at school – how much of what you learnt you still explicitly use today.

We are convinced that the most important part of education has to do with what happens outside the classroom – the socialisation and the life skills learnt. Yet many schools focus on the information and facts more than these other issues.

Our objective in this section is not to cast a poor light on schools, but rather to convince you of the important need for parents to partner schools in their children's education. Of course, there are many schools that understand what we are saying in this section, and do their best to provide holistic education for children. If you are fortunate enough to be a member of one of these schools, make sure that you support it wholeheartedly. There are many educators who understand these issues too. Many labour on in love, handling almost constant frustration with the educational system they are forced into, but nevertheless making an impact on the children they teach.

The bottom line, however, is that parents must be involved.

Not as defenders of their children and critics of the teachers, but as active partners in the education of their children. It's the only way that our children will be prepared for the realities of the world of work in 2020 and beyond. Schools and teachers cannot do it alone – not even the best ones. The need for teamwork in education has never been more critical – for the sake of our children. We need to combine the best of what schools have to offer with the best of what parents have to offer to achieve a meaningful result.

The role of the parent

I've learned many things in my attempts to work with schools, and the first among them is that if parents want to raise smarter kids, they have to take responsibility for this critical task themselves. Not only won't schools do it, but you can't delegate this job to tutors, nannies, or anyone else. I'm not suggesting that you home-school your child – although this is not a terrible idea – but that you take charge of helping your child become a true learner. This has nothing to do with teaching him specific subjects and everything to do with developing the traits characteristic of intelligent, productive, and successful people.

(Roger Schank, Institute for the Learning Sciences at Northwestern University, USA, 2001)

Parents have a new role to play. No longer are they the sage on stage, but rather the guide alongside. This means that we co-create life with our children. We collaborate with each other and learn together.

Your focus should be on developing your children holistically, not just on training them to perform in tests. Meg Fargher, the headmistress of Graeme's girls' school, explains that we need to stop preparing our children for 'just in case'[83] When they need something, they will go out and get it. And because there is so much to be learnt, children will cherry-pick only the learnings that link directly to their current life tasks and projects.

So, some bold decisions are required. The good news is that every single piece of research tells us that even if your child fails within the education system itself, but you manage to instil the X-factors outlined in the next section in the process, then your child will be successful.

The past few decades have belonged to a certain kind of person with a certain kind of mind – computer programmers who could crank code, lawyers who could craft contracts, MBAs who could crunch numbers. But the keys to the kingdom are changing hands. The future belongs to a very different kind of person with a very different kind of mind – creators and empathizers, pattern recognizers and meaning makers. These people – artists, inventors, designers, storytellers, caregivers, consolers, big picture thinkers – will now reap society's richest rewards and share its greatest joys.

(Daniel Pink in *A Whole New Mind*, 2006)

X-FACTORS FOR SUCCESS

We are in the twilight of a society based on data. As information and intelligence become the domain of computers, society will place more value on the one human ability that cannot be automated: emotion. Imagination, myth, ritual – the language of emotion – will affect everything from our purchasing decisions to how we work with others. Companies will thrive on the basis of their stories and myths. Companies will need to understand that their products are less important than their stories.

(Rolf Jensen, Copenhagen Institute for Future Studies, and author of *The Dream Society*, 2001)

If even a fraction of what we have said so far comes to pass, it is critical for us to attempt to develop in our children the characteristics of successful talented people from as early as possible. After all, they hold much of this blueprint for success in their preschool years, before they start to lose it in traditional education systems that are not changing with the times. There is no single definitive profile of a successful person. Every book you read on success – and there are many! – will highlight slightly different characteristics. It is not our intention to create yet another such unique list for you. Our goal in this section is to encourage you to think about what future success might require; to inspire you to be proactive and intentional in your parenting; and to provide you with highly practical suggestions about what you might do *with* and *for* your children to give them every chance of future success. We will supply references to a variety of the works that we have found helpful along the way, but these are by no means the only sources that we recommend on this important issue.

Conversations, connections, choices

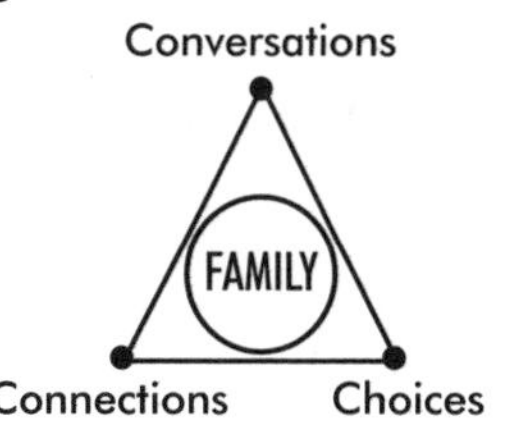

The many practical ideas in this section will help you to equip your children for future success. This is the menu that we spoke about at the end of Section 1. Select items from this menu to flesh out your parenting framework, which should always consist of the cornerstones of conversation, connection and choice. You will find these key words and concepts scattered liberally throughout this section.

Survival of the talented

Our children are going to find increasing competition in a global war for talent. If you think about the vast number of talented people in the world, then it will be evident that each of us has to find our own unique way to shine by discovering how we can add value. In our connected world, the playing fields have been flattened, enabling people around the globe to operate from the same web-based platform, increasingly offering a similar array of goods and services. This is why *who* you are and *how* you do things is becoming more important than *what* you do. To stand out, you need to do things in a highly unique and effective way. And, not only that, you will have to keep on reinventing yourself, re-engineering the way you do things, and re-defining yourself by your creativity and originality. This is your personal brand – **Brand You.**[84] We will look at how to present your brand to the world in Section 5.

If there is nothing very special about your work, no matter how hard you apply yourself, you won't get noticed, and that increasingly means you won't get paid much either.
(Michael Goldhaber, 'The attention economy and the Net', 1997)

Fact: 25% of the population with the highest IQs in China equates to more than the entire population of North America (USA and Canada combined).[85]

Fact: There are more dollar millionaires in India than there are people in Australia.

Sections 1 and 3 have provided the outlines of a framework for thinking about the future. One thing should be clear: we are unclear about what the future holds. But this should not lead us to despair. Whatever the future holds, we know that talented people will be successful. They will give themselves the best chance of choosing happiness for themselves and those they love.

This may be simple to say, but what does it mean?

The biggest problem with the concept of talent is that it defies definition. Ask anyone to give you a definition of talent and, the best that they're likely to come up with is, 'I'll know it when I see it'. This is unhelpful for us as parents as we try to nurture the next generation of talent. What are we aiming at? What characteristics must we instil in our children? Can we even teach talent? There are many who believe that we can.

Through extensive research, Harvard psychologist Howard Gardner identified three key characteristics that make exceptional individuals noteworthy:[86]

1. They reflect on their experiences far more than most people.
2. They are distinguished not so much by any innate abilities, but rather by the way they identify and exploit their strengths – they are strongly self-aware.
3. They are assiduous learners, especially from their failures – they learn from setbacks and turn them into opportunities.

These characteristics can be developed and nurtured. They can be made into habits. Probably the easiest way to do this is to nurture them in your self – they are most likely to be caught, rather than taught. But, to be proactive about developing the characteristics of talented people, you can build specific activities and experiences into your life and the lives of your children.

Those new sources of value-added are [all] about ... Creativity! ... Imagination! ... Intellectual Capital! And that stuff is all about ... Talent.

(Tom Peters in *Re-Imagine!*, 2006)

In their book, *The New Learning Revolution*, Gordon Dryden and Jeanette Vos quote the results of two mammoth research studies by Gallup, the world's largest polling organisation:

- Everyone has the talent to be good at something, but not good at everything. The trick is to find that something, and then to develop the skills and abilities so that talent can flourish.
- But talent is not merely a vocational skill. Rather it is a mixture of each person's personality, behavioural traits and passions.
- Great managers select for talent, and then train for skills. But that's also a great lesson for parents, teachers and students: learn how to identify talent, and then develop the skills and abilities to let it flower.

Talent X-factors

In the past few years, reality TV shows have become increasingly popular. The most watched shows are those that try to find the latest pop star. Week after week, as the judges make comments on the young people in front of them, they constantly refer to the 'X-factor'. Either you have 'it' or you don't – and 'it' determines your success in the music industry. 'It' is the difference between being good and being extraordinary. Not everyone desires to be successful in such a competitive environment, yet each of us needs to identify and cultivate the X-factors that will aid success in our chosen jobs and careers. This is what we want to help you to develop in your children.

To make it in this new world, we need to model talent for our children so that they can become talented. You cannot study to become talented since talent is borne of *who* you are, *how* and *why* you do things – and not necessarily just *what* you do. It is based on the acquisition of X-factors, not grades. X-factors for success are mostly caught and not taught – via role-modelling and a process of osmosis – from parents, mentors, coaches and other significant people in our lives and those of our children.

The factors discussed below are critical to your children's future success, regardless of what industry or field they select, and irrespective of their personalities and characters. We have given some very practical suggestions with which you can experiment. These lists should be seen as mere starting points for your own imaginative interactions with your children.

The most important 'talent X-factors' for developing exceptional young people include teaching our children:

- to break conventions
- to be resilient
- to learn
- to know themselves
- to relate to others

> We are giving a lot of tips for developing X-factors here, some of which may turn into family rules. Bear in mind that the best rules are those which apply to every family member. For example, if your children are not allowed to make calls on their cellphones during family meal times, then neither should you!

Breaking conventions (creativity by another name)

We cannot continue to do what we have always done, or just follow conventional rules if we are to survive and thrive in the future. This is a time to connect the dots differently and to think out the box, a cliché which refers to looking at a problem from a new perspective, without preconceptions. Because the world has never looked this way before, we must apply different thinking to a whole new set of problems and challenges. This may involve breaking old rules (when it makes intelligent sense to do so) and making up new ones, as well as piecing together information and experiences differently.

The concept of breaking conventions has nothing to do with bringing up children without limits or boundaries. Indeed, we believe that these are essential to raising children in a constantly shifting and changing world. Here 'breaking conventions' means developing a way of thinking outside the dots.

THINKING OUT THE BOX

Thinking out the box is a consultant's favourite phrase, which probably originated from the nine dots puzzle in the 1980s. The challenge is to connect the dots by drawing four straight, continuous lines without lifting the pencil from the paper.

The puzzle is easily solved, but only if you draw the lines outside the confines of the square area defined by the nine dots themselves. Here is one possible solution:

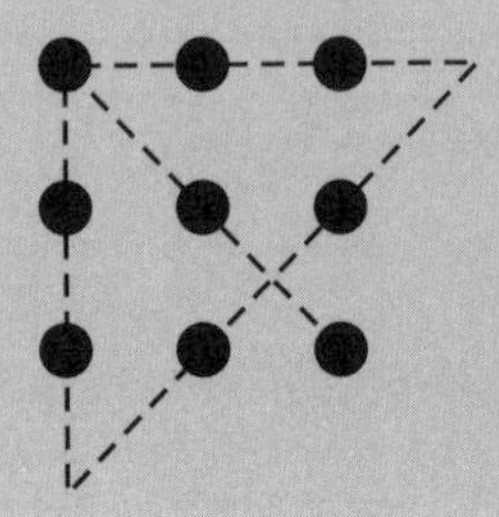

A key defining factor of talented people, in any industry or arena, is their ability to break conventions, push boundaries, stretch the limits of performance and change the game. This may be the toughest skill to teach our children. The skills discussed below will be helpful in building a foundation for breaking conventions.

Imagination and play

Great inventors, scientists and sportspeople never stop at the known limits presented by the world around them. They push the barriers because, as Mind Power specialist John Kehoe comments, whenever there is a conflict between the willpower and the imagination, the imagination always wins.[87] All great discoveries have been made and records set by an individual posing a question, pursuing a dream, or wanting to do the seemingly impossible.

The emotion economy has another name – the Dream Society, in which products and ideas will be sold by the stories that are told around them. You will need to create a company dream to enable you to develop a company or product story. One of the most sought-after skills in this new society will be storytelling. Successful companies will sell stories – the products will come second. Good stories are memorable and they sell. Human beings love to be actors or players in a story, but most have never had the opportunity to be part of an unfolding dream. So we need to create dreams in our businesses. Says Rolf Jensen, 'The future's realm of possibilities is always bigger than you imagine.' Whoever would have imagined, for instance, that there could be a market for Ice Age ice cubes made from imported pieces of the Greenland ice cap? By making this story the product in 1996, Copenhagen Airport single-handedly expanded the ice cube market.[88]

The Dream Society will demand the ability to visualise, to form images and ideas in the mind, especially of things never seen or not yet experienced personally. Imagination leads to original thought and is often driven by the dual thoughts 'Why?' and 'Why not?' Our children will need original thoughts and ideas to solve the problems and challenges of the world – problems which do not yet exist!

You hardly need to develop this ability in most children. The key is to ensure that you don't stifle it.

Tips for developing imagination

For all

- Tell stories. Tell the good old favourites – the fairy tales. Tell modern stories. Make up your own. Just tell stories. Avoid the shortened, abridged versions and look for the lengthy originals. Make sure your children *hear* stories. Note the word 'hear'. Television and movies strip away the creative, imaginative power of turning words into mental pictures.
- Tell ghost stories in the dark. It's great fun. Just make them up as you go along. These stories should obviously be age-appropriate and not unduly frighten younger children!
- Make up stories in the car. Each person gets to add another detail to the story.
- Keep a dress-up box at home for children to engage in fantasy play. They love different hats, old clothes, adult shoes, jewellery, pirate swords, masks, fireman and nurse outfits, fairy and king accessories, etc.

> Nikki once came upon her husband, Simon, with three-year-old Ryan on his lap, telling him an imaginative story about the small engine embroidered on his slippers. Ryan was enthralled.

For younger children (1–5 years)

- Before going on holiday, instead of telling your children a bedtime story, tell them to close their eyes. Then make up a story, with the family as the main characters, going on a holiday to the exact place where you are heading. Obviously this works particularly well if you are going back to a place you have previously visited. Get your children to visualise what you are saying and to imagine themselves helping to pack the car, on the journey, arriving at the destination, smelling the air on the beach, feeling the sand between their toes, etc. You could do something similar a day or two after your return from a holiday or from a visit to a particularly interesting place.
- Encourage your children's artistic efforts from the time they pick up their first podgy crayon. Never criticise their artwork or label it for them. What looks to you like an aeroplane may be something entirely different. Encourage the process with comments such as 'I love all the colours you've used', or 'Look at how you've covered your whole page with your drawing'. Stunting your children's imagination and creativity at an early age is interrupting a highly important natural developmental process that will enable them to come up with original thoughts and creative solutions to life's problems at a later stage.
- Discourage the use of colouring-in books and worksheets in the early years. Large pieces of blank paper are the best canvas for a child's imagination.
- When choosing a preschool for your child, enquire if there is a creative art *and* a creative crafts programme, and ask what the difference is. Many schools churn out crafts at an impressive rate, but this is prescriptive. It does not allow children to exercise their imagination and creativity in the same way as art does.
- Always look at the art on the walls in a preschool. It will give you a very good idea as to whether or not children

are being encouraged to use their own imagination. It's a good sign if all the art looks different. Also make sure that the children are being given large sheets of paper to work on. This is very important!
- Look for a play-based preschool programme, not one in which worksheets abound. Children in this phase learn best through concrete, real-life play experiences and not through abstract learning, which is boring and fails to stimulate the imagination.

For older children (6–14 years)
- Encourage your children to become avid readers. (Yes, we know some children are and some aren't, but give it a go – and persevere!)
- The Harry Potter series and *The Chronicles of Narnia* are examples of books and movies that could stimulate an older child's imagination.
- Encourage your children to express themselves through creative pursuits such as art, music and drama.
- Have fun by playing word association and problem-solving games in the car instead of constantly talking on your cellphone, or allowing your child to watch DVDs on the way to school.
- Playstation and strategy computer games such as Star Wars, SIMS or Age of Empires can enable older children to play in an imaginary world. Play the odd game with your children. It's a way of accessing their world.

You will have noticed that play has been mentioned often in this section, so it would be appropriate to say a little more about here. Play is the language of childhood. It is a child's work, the way children learn, and the least stressful way of learning for children. Play can help a child to achieve almost anything. It is often multi-sensory and appeals to a variety of different intelligences at the same time. From this you will understand why play becomes a memorable experience and makes learning fun.

The ancient philosopher Plato said: 'It is the essential nature of man to play.' To play is part of human nature – we were born to do it; it is hardwired into the very core of who and what we are. Yet, in our high-tech world, we seem to have lost the software to access play. Our shift from the information economy into the connection economy allows us to acknowledge that play is a basic human need. Indeed, some commentators go as far as to say that our very survival on this planet depends upon play because it is the basis of discovery of self and life; it is the bridge that connects mere thought with experience, that integrates new experiences with old, that opens up new possibilities and new ways of being, and that enables us to transfer learned skills or ideas into new contexts.

The definition of play from the *Collins Concise English Dictionary* is: 'To occupy or amuse oneself. To fulfil a participative role in a team. To give a dramatic performance. Fun and light-heartedness. Games and diversions.' Play is all these things and so much more. It is truly multidimensional with mental, physical, emotional and even spiritual significance. It reflects the holistic nature of our beings, our interconnectedness within our selves and with our world as a whole.

Through play, small children begin to understand their physical world. They become aware of their bodies and learn to communicate. Play helps them to solve problems and enriches their creativity and leadership skills. Play, or stimulation through the medium of play, actually grows and wires their brains.

Then children go to school. There they are told to sit still, keep quiet, and do repetitive tasks in rooms often devoid of art, music or human comfort. 'In effect, to learn with their brains tied behind their backs. Or worse, in suspended animation,' says Laurel Schmidt, author of *Seven Times Smarter*. We all experienced this in our industrial age schools. Today, to a very large extent, our children are in an education system that renowned business consultant Tom Peters rants about. In his best-selling book, *Re-Imagine* (2006), he states:

- Our school system is a thinly disguised conspiracy to quash creativity.
- We are at an inflection point. We seem to be reinventing everything – except the school system, which should (in theory) underpin, even lead, the rest.
- The main crisis in schools today is irrelevance.
- Our education system is a second-rate, factory-style organisation pumping out obsolete information in obsolete ways.
- Our educational thinking is concerned with 'what is'. It is not good at designing 'what can be'.
- Every time I pass a jailhouse or a school, I feel sorry for the people inside.

Compare this to the positive experience of young preschoolers who learn:

- through play
- by using all their senses during hands-on, concrete experiences
- language and communication by engaging in real-life conversations with other children and adults
- about life by solving real problems – from a crawling baby negotiating a chair blocking the way, to how to reach the biscuit tin on the third shelf in the pantry
- through exploration and discovery. The driving force is 'What if . . .?' and 'I wonder . . .'

Creativity

You see things; and you say, 'Why?' But I dream things that never were; and I say, 'Why not?'

(George Bernard Shaw, renowned Irish playwright, 1850–1956)

We live in what some are calling 'the imagination economy'[89], in which imagination, innovation and creativity are rewarded as never before. Advances in technology will not guarantee success in the future since they travel around the globe almost instantaneously, and are difficult to protect from the copyright breakers of the world. As Geoffrey Colvin (2006) says: 'The very basis of value creation is shifting from the disciplines of logic and linear thinking to the intuitive, nonlinear processes of creativity and imagination.'[90]

> Exhibit A in this argument is the iPod. Its success was based on imagination as much as technology. MP3 players had been around for years and had never done much commercially. Apple's achievement was creating an appealing design and extraordinary software that yielded a superior, intuitive interface – plus the business innovation of the iTunes online music store. The company then imbued the whole thing with an undeniable coolness. The result is an overwhelmingly dominant business, with about 75% of the MP3-player market and the online-music market – all based on existing basic technology plus a lot of ingenious creativity.
>
> (Geoffrey Colvin, 'The Imagination Economy', 2006)

We often think of creativity as an attribute of mad scientists, designers or artists. However, the ability to think out of the box and to employ original thinking to problem solve are critical life skills for any career today. We would go so far as to say that creativity is a core element of our very survival! It is a vital way of expressing who we are since we all do things differently and for different reasons.

THE BUTTERFLY OF FREEDOM

'Why do you fly outside the box?'
'I fly outside the box because I can.'
'But we *know* the box. We are *safe* inside the box.'
'That, my friend, is why I leave it. For you may be safe, but I am *free*.'

(Edward Monkton in *Happiness*, 2007)

One of the myths about giving children creative freedom is that no boundaries should be imposed. On the contrary, however, true creativity is being creative within given boundaries. If you say to kids, 'Go and play a game', more often than not they will reply, 'I don't know what to play or what to do.' But if you change the instruction to 'Try to create a game that uses these three balls and a stick', you gain a much better result. Boundaries can enhance creativity because children are forced to use their imagination. In a room full of toys, no imagination or creativity is required to work out how to have a fun-filled afternoon – you need just flit from toy to toy, window shopping. But having only one toy to play with for a few hours ensures that, out of necessity, creativity and the imagination are engaged to alleviate boredom.

Nikki asked her son the following question: 'If I gave you a box of Lego and said you have one hour to build a military vehicle without an instruction booklet, would you find that fun?' His eyes lit up and he said excitedly, 'It would be such fun because it's not what other people think you should build, it's what *you* think you should do. It's using your own ideas.' Much more fun indeed than using a Lego kit with an instruction booklet!

When playing with a friend's six-year-old daughter, Jenna, recently, Nikki asked her to build a fairy castle out of a bag of wooden blocks, with the specific instruction that it was to have two towers. Jenna tackled the project with gusto, taking great pride in showing Nikki her masterpiece fifteen minutes later. It was a stimulating and absorbing whole-brain exercise, which required Jenna to use her left brain to problem solve by designing within the parameters of a bag of blocks and two towers, but allowed her right brain to be as creative as it liked.

School encourages creativity within very specific norms and structures, and few worthwhile things have been invented within standard norms and given structures.

'The Wright brothers invented the airplane because they were willing to fly off a cliff hundreds of times. Edison invented the light bulb because he played around with all those different filaments. The truly creative person has an insane devotion to an idea, banging away at it from all sorts of angles in all sorts of ways. School doesn't permit this ... Teaching to the test, the inflexibility of [curriculums] and policies, and the mass production of students stifles creativity.'

(*Coloring Outside the Lines* by Roger Schank, 2001)

It is up to parents to create spaces for creativity to develop.

Tips for developing creativity

Children are full of wacky ideas. Take them seriously. Ask a lot of questions about them, get your children to think them through and to verbalise them. Just as you play games with your child, you can play with his or her ideas too. Fantasy play in which children make up their own roles and rules is great for creativity.

Here are some more very doable ideas:

For all

- Don't always answer all of your children's questions. Help them to find the answers for themselves.[91]
- Create reasons for different family celebrations, in addition to the usual birthdays or religious festivals. For example, have a rugby World Cup dinner just because dad is a rugby fanatic and it's World Cup month.
- Play word games in the car instead of talking on your cellphone, or becoming frustrated with the traffic, or allowing your children to watch a DVD or listen to the news on the car radio (usually fairly negative content).
- Cook or bake together.
- Grow a garden together.
- Play a wide variety of games – some with toys and some without.
- Prolong childhood by allowing children time to engage in unsupervised free play. Children need time out in nature or at home to be alone with themselves. This enables them to process all the input they receive in order to create meaning. Children today move so quickly from wearing fantasy costumes to dressing like adults, and from playing like children to acting like adults. They need the time and freedom to be children. A longer childhood is preferable in terms of adjusting to adolescence.
- Don't over-schedule children with too many organised, supervised, prescriptive activities. Play dates and free play are essential to their development.

For younger children (1–5 years)

- Provide your children with plenty of opportunities to create their own artwork in their own way. From shaving cream on the bathroom mirror or on the glass of the sliding patio door, to pavement chalk for use on the driveway, to paper, paint, pastels, play dough, etc. But there are two rules – Rule 1: Your child should work on the surface provided, and nowhere else; Rule 2: Do not interfere with your child's creative process. Encourage the process more than you praise the outcome, for example: 'I just love the colours you are using'; 'Do you have a name for what you have painted?'; 'I can see how much thought you have put into your drawing.'

Don't ever label children's works of art for them. Allow them to tell you what they are all about (what looks like a fish to you may be the sun to them). You should not disturb or unsettle their creative process.

- Look for a preschool that runs a play-based curriculum, pays attention to creativity and movement, and is not dominated by worksheets and prescriptive art. (As mentioned previously, it's always a good idea to look at the art on the walls when shopping for a school. If every child's art looks different, it's a good sign that children are being allowed to express themselves.)
- Turn ordinary time or activities into special experiences that reinforce your connection with your children while, at the same time, stimulating their skills. For example, lay the table together, play games in the car or do spelling homework in shaving cream on the bathroom mirror.

For older children (6–14 years)

- Serve a Perseverance Breakfast (or Lunch or Dinner) for your child who has been working really hard to improve a grade (or a skill), in recognition of his or her effort. A little creativity can go a long way to engender excitement and anticipation in children in what would normally be rather mundane situations.
- Create family adventures and holidays together. The older

children become, the more involved they can be in the planning and decision making.

- Encourage your children to put together plays with their friends and siblings for special occasions.
- Organise creative birthday parties for your children – you do not have to do what everyone else is doing. If you want a good party, just base it on play. For example, plan a Mad Food Party with a cryptic menu. Children might land up ordering a knife, fork, spoon, salt and pepper for their first course, and ice cream with mayonnaise and rice for their main course, etc. Children are attracted to, and delighted by, creativity.
- Encourage your children to play with shape games and to make their own picture or design out of shapes without copying a picture card. Construction toys such as Lego are great for creativity when they are used without instructions and children are left to pursue their own ideas.
- Ask your children what they think about current world problems and if they have any solutions. You will be amazed at how creative their solutions can be!

Experimentation

Children are naturally adventurous. The best way to learn at a young age is by trial and error (personal experience), so experimenting is natural to them. We slowly shut down our children's curiosity through our fears about their health and safety, and as we become irritated with their constant tinkering which fails to fit into our busy schedules. This is a serious error on our parts since the skills of experimentation and investigation are both critical for success in the 21st century, as well as essential characteristics in talented people.

Tips for developing an experimental mindset

For all

- The easiest way to encourage an experimental mindset is to consciously experiment on an ongoing basis. For example, tell your family: 'Tonight we are going to experiment with some new tastes and smells' as you prepare an extraordinary dinner with unusual ingredients. You could even start with dessert first!
- Do actual experiments with your children. Safe and fun science experiments are available at all good toy stores. These can do many things, from firing rockets, to testing wind speed, to building a home volcano. Various books packed with ideas for science experiments can also be purchased at good book stores. Your local library might have a useful selection of ideas too.
- Ensure your children have a variety of different construction toys and brain-teaser games. These allow them to experiment with different solutions to find the one that works through trial and error. A tower of blocks will fall down if the base is not wide enough – but you only learn that through experience! This is a safe way of allowing children to experiment and, the more they are encouraged in this area, the more confident they will be when challenged by real-life situations that require creative solutions.

For younger children (1–5 years)

- When driving to preschool or the shops, take a different route. Take random turnings and see where you end up. Make sure you get your children involved in the fun of this experiment.
- Let your children bake with you. Baking is always a wonderful experiment. Next time you use the same recipe, add another ingredient just to experiment, such as raisins to bran muffins.

- Make jelly. It's the perfect science experiment, changing state from solid to liquid to solid.
- Making fruit smoothies also fascinates children as different ingredients create a different result in taste and appearance.

For older children (6–14 years)

- Eat out at a variety of different restaurants, exposing children to food from different countries.
- Teach your children to test the swimming pool water to learn about acidity and alkalinity.
- Water-skiing and snow-skiing demand physical experimentation to develop the necessary skills to master the particular environment and equipment.
- En route to your family holidays, try to stop at a different national monument or tourist attraction each year.
- Encourage your children to plan family days once a quarter. Give them a budget, but very few other limits to restrict them. The only rule should be that they should do something none of the family has ever done before.

> In Graeme's family there is a simple rule at restaurants. You have to try at least one bite of every new food that is on the table. You can't say 'No, I don't like it' until you've actually tried it! It was through this simple rule that Amy, at age six, discovered she was a sushi fan. And she even mastered using chopsticks. But Amy doesn't like tomato sauce. That's Hannah's favourite, and she'd have it on anything. As long as you try, you can then make your own decision about your likes and dislikes. But you can't decide until you've tried.

Initiative and proactivity

A core characteristic of talented people, which is most prized by their managers, is the fact that they go beyond what is expected of them without being told to do so – they take the initiative and are proactive. This links in specifically with the aptitudes of experimentation and imagination, but it also refers to leadership in that talented people make determined efforts to find solutions to problems.

At times modern parents have been labelled as helicopter parents – they are overprotective of their children and hover over them. Ironically, in fact, children who are highly mollycoddled and brought up almost risk-free are at greater risk. Children need a certain amount of risk in their lives to help them to solve problems and develop personal initiative and coping skills. This starts from toddlerhood. For example, allow small children to navigate the stairs so that they learn how to do it for themselves. Children who are always carried up and down stairs for fear that they will fall are at greater risk of falling down the stairs because they haven't had the chance to experiment and work out the skill for themselves. This is not to say you should be negligent, but you need to find the balance between allowing your child to develop and use his or her initiative, and protecting your child from all the bumps and bruises that accompany learning.

Tips for developing initiative and proactivity

For all

- Let children try things for themselves as much as possible.
- Allow children to help you prepare and cook meals, lay the table, make beds, and do everyday household activities. Non-verbally, you are expressing your belief in their capability by encouraging and permitting their involvement, instead of sending them to watch TV while you do it all by yourself. This instils an 'I can' mentality, which fuels initiative and proactivity.
- Say 'yes' to as many of your children's ideas, suggestions or

requests as possible when it comes to showing initiative and being proactive. If it is not convenient or practical at that particular moment, then say, 'Yes, but not right now'.

For younger children (1–5 years)

- Teach your children how to do things for themselves, such as fastening their seatbelt, doing up their own buttons and tying shoelaces. Make sure that you give them enough time in your busy schedule to do these things without rushing them, showing irritation, or winding up doing it for them anyway because you have run out of time.
- Give children the responsibility of watering plants and feeding pets.
- Encourage your children to become involved in art and other creative outlets such as drama, music or pottery.

For older children (6–14 years)

- Teach your children to pack their own school bag from Grade 1 so that it becomes habit. In this way they learn to plan ahead and prepare for the next day, which shows initiative and proactivity.
- Encourage your children to do homework when there are gaps in their daily schedule, such as half an hour between extramural activities. This will save them time later and teach them effective time management skills.
- Give your children the opportunity to make decisions or to help you with the decision-making process. If you are planning a holiday, for example, ask your children what they think needs to be packed.
- From time to time, ask your children how they think things should be done. Then try them in your child's suggested way for a change.
- Teach your children to switch off lights when they leave a room that will not be in immediate use thereafter. (The energy crisis has provided a great opportunity for

implementing this lesson!)

Resilience

Resilience is knowing what to do when you don't know what to do.

(Jean Piaget in *Child Psychology,* 1986)

Resilience is simply defined as successful adaptation to risk and adversity. Some would define it as survival in the face of multiple challenges, while others would describe it as coping with trauma.[92] Resilience is the new mantra for the Millennial generation. As members of an era experiencing unprecedented levels of change and shift, they will need to be the most resilient generation ever. Resilience and constant flexibility will help Millennials to adapt and survive.

There is a lot of debate about whether resilience can be taught or not. Some experts assert that you either have resilience or you don't. Others argue that various skills can be learnt which result in resilience. We believe that you can nurture resilience in yourself and your children, realising that your resilience quotient is impacted upon by a multitude of factors, including personality, health, self-esteem and your environment.

In *The Secure Child* (2003), Stanley Greenspan describes a study of Hawaiian children who had grown up in adversity. Those children who managed, despite the difficulties they encountered, all had one thing in common. The 'hidden strength', as Greenspan called it, was neither physical nor intellectual. It was access to a nurturing and supportive relationship with a relative or other person in the community. According to Greenspan, resilience emerged not as a state of mind, but as a reflection of the relationships available to the child.

Annie Greeff, author, educator and trainer, explains that we are born with an innate capacity for resilience, a so-called 'self-righting capability' which enables us to adapt to changing circumstances and to develop:

- social skills
- problem-solving skills
- analytical thinking skills
- autonomy
- a sense of purpose

Resilience also involves:

- having strategies for getting the best out of yourself – assuming that you live in a multiple intelligence world and it is possible to develop the full range of your talents
- loving learning
- being able to keep going when things get tough
- being resourceful (having a good, full 'toolkit' of techniques)
- adapting and responding to circumstances
- having self-knowledge, or knowing yourself.

Research shows that resilience leads to happiness. One of the traps that parents of Millennial children have fallen into is striving to keep their children happy and stress-free from an early age, which does not help them to develop resilience. In fact, overprotection is a form of deprivation.

The idea that a child should avoid misery at all costs distorts both the reality of life and the ways children learn to find happiness ... Learning to build these inner resources for a happier life demands that we endure the hard knocks of the playground – boot camp for the inevitable upsets of everyday relationships. Given how the brain masters social resilience,

children need to rehearse for the ups and downs of social life, not experience a steady monotone of delight. When a child gets upset, the value lies in attaining some mastery over that reaction.

(Daniel Goleman in *Social Intelligence: The New Science of Human Relationships*, 2006)

Tips for developing resilience

For all

- Research shows that the most important component of resilience is a solid emotional base for every individual, and knowing that you are loved unconditionally by others. Therefore, it is essential to give your children regular, focused, undivided attention. This, more than anything else, communicates your unconditional love to them. They also need to know that your love for them is not related to their performance, but simply to who they are.
- Resilience emerges out of self-awareness and self-esteem. See the section 'Know yourself' (page 237) for practical tips on developing self-awareness in your children. When they fail or are stressed, help them to understand the link between the situation they are currently facing and their strengths and weaknesses.
- Girls tend to become resilient by building strong, caring relationships. Boys usually bounce back by learning how to problem solve.

For younger children (1–5 years)

- As children get older, start taking them on family walks and slowly progress to hikes. It's good to push them every now and then to break their own personal best. Small children can walk by themselves without being picked up for 15 minutes or so, but they can learn to extend this if they are encouraged.

- Allow children to get dirty and climb trees.
- Obviously keep a watchful eye on your child's antics, but don't always rush over the moment he or she trips or falls. On most occasions, if children think you aren't looking, they will pick themselves up, dust themselves off, and carry on as if nothing had happened. They often cry for effect. (Of course, we are *not* encouraging you to be irresponsible parents here!)
- Allow your children to sort out their differences with their siblings with as little interference as possible. Obviously there are times when you must step in, but sibling rivalry is also a way of learning to be socially resilient.

For older children (6–14 years)

- Today's teenagers are more at risk of anxiety and depression than any generation in history, says Andrew Shatte, co-director of the Resiliency Project at the University of Pennsylvania, Philadelphia. 'Yet our ongoing studies for the last 10 years show we can cut the adolescent depression rate in half and make kids more resilient by teaching better thinking skills.' For 12 weeks the Penn researchers taught children how to tell the difference between productive and self-defeating thinking. They used the story of *The Little Engine That Could* to illustrate the importance of a positive attitude, and of *Chicken Little* to illustrate the pitfalls of catastrophic thinking. Researchers then instructed the children to look at their own fears and ask themselves, 'What's the worst that can happen?' and 'How likely is it that this will pan out?'[93]
- It's never too early to teach children physical and mental relaxation exercises. These include breathing techniques, some forms of meditation, mental imagery, and muscle relaxation exercises. Help your children learn to recognise their own stress triggers and responses, and to identify which relaxation methods work best for them.

- Encourage your children to laugh – read funny stories, watch age-appropriate comedies, laugh at their jokes, play the fool with them sometimes, and find the humour in various people and situations.
- Avoid rushing in to fix what is not working for your children emotionally. Where possible, try to help them to develop coping skills for next time rather than fixing things for them every time.

Flexibility

If the world is going to continue changing as much as we suggest, then a critical skill will be the ability to change and be adaptable. We prefer to think of this as flexibility because we are not advocating change for the sake of change. Think of a stiff piece of plastic – it is flexible because it can bend into a different shape but, when it is let go, it springs back to its original shape. Our children need the structure of routine as the basis for a consistent and calm life. But they also need to develop an ability to change and be flexible when required.

> **It means that you stay permanently flexible, because it is only by being so that you can achieve synchronicity with a world that has, itself, entered into a state of permanent flexibility, a world that is being subtly and meaningfully altered every single day. Here's the real secret of successful people and businesses: They are different every day of their lives.**
>
> (Watts Wacker and Jim Taylor in *The 500 Year Delta*, 1998)

Tips for developing flexibility

For all

- It's important for children (both young and old) to have a routine. However, you can stretch them a bit by following the same routine but in a different environment, such as while away on a holiday or when visiting a friend. This gives you so much more flexibility as a family and ensures that your children learn how to adjust and adapt when situations and circumstances change.

- Develop a trusted circle of friends and family with whom you can leave your children from time to time. Life is a journey to independence and children need to learn such skills from an early age if you want them to be flexible.
- Always have a plan B in mind. If there is a fairly good chance that you may need to use it, then talk your children through the options before they happen. In this way, they are mentally prepared for change and will not be taken by surprise. For example, if you are going to a meeting which has the potential to run longer than your time schedule allows, resulting in you picking up your child late from school, then warn your child that he or she may receive a message to go to aftercare, and that you will pick him or her up there. Or, you may have a friend who will pick your child up for you if necessary – just make sure that your child knows the plan, if possible. If children feel well prepared and that you are in control, they panic less if situations or circumstances change.
- Remember that some children are more flexible and adaptable than others. Those to whom this does not come naturally need encouragement, but they may also need some time to develop this trait.

For younger children (1–5 years)

- When children start to attend school, they learn to be sociable, to play with each other, and to get along. This demands a certain amount of flexibility and adaptability, especially when it comes to sharing.
- Avoid giving in to your children's demands and whines all the time. This teaches them to try to shape the world

around their own wants and desires. Imposing discipline and saying 'no' to your children will help them to develop critical life skills. Focus on the bigger picture next time you feel that it's just easier to give in to a whining child.

For older children (6–14 years)

- Children can also learn flexibility by adapting their skills and abilities to suit various platforms and different media, such as Gameboys, Playstations, computers, cellphones, etc.
- Watch from a distance as your children play with siblings and friends. Later, chat to them about their interactions and give positive suggestions and practical examples of what they could have done differently. This is not about discipline or correcting behaviour, but rather a form of training and discussion around options and possibilities.

Persistence and perseverance

A 'never give up' attitude is typical of those who are identified as talented. Having said that, however, it is generally true that these individuals are quick to give up things they know they're not good at, and unbelievably tenacious in those things they want to succeed at.

In a world in which we are spoilt for choices, so too are our children. From the multitude of extramural activities on offer from the time that they enter nursery school, to the plethora of games and toys they have to choose from, and the variety of media they have access to, it's easy to see why our children may want to have their cake and eat it too! It is essential that parents act as guides and mentors in helping children to make wise choices. This also includes sticking to choices that have been made. For example, if your daughter decides she would like to do ballet but, after the first class, makes up her mind that she dislikes this activity, do you – as parent – allow her to give it up immediately, or do you insist that she continues for the first full month or the first full term to get a proper feel for it?

Stickability is a wonderful word to associate with persistence and perseverance. Sticking to the task at hand teaches self-discipline and commitment, both highly important qualities for 21st-century living. It usually takes a lot of time and practice to become good at something. Perseverance is a core character trait to have. It shows grit and determination, which will help a person to succeed alone or as a team player.

Life is rarely straightforward. It will often be unpredictable and will always toss ups and downs at you. It rarely follows a linear path. Therefore, part of any good future-proofing plan involves making sure that your children develop persistence and perseverance.

Tips for developing persistence and perseverance

For all

- Share inspirational stories (tell them, read them, watch movies about them) of people who have persevered in the face of adversity.
- As with all of the aptitudes and skills that we have outlined in this section, it will help enormously to praise your children for the behaviour you are trying to develop in them, especially at times when they are playing games, learning new sports, and completing unpopular chores.
- Encourage your children to save up for things they want. Avoid fulfilling all their desires immediately, or they will have little to look forward to, or to strive for.
- Bringing children up with a positive *I can, I am, I will* mentality will assist them greatly in the development of perseverance and persistence. It's all about being committed.

For younger children (1–5 years)

- Don't give up on potty training. Show your enthusiasm and support for your child's efforts.
- Allow your child to become frustrated – it is good for development and pushes him or her to the next level, for example sitting up and falling over, standing up and falling down, or battling to push shapes into a shape sorter, or a key into a lock.
- Throwing a ball to a child over and over again to help him or her master the skills involved develops persistence and perseverance.

For older children (6–14 years)

- Encourage your children to share their own stories (by telling them, writing or drawing them) about times when they did not persevere and the outcomes that resulted and vice versa.
- Encourage your children to keep a journal. If they wish, it could focus on experiences that have required them to persevere and which have taken place over an extended period of time.
- If at first your child does not make a sports or cultural team, encourage him or her to keep trying. Children need to practise to improve.

Learning from failure

If we develop creative children who are prepared to experiment, then we must expect them to fail. Failure is part of the process of innovation. Obviously we do not reward or encourage failure, but we do reward effort and learning from failure.

This point is linked to 'Experimentation' on page 190, but let's take it a step further. The only way to push our boundaries is to fail along the way. But we should guide our children to 'fail forwards' and not backwards, as the renowned leadership expert John Maxwell famously says.[94] We must help our children to see that mistakes are stepping stones to success. This is the difference between achievers and average people, which is also linked to persistence and perseverance. One of the most well-known examples of this is Thomas Edison and his invention of the light bulb. Edison tried and failed thousands of times, but still he did not give up. Rather, he chose to see each failure as just another way of how *not* to make a light bulb!

We need to help our children to shape their perception of, and response to failure, and to master their fear of failure. This starts right from the moment they first learn to sit.

Tips for mastering the fear of failure

For all

- Be a positive role model. Let your children see *you* experiencing successes and failures. They will learn how you handle the emotions that accompany success and failure when they see these in you. Don't hide your disappointment and pain from your children when you experience failure. But also teach them how to be an honourable winner and a gracious loser.
- Celebrate successes to help your children see what they have done well. When children fail, do not try to cover up the failure – allow them to grieve the failure and help them to process it. Too many parents try to pretend that a failure did not happen, or they tend to apportion blame and deflect the failure from the child – 'It wasn't you darling, it was that silly referee'. Not enough parents acknowledge failure, while remaining positive and affirming.
- Provide structured routine at home. The daily routine can be reassuring for your children after things have not gone well.

- Put your children in situations in which they are bound to fail or mess up in some way, such as playing sport. Everyone makes mistakes and you simply cannot win all the time. This is how you get good at what you do.

For younger children (1–5 years)

- From babyhood, when your children first learn to sit and then overbalance, or take their first steps and stumble, do not make a fuss of their falls. Have you noticed that when you pretend not to have seen your children take a tumble, they do not cry – they just get up and carry on? However, if they are aware that you have seen them fall, they often produce a spectacular display of tears and really play up the situation. Your response to their failures and mistakes is very important.
- Play games that require taking turns, and both winning and losing.

For older children (6–14 years)

- As children get older (from five upwards) and make mistakes, you can chat about them. Say things such as, 'All of us make mistakes often – that's how we learn. So what did you learn from this today? And what will you do differently next time?'
- Play board games to expose children to winning and losing.
- Play team sports in which good sportsmanship must be displayed when winning or losing.
- Role-model good sportsmanship for your children.
- Watch famous sportspeople and discuss their behaviour – good and bad.

Self-discipline and delayed gratification

Self-discipline is the ability to take action, regardless of your emotional state. Deferred or delayed gratification is the ability to wait in order to obtain something that you want.

In a landmark 1960s Stanford University study by Walter Mischel, four-year-old children were each given a marshmallow and left in a room. They were given the choice of eating it immediately, or waiting 20 minutes when they were promised an additional marshmallow as an extra reward for waiting. In videos of the experiment, you can see the children squirming, kicking, hiding their eyes – desperately trying to exercise self-control and to wait in order to get two marshmallows. Some children simply couldn't wait and ate their marshmallow right away. Others waited and received an additional marshmallow. The study's real significance came 14 years later. The researchers found that the 'grabbers' suffered low self-esteem and were viewed by others as stubborn, prone to envy and easily frustrated. The 'waiters' had better coping skills and were more socially competent and self-assertive, as well as more trustworthy, dependable and academically successful. This group scored about 210 points higher on average on their SATs (US scholastic aptitude/assessment tests, required to be taken before entering college).[95]

Tips for developing self-discipline and an ability to delay gratification

For all

- Practise doing some disagreeable things in your daily life. This may be tough to force on your children, but it is worth doing. Your mind and feelings will oppose doing these activities, but nevertheless they should be done. Just as muscles become stronger by resisting the power of weights, so inner strength is attained by overcoming inner resistance. Some mornings brushing teeth can be as disagreeable to a child as tidying up all the toys he or she played with when a friend came to visit and didn't help to tidy up.

- Make sure your children assist you with daily household chores. Don't allow them to procrastinate or grumble about doing them either – they are part of life.
- Be consistent with the dos and don'ts. By making these rules, you are instilling in your children a lifelong habit of self-discipline which will help them to develop a strong personality and a positive attitude.

> Nikki's eldest son, Ryan, saved up for an iPod. A while before his birthday, they went shopping to check out the best prices. Ryan fell in love with a limited edition red iPod – red in support of people living with HIV/Aids. But there were none to be found in the shops. No problem – Ryan used the Internet to source an online supplier based in Cape Town. His birthday was about a week thereafter so, with a five-day delivery promise, timing was not going to be an issue. Waiting for delivery is about delayed gratification, especially if the item is something that you want desperately and have spent a long time waiting for. The day of Ryan's birthday arrived and Nikki collected the promised parcel from the post office, only to find that a highly inadequate half of the delivery had been made – the speakers and silicone cover. The iPod itself, in a separate parcel, had been mislaid! Would you believe that it took another three weeks for a new iPod to arrive? Ryan's patience was impressive, and a lot better than that of his parents! There is no chance that they will ever use the same supplier again!

- Practise the Christian tradition of Lent, or some similar form of ritual, at least once a year. For the 40-odd days leading up to Easter[96] every year, many Christians will give up something they really enjoy (such as sugar in their tea, or chocolates, or even a bad habit such as sulking).

Doing this as a family and holding each other accountable builds self-discipline. Different religions and cultures have diverse practices.

- On Christmas Day, or any other religious festivals during which gifts are shared, teach your children not to rip open all the wrappings on their presents immediately, but to savour and enjoy each gift, slowly and patiently. Families have different rituals which help small children with this process. For example, on 25 December, Christian families may open presents in Christmas stockings before breakfast, go to church, then open family presents around the Christmas tree on their return from church. What is your tradition of giving?

For younger children (1–5 years)

- Let your children make jelly – often. Apart from being a great science experiment that they never tire of, jelly takes a few hours to set which requires waiting and patience. Either make it at lunch time to eat in the evening, or make it the day before you need it. This is an excellent activity for teaching delayed gratification.
- Allow children to keep silkworms. This will require many weeks of picking and gathering leaves, feeding and waiting for the silkworms to grow and fatten up before they start spinning their cocoons.
- Encourage your children to grow beans. They will have to remember to water them every day while watching the natural growing process with wonder.
- Take your children to restaurants – proper restaurants, not just fast-food outlets – where they have to sit and wait patiently for their food. Ensure that you find ways to keep your children occupied, distracted and well-behaved while waiting for their meal to arrive.

For older children (6–14 years)

- Saving for something special takes a lot of self-discipline

because it takes a long time to save enough for the purchase.
- This point should be obvious – simply do *not* give your children everything they ask for when they ask for it.

A sense of humour

By 'sense of humour' we do not mean the ability to tell good jokes. Rather, we believe that the ability to laugh self-deprecatingly at yourself and not to take your own experiments and failures too seriously is critical to being exceptionally talented. Every truly successful individual will be able to point back to moments of failure and disappointment. What makes these individuals successful is how they respond in these moments, and how they pick themselves up and use the failures to develop. We discussed learning from failure earlier, but part of the process is to be able to laugh at yourself and not take life too seriously.

A good sense of humour is a tool that your children can rely on throughout life to help them:

- deal with failure and disappointment
- see things from many perspectives rather than just the most obvious
- be spontaneous
- grasp unconventional ideas or ways of thinking
- see beyond the surface of things
- connect better with others
- enjoy and participate in the playful and fun aspects of life
- not take themselves too seriously.

The experts agree that our children need a healthy and well-developed sense of humour if they are to manage everyday life happily and successfully. Our children are not born with a sense of humour – it is something they learn, and their ability to find 'the amusing, the funny, the hilarious' is based on what they know. Children with a sense of humour grow up to be adults with a sense of humour. And adults with a sense of humour enjoy life more – their relationships are more successful, they enjoy better health, and they are better able to deal with stress and difficulties.[97]

> One of the young girls in Nikki's lift club spent the whole of last year in and out of hospital, undergoing chemotherapy for lymphoma. Her mum tells the story of the two duty doctors, who they nicknamed Dr Yes, Yes, Yes and Dr No, No, No. If they wanted to ask a favour, they always made sure that they asked when Dr Yes, Yes, Yes was on duty because – yep, you got it – he was more likely to say yes! These little labels added a touch of lightness and humour to an otherwise incredibly stressful and serious situation.

Tips for developing a sense of humour[98]

For all

- As with all of the tips throughout these sections, your example is probably the best teacher. Don't be scared to laugh at yourself in front of your kids.
- Children love to make jokes because this is a wonderful, fun way for them to demonstrate new skills and knowledge. They also love to laugh at your jokes. With any luck, the jokes will improve as your child gets older!
- Take your child's humour seriously. Encourage your child's attempts at humour, whether they entail reading (potentially unfunny) jokes from a book, or drawing 'funny' pictures of the family dog. Praise your child for trying to be funny, and be open to surprise — the first time (and the next, and the next …) that your child makes you laugh is one of life's great pleasures.

- Teach children that adults are funny – and that they can be too. Make humour a part of your day-to-day interactions with your children and encourage them to share amusing observations or reactions, even when you are around other adults.
- Making up stories when travelling in the car can be a good source of instant humour (and an excellent way of passing the time). Someone starts with 'Once upon a time ...' and you go round the car in a circle, with each person adding some colourful detail to the story. The story doesn't have to make sense, but it will certainly be fun!

> The children in Nikki's lift club know that they will always play a word game or two on the way to school. Storytelling is something they all love to do just before arriving at school because they usually end up in hysterics. Children often come up with off-the-wall, sometimes quite bizarre, and frequently hilarious ideas. One of the latest stories involved a tall oak tree falling down after being struck by lightning, squashing a hapless squirrel, being hit by a taxi, and having a flying bunny jump out of its branches!

For younger children (1–5 years)

- Create a humour-rich environment and surround your children with funny books. For toddlers and preschoolers, these include picture books or nonsense rhymes.
- Make silly jokes. For example, try calling Daddy 'Mommy' and watch how your three-year-old howls with delight.
- Tickle each other and make funny faces.
- Surprise your child by jumping out from behind the door or doing other nonsense but fun activities.

For older children (6–14 years)

- Older children tend to love joke books and comics. There are also many amusing television shows, hilarious movies and funny websites for all age groups. Help your children to make good choices, then enjoy them too.

- Buy your children joke books and make sure you listen to their jokes. Also teach them how to deliver a good joke, with a pause and a great punchline.
- Have a family prize for the joke of the week. Write it out and put it up on the fridge.
- Go on family adventures that you can talk and laugh about later.

Optimism

> **Over the last three decades a major cultural shift has taken place in the attitudes of Western societies toward the future. Optimism has given way to a sense of ambiguity ... [which] threatens to stifle hope at a personal as well as a social level.**
> (Miroslav Volf and William H Katerberg in *The Future of Hope: Christian Tradition Amid Modernity and Postmodernity*, 2004)

Optimism is being able to expect the best from life's experiences. It means nurturing hope and having confidence and a strong belief in your ability to deal with situations. Optimism is about thinking positively. Being able to look on the bright side helps all of us to surmount challenges and manage life's difficulties. Optimism is not about being foolish or unrealistic.

Without optimism, we often become a victim of life's circumstances. We simply react to what is, rather than take part in shaping our own reality. Complaining about how tough life is does nothing to help our children grow up with a sense that their destiny lies in their own hands and they have the power to choose and shape their lives. Living in an Age of Possibility means it is essential to empower our children from a young age. They must learn early that all choices carry with them responsibility and consequences.

If we don't have optimism for the future, our children are in danger of growing up with a sense of hopelessness. This is easy when you take into account the staggering amount of negative press that surrounds them in every country of the world. It is our involvement with, and influence on, our children that can transform this negative into a positive.

Tips for developing optimism[99]

For all

- When dealing with success, focus on what traits in your child made the success possible, and examine other successes that might stem from these traits. In this way, you keep a future focus and link it to success that your child has just achieved.
- Don't praise indiscriminately. Telling children that everything they do is great, rather than helping them to experience real successes and persist in the face of reasonable obstacles, puts them at a disadvantage. It creates an overly strong self-focus and often makes them more vulnerable to depression. So validate success, but also acknowledge when your children's efforts are not successful. Children learn to recognise empty praise.
- Help your child to see that there is good and bad in most situations. Make a game of looking for the silver linings in seemingly negative situations. For example, if your child can't play outside because it's raining, look at the positives of indoor play, or highlight the advantages of having extra time to study. Even a broken leg can bring the fun of having friends sign the plaster cast! The game can get silly, but that's okay – it's a good habit to form.
- Re-phrase what your child says in order to accentuate the positive. Use different words to make more positive sense out of a situation. For example, your child might say: 'I

never have anyone to play with.' You, as parent, might reply: 'Sometimes it's hard to find a friend, but last week you had a good time with Mary.'

- Tell your own stories of overcoming hardships: 'When I was a child, I thought … but then I realised …'
- Use stories or movies to inspire. There are many great examples, such as *The Tortoise and the Hare*, *Chicken Little*, *The Lion King* and *Charlotte's Web* for younger children, and *The Karate Kid* and *Free Willy* for older children. This is a genre that will always have new releases. The Discovery channel on DStv, among others, shows excellent real-life stories of people overcoming adversity.

For younger children (1–5 years)

- Play with your children as often as possible. It creates that 'feel good' sense for both of you and increases their happiness quotient.
- Involve your children in household chores – from making beds to cooking. This is a way of giving them positive strokes because they feel included, useful, capable and part of the exercise. It engenders an 'I can' positive feeling, which is also good for building their self-esteem.

For older children (6–14 years)

- Optimistic thinking does not mean downplaying your child's responsibility where failure is concerned. It is perfectly acceptable – and certainly instils optimism – to look at external circumstances that may have contributed to things going awry. But it's also important to assess where your child went wrong and to ensure that he or she takes responsibility for the error or failure. Instead of a self-blame session for your child, however, it's affirming – and optimistic – to discuss what your child can do personally in the future to improve next time. See this as a 'looking for opportunities to do better' approach.

- The ways in which adults *think* and *express themselves* about a child's experiences are very powerful in shaping the child's beliefs about the reasons for success or failure. For example, an optimist might say: 'It seems to me that you usually get good results when you give yourself enough time and really try hard with your maths homework.' A negative person, who fails to boost his or her child's self-esteem, is more likely to say: 'You see! You *never* allow yourself enough time and you just don't try hard enough with your maths homework.'

Self-confidence

> **So if you want a person to achieve his utmost and to persist in the face of resistance, reinforce his belief in his strengths, even overemphasize these strengths, give him an almost unreasonable confidence that he has what it takes to succeed ... And if this person succeeds, should you praise him for his hard work or for his unique strengths? Always the latter. Tell him he succeeded because his strengths carried the day ... It doesn't matter if this assessment is, in part, an illusion because it is an illusion that will serve to create a better reality. It will reinforce the self-assurance he needs to be resolute and persistent when taking on the next challenge, and the next.**
>
> (Marcus Buckingham in *The One Thing You Need to Know*, 2005)

Self-confidence usually grows out of mastery. Young children learn to master skills and learning areas through repetition. Whether it's learning to walk, talk, match shapes, identify colours or play a sport, practice and plenty of failure lead to learning and ultimately success. And, of course, the better you get at something, the more confident you become in your ability and in yourself.

Self-confidence within one aspect of your child's life can

easily transfer to other aspects. There can be a positive knock-on effect.

It seems that some children are just born plain confident while others acquire confidence over time. There is plenty that parents can do to help build their child's self-confidence, which is a highly desirable trait to possess during school and in later life. Self-confidence does not manifest itself in arrogance or boastfulness. It is a secure sense of self, a sense that 'I am able' and 'I am worth it'.

Tips for developing self-confidence

For all

- Encourage your children to ask for what they want assertively and clearly, pointing out that there is no guarantee they will always get it. Acknowledge them for asking, and avoid anticipating their desires. (This is different to anticipating and fulfilling their basic needs for food, water, sleep, stimulation and appropriate attention.)
- Teach children to change their demands to preferences. Point out to children that it is not possible or good for them to get everything that they want, and it is pointless to display anger in this regard. Encourage them to work against anger by setting a good example. Reinforce their behaviour when they display appropriate irritation rather than anger.[100]
- Teach your children life skills such as how to swim, how to cross the road safely, how to build a fire and light it, how to make a sandwich, and how to answer the telephone or make calls themselves. (These are just a few ideas among a plethora of possibilities.)
- Encourage other significant adults in your circle to play social sport with your children and even family board games. Children's self-confidence gains an additional

boost when other adults show interest and confidence in their abilities.

- Celebrate and acknowledge your children's achievements and strengths. For example, acquire or make a family celebration plate that is brought out at dinner time for a particular family member to eat from on any day when he or she has won a race, been especially compassionate towards a friend in need, been extraordinarily helpful, etc. Remember to celebrate not just achievements or birthdays – the 'what', but more importantly, anything that comprises the good inner nature of your child – the 'who'. And mum and dad get to use the plate too!
- Always have a plan B up your sleeve just in case you need it, and teach your children about this important secret to success too. Knowing there is another plan to fall back on certainly provides a modicum of self-confidence.
- Stick to your promises. If your children have confidence in you, they also develop self-confidence.

For younger children (1–5 years)

- Show your belief in your children's capabilities by giving them responsibilities, such as feeding the goldfish each morning, setting the table, helping you to maintain the garden, or assisting you with preparation for meals.
- Arrange playdates for your children. When they are small, you will need to 'play and stay instead of drop and run' to role-model for your child how playdates work and to build their confidence in this area. The older they get, the more confident they will become when you drop them off to play with a friend.
- Attending playgroup and preschool builds social skills and self-confidence.
- Play perceptual games, simple card games and basic board games with your children. As they learn 'how', they develop confidence.

For older children (6–14 years)

- From the age of six, allow your children to walk to their classroom by themselves from the school gate. Children are on a pathway to independence from the time they are born. When we let them go, little by little, we are showing our confidence in them.
- Together with your child, work out the study method that suits him or her best. When you hit the correct button here, your child's self-confidence improves as well as his or her marks.
- Help your child to know himself or herself – see 'Help your child to build a Talent Profile' on page 271.

Health

It makes sense that the biggest asset you have is yourself. It follows then that the more care you take of that asset, the easier learning will be. Physical health is becoming increasingly important. We live longer than people in ages past, and we need our bodies to function effectively for many more years than previous generations did. At the same time, food has become less healthy and nutritious, poorly affected by mass farming techniques and relentless refining and processing.

Of course, health is holistic. It's not just about keeping your body healthy, but your mind, emotions and spirit too. Stress and strong emotional reactions can all interfere with our ability to learn, to absorb and process information, and to use it efficiently and sensibly. Teach your children to honour their bodies. And teach them to get in touch and in tune with themselves, to know when they need to take a break, and when enough is enough.

Health is so important that it will be taken into account when your children negotiate a contract for work in the future.

Tips for keeping your children healthy

It is not our intention to provide you with comprehensive information on health and nutrition – that would be a book in itself. We recommend that you read various books on the physical development of children, as well as on child health and nutrition, to assist you in understanding what is happening (and what is *supposed* to happen) within your child's body during the first decade of his or her life. Most good book stores carry a useful selection of titles by leading authors in this field. In addition, do not hesitate to seek expert professional advice about anything that concerns you, for example from occupational therapists and developmental specialists.

For all

- Good nutrition optimises the way your mind and body works. A well-functioning mind and healthy body increase self-esteem and resilience.
- Buy a good water filter and guide your children into a habit of water being the drink of choice to quench their thirst. Educate your children about the side effects of drinking high sugar cool-drinks and energy sports drinks. The first organ to dehydrate when the body needs water is the brain, which will make your children irritable. They will also find it difficult to concentrate, which will interfere with their performance and ability to learn.
- Make exercise and recreation a family affair. If your children see you exercise, they are more likely to take it up themselves and to develop a lifelong positive habit.
- Bring your children up with some form of spiritual life. We are multidimensional beings and spirituality is part of who we are. This will enable your children to make decisions about their beliefs and meaningful sources of spiritual nourishment when they are older and better informed. Encourage tolerance of all faiths and creeds.

- Teach your children to honour the planet and take care of the environment. This is the world they will inherit. Good habits start young, such as sorting the household refuse into recyclables, glass, plastic, cans and garden waste.

For younger children (1–5 years)

- Teach your children healthy media habits from a young age. This will help them to protect their minds from 'media pollution', and their bodies from radiation from one screen or electronic device or another.
- Part of a good routine is that there is a time to eat and a time to sleep.
- Teach your children about blood safety from an early age, which is important owing to the prevalence of HIV/Aids. There is no need for hysteria, but children must learn to call an adult for assistance rather than touch another person's blood.

For older children (6–14 years)

- Inform and educate your children about drugs and their effects from an early age by having frank and honest conversations and discussions with them.
- Teach children to 'read' their own bodies so that they can tell you when they have a headache, need a doctor or physiotherapist, feel down, etc.
- Do not over-schedule your children so that their days are literally spent going from one organised activity to another. Bear in mind that while extramural activities are an essential part of your children's lives, they still need time to play, socialise and 'chill'. They need down time to simply 'be'.

Learning

In a world in which information is being generated at an unprecedented rate, it is absolutely essential to continue to learn throughout your life. A love of learning, in addition to the skills and competencies required to learn, will be among the most important characteristics we can instil within our children to ensure that they remain continually relevant – as well as continually intrigued and engaged by life. Regardless of what life throws at our children, if they are willing and eager to learn, they will be able to work out how to cope. We need to stop trying to educate and overwhelm our children with a whole lot of information they may only possibly need. We really need to start instilling within them an ability and desire to learn what they need to learn, when they need to learn it.

Curiosity

This remains the best toy in the store.[101] It's about exploring and searching for new ways, ideas or approaches to accomplish things. Asking why is an innate human drive that we need to protect and encourage. Accepting the status quo today does not signify progress. We need to support our children's quest to explore and discover their world. 'Encouraging kids to explore their ideas – no matter how unusual or strange those ideas might seem – is within the power of all parents. The key here is creating a relationship and an environment in which questioning becomes second nature,' comments eminent psychologist Roger Schank in *Coloring Outside the Lines* (2001), which we highly recommend you read.

> A friend of Nikki's overheard her six-year-old daughter, Claudia, and a friend discussing why big people have children. This is how the conversation went:
>
> So that big people can play [with the children].
> So that big people can love.
> So that trees are climbed.

So that big people can go out and work to earn money for the little people.
So that big people can have big houses.

Out of the mouths of babes!

Why forms the basis for all human enquiry. It indicates a passion for life, a quest for knowledge and understanding that fuels all learning. If you have a preschooler, you will be all too familiar with the constant stream of 'why' questions. It's fascinating to listen to what young children ask about, but it can sometimes become rather irritating because they ask so many questions so often. According to neurophysiologist and educator, Carla Hannaford, once speech is in place, the child will process thought through outer speech until about the age of seven. This stream-of-consciousness speech (as children think, so they say it) is the problem-solving tool of four- to six-year-olds. 'Why' becomes the generator of that process.

'This stream of consciousness speech, in varying degrees, is essential to language and thought development. Inner speech development (when children think before they speak) doesn't normally occur until around age seven, so children literally think aloud. I'm sure children of this age wonder if adults ever think because we are so quiet!' Hannaford comments in her book, *Smart Moves*. So next time your child asks another 'why' question, know that it is a vitally important part of his or her intellectual development.

Tips for developing curiosity

For all

- Take your children to visit places of interest such as the planetarium, museums, zoos, game reserves, etc. These places provide a variety of contexts for the 'why' questions as well as opportunities to connect information between experiences.

- Go on holiday to different places so that your children can start to compare their holiday experiences.
- Most children are curious about where their parents disappear to each day when they go to work. If you work away from home in an office, then make sure you take your child to you place of work for a visit. When your child is old enough – from around age six – let him or her sit in with you for half a day or so to see you in action.
- As mentioned previously, do not always provide your children with answers to their questions. Rather help them to discover the answers for themselves. Psychologist Roger Schank has a great deal to say on this subject:

> **When children ask questions, they're expressing interest in a subject and setting the stage for a true teachable moment ... Most children (and most people in general) don't ask questions to receive answers. They ask them because they're intrigued, puzzled, and provoked. They want the chance to bounce ideas off an expert, to get some guidance so they can find the answer themselves. This is especially true when children ask open-ended questions ('Why do we die?', 'Why do birds have wings and we don't?'), but it's also true when they ask factual questions.**
>
> (Roger Schank in *Coloring Outside the Lines*, 2001)

So engage your children in discussions. Ask them questions in return, such as 'What do you think?', 'What do you know about birds?', 'Why would they need wings?', etc.

On National Women's Day 2007, seven-year-old Matthew asked Nikki why it was a public holiday. When she answered that it was Women's Day, he said, 'Does that mean we need to buy you something?' She said no, and he countered with 'Don't you think we should at least buy you a bunch of flowers?' Very dear. Later in the day, both boys wanted to know why there was a Women's Day and not a Men's Day. Instead of answering, Nikki asked them why they felt women were important in the world. Matthew jumped in by saying that if there weren't any women then there wouldn't be any babies, and if there weren't any babies then eventually no people would be left on earth! This topic can – and indeed it did – lead to a long discussion on many issues related to women, for instance the courage of the marching women who protested against carrying passes in apartheid South Africa; the fact that not long ago women were not permitted to vote and many were expected to do menial labour; the fact that, even today, comparatively few women hold leadership positions in politics, commerce and industry; and so forth.

- When your children come home from school, ask them some additional questions. For example, what did they find interesting in the classroom that day, or did anything bother them or seem unclear about what they learnt, or did they ask any interesting questions?
- Use books or television as a springboard for thinking. You can encourage an enquiring mind by asking children interesting questions about characters in books or on TV, such as 'I wonder why that person did or thought that?', and wait for their answers.
- Don't be judgemental about your children's questions. If you tell them that their questions are silly, then they may lose confidence and avoid asking more questions. In the same vein, don't be critical about their answers. If need be, ask a follow-up question such as 'Why do you think that?'
- Don't be afraid to say 'I don't know' – you can't have all the answers! But do follow up your 'don't know' with an

expression of curiosity and interest, such as 'When we get home, let's check on the Internet or in the dictionary', or 'Let's ask your aunt because she's interested in this topic and is sure to know.' Encourage the process of enquiry to find the answer rather than dead-ending the thought process. This will develop a love of learning and insatiable curiosity.

For younger children (1–5 years)

- Allow your children to explore their environment – the house and garden, instead of sitting them down in front of the TV.
- Play hide and seek with your children, or hide objects around the house for them to find.
- Play peek-a-boo with a baby.
- Do not do everything for your children, or teach them everything. Let them learn through exploration – make time for this.

For older children (6–14 years)

- Remember that the best learning experiences for children under the age of 12 are real, concrete experiences (with people, toys and equipment, and through their own body movements and senses, etc.) and not virtual ones. Concrete learning enables children to create meaning and real understanding about the world around them.
- Make a conversation jar (or basket). This works well with older children, say from the age of seven upwards. Whenever a family member has a question or an interesting thought, he or she can write it on a piece of paper and put it into the jar. From time to time the conversation jar can be brought to the dinner table. Each person has a chance to pick a piece of paper out of the jar and to answer the question. Then everyone else at the table can add to the answer, person by person, going around the table.

Questions could be about anything, for example 'What makes us hiccup?', 'Who is God?', 'If you weren't yourself, who would you like to be?', 'What happens when you die?' A conversation jar creates interesting discussions, shows that the family values curiosity, enables different members of the family to share their knowledge, and encourages them to find out more about the things that interest them.[102]

Hard work and focus

Talented people stand out from the crowd by being prepared to work harder and longer than their peers. Of course, they also work smarter, so it's not just about putting in extra hours – it's about adding more value.

There is no doubt that whatever we focus our attention on grows, expands, blossoms and flourishes. It is a universal law of life. If you want to become an expert in a particular area, focus on it, study it, write about it, talk about it, live it – and you will become a specialist. Often this means making various sacrifices, such as working extra long hours to get an idea off the ground, or being prepared to do things that others wouldn't normally do.

It is easy to put enormous effort into something that you are passionate about. So, if you have an emotional attachment to making something happen, it stands to reason that you are far more likely to invest quality time, huge effort and clear-cut focus.

Tips to encourage focus and effort in your children

For all

- Help your children to understand that every child is different. This means there is no need for children to compare themselves to others.

- Focus on and put effort into your relationship with your children. By showing them *how*, we teach children to concentrate and put in hard work.
- Teach children that there are times to multitask and there are times to focus in order to get the job done, and done well.

For younger children (1–5 years)

- Teach your children to complete tasks – simple tasks when they are small, and bigger ones as they get older.
- Extend your children's ability to concentrate by being part of the play experience yourself. The more involved you are in their games, the longer they will be able to play without losing interest or getting bored. Teach your children well and they will learn how to play by themselves and to concentrate for longer periods.

For older children (6–14 years)

- Create a positive, regular homework habit from Grade 1 – preferably homework at the same time every day in the same place. This regular focus and consistent effort will ensure that your child achieves some rewards and learning will become easier with more practise.
- Work out your children's preferred learning style so that they learn in the best way for them. This means that taking in, storing and retrieving information for later use will be easier and more effective, yielding results and increasing confidence. Putting in focus and effort will make far more sense if learning is not a constant battle.
- Discover your children's interests and passions. Create projects for them in this area and, when they are older, allow them to develop their own projects. Support these with enthusiasm and watch how easy it is for them to invest their attention and effort. If they experience the rewards of their commitment, then they will be more

willing to put focus and effort into things about which they are less enthusiastic because they will have worked out that there is always a return.

- Help your children to develop some real and meaningful goals based on their strengths, interests and passions. Often goals set in the school environment are fairly artificial and don't relate to real life. You may need to look at non-academic activities here, such as photography, building model aeroplanes, scrapbooking, etc.

Information processing and filtering

Here are some rather mind-boggling facts about information overload:[103]

- The amount of technological information is currently doubling every two years. By 2010 it could be doubling every 72 hours! As mentioned previously, this means that half of what students studying a four-year technical degree learn will be outdated by the third year.
- In a recent test it was found that fibre optic cables – the information superhighway – can transmit 10 trillion bytes of information per second down one strand of fibre. This is equivalent to 1 900 CDs and 150 million simultaneous phone calls every second. This will triple every six months for the next 20 years because fibre optic cable becomes more efficient the more it is used – at no extra cost.
- Daily, 3 000 new books are published around the world.
- In January 2007, there were 106 million registered MySpace users and the average MySpace page was visited 30 times per day. If MySpace were a country, it would be the 11th largest (between Japan and Mexico).

- In 2006, 2.7 billion Google searches were conducted per month. The question remains – to whom were these enquiries addressed Before Google (BG)?
- The number of text messages sent per day now exceeds the number of people on the planet.

Clearly our children are growing up digital and they appear to be extremely comfortable navigating the world with technology. They will live with constant information overload, and much of that information will be changing and becoming outdated as quickly as it arrives. When faced with this inundation of information, in a world that plugs in 24/7, Millennial children need strong traditional reading, writing and spelling skills as well as good old-fashioned comprehension skills. To be able to make sense – quickly – of so much information, solid foundations in all these disciplines will be essential.

The development of all these skills can only be achieved effectively if there is a solid foundation of school readiness skills. The building blocks of preschool learning are shape, colour and quantity. As far as possible, a child should experience these concepts in concrete, real-life form through the medium of play. Reading, writing, spelling and maths are semi-concrete and abstract principles, which are built on seemingly unrelated perceptual skills. Parents of preschoolers would do well to improve their knowledge in this regard. Preschool learning is a miraculous process that unequivocally demonstrates the powerful and almost magical connection between the brain and the body. The body is quite literally the architect of the brain, adding weight to the importance of balancing a child's real and virtual play experiences. (See Section 2 for more detail.)

Tips for developing information-processing abilities

For all

- Talk your children clever. Language is the way in which we communicate with the world. Children need to learn this from you.
- Develop a love for books and reading.
- When you have finished reading your child a story, or even the next day, ask your child questions about the story you read together, or the setwork the class is reading at school, just to test his or her comprehension skills. These skills are of vital importance in a world of information overload.
- Play with your children often, to improve their concentration skills. Children need to be able to concentrate in order to read, write, spell and do maths. A child only has about a minute's concentration for each year of his or her life, so it is up to parents to increase this by engaging their children in fun and stimulating activities.

For younger children (1–5 years)

- When your children are small, keep them socially active with children you would like them to spend time with. Children learn and gain a great deal from face-to-face socialising, including language development which is the foundation for information processing. What children learn face to face, they cannot acquire from on-screen activities. At this age, choose friends for your children whose parents have a similar outlook to yours. Obviously, as children become older, they make and choose their own friends. But gently continue to guide them, and keep an eye on whether or not they are choosing friends with similar value systems.
- Ensure your child moves a lot and has opportunities to play outdoors on jungle gyms, with balls, and with other

children too. Movement not only strengthens the body, which will help a child to sit comfortably in a chair at school for lengthy periods of time, but it also stimulates and strengthens the visual system, which is so important for reading and writing activities.

For older children (6–14 years)

- Choosing friends with similar value systems becomes even more important the older your child gets, and the more he or she interacts with technology. In other words, do you know whether or not your child is playing on-screen activities when visiting his or her friends? Do you know what type of TV programmes, DVDs, computer or Playstation games your child is being exposed to at friends' homes?
- Create family rules about emails, SMSes, phone calls, etc. As your children become older, they will spend more and more time interacting with on-screen media. This time will need to be managed. In order for your family rules to be effective, however, you as parents will have to adhere to them too. Create phone-free and email-free zones or times.
- Encourage your children to play with games that stimulate their intellect, thinking skills, reasoning and problem solving. Encourage them to 'fact check' TV programmes that interest them by accessing the Internet to do follow-up learning.
- Before computers, we researched topics by starting with the general and working towards the specific. We would find a general encyclopaedia entry and work our way towards more detailed information. Today, however, if we tried to start with the general in a Google search, we might get over one million websites to consider! As a result, the new approach to research today is to be as specific as possible in an online search request. In this way, we generally find

the specific information we are looking for. The downside, however, is that we often end up with loads of interesting facts, but no context for that information. In addition, not all the information that we find in these searches is necessarily factually correct or sound.

- Speed reading and touch typing are excellent skills for greater efficiency in life. Being able to operate and navigate technology confidently – from cellphones to computers to the Internet and other electronic gadgets – will enable learners to manipulate, disseminate and acquire information quickly. Competence in this area will assist with time management and enhance communication and presentation skills. (It will also bolster your own marketing plug!) You will find that your children are far more intuitive about these things than you are. Allow them to teach you to be technologically literate too.

Mastery of technology

It probably goes without saying that it is critical to be confident and skilled with technology (both hardware and software) in today's world, otherwise you will simply be left behind. This confidence and ability goes beyond computers to include mobile phones, multimedia devices, biotechnology, nanotechnology – and all sorts of technologies we can't even imagine.

Understand that technology itself is neutral – it's what we can do with it that either assists us or leads us into trouble. So don't blame the medium or channel for getting children into trouble, as we have seen with applications such as MXit and Facebook. It is essential to put firm rules in place, with consequences if these are broken. In addition, spend time connecting and communicating with your children. Invest your time in them to develop their values, their moral compass, their passions and good media habits to prevent technology from filling a void and being abused.

Tips for developing a mastery of technology

For all

- Very young children under the age of two do not need to watch TV. Far better stimulation can be obtained through play, exploration of their world and interaction with their parents and other people.
- As they get older (between the ages of four and five), allow your children to play on the computer and to experiment. This may mean you need to buy an old computer that won't cost you too much if it gets broken – but do it! This generation is naturally wired and interacts intuitively with technology.
- From time to time, play computer and Playstation games *with* your children so that you know what they are being exposed to. This will also enable you to better appreciate the attraction of these programs.
- There is absolutely no reason why parents cannot master the technologies available. Most parents get left behind, not because of lack of ability, but rather from a conscious decision that this is all too much. Such an attitude is not good for your children – keep up, stay in the loop, and they will reap the benefits!
- Over time, expose your children to a variety of technology and media –from digital cameras and cellphones (which does *not* mean they must own their own!) to computers and gaming platforms, etc. They need to be able to apply their skills across a multitude of applications.

For younger children (1–5 years)

- Limit TV viewing and computer access.
- Be careful about the content that your children watch on TV and play on computers. There is some really good stuff out there, as well as some pretty meaningless and even harmful content.

- Children love repetition, which is how they master something. Your child will want to watch the same DVD over and over again, as well as play the same computer games again and again. You will need to gauge when your child is ready for something new and more challenging, which is one of the reasons why you need to watch or play with your child from time to time.
- When playing educational computer games, your child is learning how to master the computer mouse and to navigate the screen, as well as a number of other basic computer functions.
- Teach your children to ask permission to switch on the TV or a computer. It's a good habit to get them into and it's also part of boundary setting.

For older children (6–14 years)

- Find out your children's school curriculum in terms of the subject of Computers or Information Technology (IT). Some schools teach children how to use specific computer programs such as Word and Excel, while others teach computer skills by allowing children to use computers for various academic subjects or extension activities.
- Encourage the use of different platforms, but also instil in your children the need to be responsible in terms of their media usage. They must understand that learning to be a discerning user of media will ultimately protect them.
- Allow your children to teach you about technology.
- Send your children on relevant training courses if possible.

Online security

Inevitably our children are going to use their information-processing skills to be increasingly online. Thus, we need to ensure that they are secure in that environment. Just as we teach them stranger danger and not to touch someone else's blood, so we must instil in our children the need for online security for their own protection.

Tips to ensure the online security of children

For all

- Ensure that your family computer is placed in a public space, with the screen facing the room. This will enable you to keep an eye on what your children are accessing.
- Activate the filters that are available through your search engines. As your children get older, invest in software that will protect them from inappropriate content.
- Do not put a TV or computer in your pre-teen's bedroom.
- When purchasing games from multimedia outlets, read the packaging carefully. Ask the shop assistant about the content of the games, take note of suggested age restrictions and, if possible, ask for a demonstration of the game.
- Teach your children to honour, value and protect their own minds. You can teach them that inappropriate content is much like pollution. Instead of polluting the planet, however, it pollutes their hearts and minds. Disturbing content is also very difficult – if not impossible – to erase, particularly in children under the age of seven who have not yet developed filters to protect themselves.
- Keep the lines of communication open and keep talking. This should ensure that your children will feel comfortable to come to you with any problems they experience online.

For younger children (1–5 years)

- Always sit with your preschool children when they are using the computer and especially if they are online or connected to other computers.

- Be aware of what your children are doing in other people's homes. When they go for playdates, are they playing with toys and children or are they playing on-screen activities? Get to know the parents of the children with whom your children are friendly to gain a sense of their values and to enable you to have open discussions with them.

For older children (6–14 years)

- Teach your children *never* to give out their personal details via their cellphone, the Internet or email to strangers or marketers, without checking with your first. Teach your children not to put too much information on their profile on any social networking sites.
- Young children should not use chat rooms – the dangers are too great. As children get older, make sure that they use well-monitored kids' chat rooms. Encourage even your teenagers to use monitored chat rooms.
- Teach your children not to trust digital persona:
    - They should always treat digital friends as strangers.
    - They should always keep in mind that photos can be created and adjusted.
- Do not overreact and 'blanket censor' access to the Internet. This will not benefit your child and is likely to encourage deception.
- Remember that you provide the access, so you also set the boundaries.
- Install filters and software to monitor usage on your home computers.
- Discuss the need for online protection with your children.
- Limit 'screen time' to a certain number of hours per day. This includes all screens – phones, TV, computer, Internet, etc. There should be no phoning after a certain time, and phones should be switched off or ignored at certain times,

such as family meals. Remember that this must apply to *everyone*!

- When your children are young, they should share the family email address rather than have an address of their own. As they get older, you can ask your Internet service provider to set up a separate email address for them, but your children's mail can still be processed through your account.
- If all your precautions fail and your child does meet an online predator, don't blame him or her. The offender must always bear full responsibility. Take decisive action to stop your child from any further contact with this person.

Know yourself

Self-awareness refers to knowing your internal states, preferences, resources and intuitions. Jonathan Cook, a psychologist at the Gordon Institute of Business Science, identifies three important components of self-awareness[104]:

- **Emotional awareness:** Recognising your emotions and their effects
- **Accurate self-assessment:** Knowing your strengths and limits
- **Self-confidence:** A strong sense of your self-worth and capabilities

These days, most people know that there are multiple intelligences. The school system measures mainly language and mathematical skills, and IQ tests do the same, with a slight emphasis on logical analysis. The problem is that these types of intelligence are no guarantee of success in most of life's arenas. Analyses of successful people show that, in addition to being 'clever', they are intelligent in other ways.

As Howard Gardner's research[105] shows, one of the critical abilities in exceptional people is the ability to know yourself. This involves knowing – and accepting – your strengths and weaknesses.

> A fascinating thing about having more than one child is seeing and experiencing just how different each child is. Nikki's youngest son, Matthew, recently had to prepare for a verbal Afrikaans test. They spent a considerable amount of time learning the names of fruit and vegetables. Matthew really knew the work and was excited about the test. However, he was less than enthusiastic with his result because he didn't achieve a merit. The thing is that Matthew is a visual learner, not an auditory one, and so of course he will do better in written tests than in verbal ones. It is so important that Matthew understands that he is not stupid – his natural strength lies in what he sees and not what he hears, and that's okay. He will pick up the marks in written work that he loses in oral tests.
>
> Nikki's eldest son Ryan, however, is an auditory learner. He finds oral tests far easier than written ones. He has had to work hard over the years to adapt his dominance profile to an education system that still favours written work. But he is winning because he understands where his strengths lie and that his weaker areas do not indicate that he is stupid. The person who did his profile at the age of eight asked Ryan if people had ever told him he was slow or stupid. He nodded his head (and mum almost burst into tears!). What the profilologist said next was the best thing to happen to Ryan in his three years of primary school: 'Ryan, let me tell you something. You have the brain profile of Einstein. Do you know that he was one of the cleverest people who ever lived? So don't ever believe anyone who tells you that you are stupid! Sometimes you just take longer to get out the

information than others. You are a very clever boy! Always remember that.' A few weeks thereafter, a full IQ test revealed that Ryan does indeed have a high IQ. It needs to be nurtured and understood by his parents and teachers, and especially by himself. This information made it far easier to make the decision about which school would be best for him.

Multiple intelligences

We discussed multiple intelligences in detail on page 62.

Just as people are different physically (some short, some tall, some fast, some slow), so too are our brains different. Each of us has a unique range of abilities in relation to our different intelligences. The most successful people in life seem to have at least one category of intelligence that is significantly more developed than normal, but they also have fair to good use of most, if not all, of the other intelligence categories as well.

Our task as parents is, first, to identify the built-in abilities of our children. Second, we must help them to develop their strengths, building their best intelligences into truly world-class capabilities. And third, we need to help them raise the status of their other intelligences so that they have a fully rounded base. At some stage in the future there may be drugs to assist in this development, just as there are drugs to enhance physical performance. We may or may not want our children using these artificial stimulants. Imagine a world in which the top students at a school were randomly drug tested in the way that athletes are today? But, in the absence of these 'short-cut' routes to intelligence, there are many things we can do as parents to develop the various intelligences that our children have – and need. We should start with getting to know our children.

Know your strengths (and weaknesses)

Your job is not to provide him with a realistic picture of the limits of strengths and the liability of his weaknesses ... Your job is to get him to perform. Stated more bluntly, your job is to build his self-assurance, not his self-awareness ... In short, the state of mind you should try to create in him is one where he has a fully realistic assessment of the difficulty of the challenge ahead of him and, at the same time, an unrealistically optimistic belief in his ability to overcome it.

(Marcus Buckingham in *The One Thing You Need to Know*, 2005)

Who am I? Where have I been? Where am I going? The answers to these questions will determine our capability to chart our own destiny and realise our potential.[106] Self-awareness includes understanding our personality and recognising our strengths and weaknesses, our likes and dislikes. Developing self-awareness can help us to realise when we are stressed or under pressure. It is also a prerequisite for effective communication and interpersonal relations. In addition, it is important in developing empathy for others.

In his book *Now Discover Your Strengths* (2001), Marcus Buckingham strongly suggests that many of us have an incorrect view of personal development. Ever since we brought home our own report cards from school, we had it drummed into us that our developmental focus should be on our areas of weakness. Remember that moment your parents read your report card? It may have displayed a few As, a B or C, but if there was one F on it, what did your parents focus on? The F, right? Buckingham suggests that we should focus instead on developing our strengths, simply ensuring that our weaknesses are not big enough to hold us back materially. No one can be good at everything, so why focus on bringing your weak areas up to 'acceptable' levels, that is, merely average? Why not focus on developing your strengths into world-class assets?

Don't waste time trying to put in what was left out. Try to draw out what was left in.

(Gallup research findings quoted in *The New Learning Revolution*, Gordon Dryden and Jeanette Vos, 2005)

Today children are being encouraged in the area of self-assessment in the school system too, often being asked to evaluate themselves and keep track of their own progress. 'This creates more awareness of their own personal progress – bettering their previous personal best and working out their own areas of strength and weakness. There is a greater sense of partnership between the child and the teacher, as there is between the parent and teacher,' comments Alison Scott, deputy head at HeronBridge College in Johannesburg.

David Kramer of Protec, educational consultants to the National Union of Educators, says that in the past we relied on tests that showed us whether learners could recall the facts and repeat actions that they had been taught. Learners who answered correctly, or who could do what was required, scored high marks. This kind of assessment does little to show whether learners understand what they have learned. There has been a shift towards assessment that demonstrates whether learners really understand what they have learned, and whether they can think about what they have learned in ways that allow them to apply their learning in different ways.

Here is an example of an end-of-term self-assessment form for a nine- or 10-year-old on which children rate how well they think they did:

Rate yourself	1	2	3	4	5
How do you rate your listening skills?					
How do you rate your concentration and focus?					
How do you rate your success in class activities?					
How do you rate your cycle test results against your personal best?					
How do you rate your preparedness to write tests?					
How do you rate your project work?					

Key: 1 = poor, 2 = fair, 3 = average, 4 = good, 5 = very good

The younger children are given something like this:

Rate yourself	Tick
I found this task easy	
I needed a little extra help with this task	
I needed a lot of help to finish this task	

We must help our children to develop an accurate and fair assessment of themselves.

Tips for developing self-awareness of strengths and weaknesses

For all

- Start with obvious and non-emotional areas of assessment in which a certain characteristic holds no distinct advantage or disadvantage. Help your children to understand the difference between an introvert and an extrovert, or an expressive or receptive person. Many people misunderstand these labels, thinking they are about confidence, loudness or being outgoing. They are actually about the sources from which an individual draws his or her energy. If you gain your energy from being alone, and are drained by being with people, then you are an introvert. If you gain your energy from being with people, and cannot spend long times alone without feeling drained, you are an extrovert. Help your children to understand these differences. Where you have a mix of introverts and extroverts in your home, teach them to respect the needs of other family members for space and for interaction.

> After Graeme's daughter Amy's second birthday party, she was sitting on the floor surrounded by her presents. The afternoon had been a whirlwind of friends, clowns and activity. Now, her grandparents were trying to engage her and to spend some quality time with her. But Amy had reached her 'people interaction limit'. She said simply and clearly, 'Granny, go home now!' Graeme didn't need a psychological profile test to know that his eldest daughter was an introvert.

- Your children cannot know what they are good at and what they are not good at just by thinking about it, or even based on their feelings. They should be encouraged to try as many activities as possible. They may surprise themselves with an aptitude for something. In their pre-teen years, especially, we should be encouraging our children to engage in as wide a variety of pursuits as possible.
- We must realise that even the best people in the world were not brilliant the first time they tried something. The greatest piano players in the world (apart from Mozart!) still had to spend a few years banging away fairly tunelessly at a keyboard. The greatest artists probably started by smearing finger paints on scraps of paper. Every successful person spends years of hard work

learning the basics required for success. As parents, we sometimes need to push our children when they want to give up, and help them to get 'over the hump' as they develop from good to great.

For younger children (1–5 years)

- When your children complain that they are not very good at something, take the opportunity to point out their strengths and to emphasise that everyone is different. Remember also to acknowledge strengths such as being a good friend and a great helper, among others.

For older children (6–14 years)

- If your children consistently display a flair, an aptitude or a passion for an activity, where possible and if you can afford it, you should involve them in some specialised coaching and tuition so that their natural ability can be nurtured and assessed by a professional in that area. However, involvement in too much of one thing could cause an imbalance. Also remember that children in this age bracket still need spare time to play.
- Allow your children to take part in cultural events that encourage participation and offer constructive feedback such as the national eisteddfod competition. In such a competition, all talent is recognised with certificates for different levels achieved. The adjudication is usually highly constructive, pointing out a child's areas of strength and weakness with practical advice on how to improve.

Around eisteddfod time in 2005, Ryan was entered for the prepared reading competition. Nikki had been extremely busy with her business at the time and had not spent much time assisting Ryan to practise his three pages from Roald Dahl's *James and the Giant Peach*. He assured her, however, that things were going well. Three days prior to his performance, Nikki finally sat down to listen to him read and was inwardly horrified at his poor delivery. There was no fluency, a lack of expression, and the entire reading passage was running over time. Drastic action was required. Working from her knowledge of Ryan's auditory strength, Nikki came up with a solution which has since become the blueprint for Ryan's study skills because it really works for him. She read the extract to him with his eyes closed, and then he read it back to her. They did this three times and the improvement was dramatic. They did this exercise twice more before D-day, and Ryan received a gold certificate for his performance.

Things happen more quickly, easily and confidently when you can harness your child's natural strengths. By using the same technique for studying subjects such as Geography and History, Ryan is more confident of doing well in his tests.

This aspect is discussed in far more detail later on in Section 4 under 'Building a Talent Profile' (page 268).

Future-focused

There is a restlessness about talented people. They are not always clear about where they want to be going, but they know that they want to be on the move.

(Alan Robertson and Graham Abbey in *Managing Talented People*, 2003)

Talented people are never satisfied with the status quo – 'Good enough never is.'[107] Their restlessness is focused on the future – on a world that they can visualise in their heads, and then set to work to turn into reality. Being future focused involves imagination, creativity, hard work and resilience, with a specific focus on what could be, and how we get there.

Tips for developing future focus

For all

- Speak to your children about the future. Create a strong interest in new inventions, in the changing world, and in the future itself. Generate excitement and a belief in their ability to create a great life for themselves further down the track as they become part of the solution for the challenges facing the planet.

For younger children (1–5 years)

- You can have discussions with your children from the fantasy stage when they voice, 'One day I want to be ...', or 'When I'm big, I want to be ...', which can be the start of some wonderful conversations. Note how these discussions change and evolve as your child discovers more and more about himself or herself and about life.
- Tell your child the same story for five days in a row. But, every day, make the ending different and explain to him or her that the same events can have different outcomes.

For older children (6–14 years)

- Encourage your children to read and watch science fiction books and movies. Discuss the content with them, and chat about the likelihood of some of the scenarios. Get them to imagine what careers they could pursue to be involved in these futurist visions.
- Bring your children's attention to various kinds of jobs and careers as they are growing and developing. We are so used to hearing about the traditional trades or professions, yet most people find employment in other spheres. As we have already discussed in Section 3, this

will increasingly be the case.

- Discuss current affairs with your children. They hear about these on the news and you should contextualise these issues for them. Current affairs can form the basis for good conversations about various industries in which your children could find a niche for themselves in the future.
- Ask your children how they would solve some of the problems of the world, such as traffic congestion, global warming and littering. Their solutions will range from the simple to the complex and might even be quite profound for their age. They need to know that we value their opinions and want to hear what they are thinking.

Emotional intelligence

Emotional intelligence is the measure of an individual's self-awareness (*intra*personal) and their ability to relate to others (*inter*personal).[108]

Children will need to be socially and emotionally mature to build and maintain the relationships that they will require to succeed in the 21st century. Academic qualifications are simply not enough to ensure success in life. Emotions and feelings play an important role in our lives as they drive our behaviour and influence our values. Emotional intelligence (EQ – emotional quotient) is the ability to recognise, understand and manage our own feelings as well as be aware of the feelings of others. It is the ability to show understanding and empathy, as well as to see things from other points of view.[109]

Emotionally intelligent people learn to control their emotions and to moderate their emotional reactions to situations. They listen effectively and are able to give constructive feedback about themselves and others. They are able to set goals and to devise plans for achieving their goals. People with EQ see problems as opportunities. They are able to communicate clearly and effectively, which helps them to deal efficiently with conflict and group situations.

Tips for developing emotional intelligence

To develop emotional intelligence in your children, you need as parents to create or take advantage of connection opportunities by making choices and having conversations.

For all

- Praise less and encourage more. Praise focuses on the outcome (winning, or the end product). Encouragement focuses on the process, or the effort involved in reaching a goal (winning is not everything, especially at any price).
- Use what is called *descriptive praise* to let your children know when they are doing something well. Of course, you will need to get into the habit of looking for situations in which your child is doing a good job or displaying a talent. When your child completes a task or chore, you could say: 'I really like the way you tidied your room. You found a place for everything and put each thing where it belongs.' When you observe your child showing a talent, you might say: 'That last piece you played sounded so good. You really have a lot of musical talent.' Don't be afraid to give praise often, even in front of family or friends. Also, use praise to point out positive character traits. For instance, 'You are a very kind person.' Or, 'I like the way you stick with things you try, even when they seem hard to do.' You can even praise a child for something he or she did not do, such as: 'I really liked how you accepted my answer of "no" and didn't lose your temper.'[110]
- Teach children that all emotions are okay, but it's their response to them that is important.

One of Graeme's friends had a feisty six-year-old daughter who had inherited her Dad's quick temper. In addition to disciplining her when she lost her temper, her smart parents got her to manage her rage. When she felt angry, she had to walk calmly to the bathroom, close the door, and stand there and scream and howl all she liked. She then had to emerge calmly from the bathroom. It was not a long-term solution, but it really helped her to work through a stage in her life, to accept her emotions and manage them appropriately.

- Children will copy you. You are their role model. It is a 'do as I do' world. Children will no longer swallow 'do as I say', especially if it does not match your behaviour! This has huge implications for parents who must now really 'walk their talk' or lose credibility. Children only want to engage with you if you offer them something authentic, which means being consistent.
- Choose caregivers well, and 'co-parent' consistently with your spouse, ex-spouse, life partner, step-parents, caregivers and other significant adults in your children's lives. It is so important that all parties agree and stand together on everything from issues of watching TV, to diet, homework time and gifts, among many other things. Consistency and a united front leave no room for children to manipulate the situation, which they are quick to do if they spot a gap or weakness.
- Do not be afraid to say sorry to your children when you have made a mistake. In fact, look for opportunities to talk to your children about why you do what you do, and help them to see your own self-awareness. For example, if – like most people – you get short and snappy when tired, then explain this to your children. If you're going through a busy patch at work, pre-empt it with your

children by asking them to point out when you are being unpleasant or somewhat irritable! You can even make it a game, awarding 'prizes' when they point out that you are not acting your normal self during this busy time.

- Teach your children how to listen well by being a good listener yourself. Teach them the importance of eye contact and face-to-face communication. It is through verbal communication in the presence of others that we best learn how our words and actions impact upon people. We see their reactions and realise that they too have feelings and emotions. In today's world of electronic and text communication, much of this learning is being missed or bypassed. We cannot gauge how we make others feel. Millennials thrive on sending text messages to each other. This needs to be balanced with real communication experiences. According to Daniel Goleman[111], whenever we connect with another individual face to face (or voice to voice or skin to skin), our social brains interlock and every interaction has an emotional subtext. Children need to experience and learn to interpret these interactions.
- Make a determined effort to be really present when you are with your children. It is so easy to be distracted, and children know instantly whether or not they have your attention. Failure to attend to your children will often lead to attention-seeking behaviour, which is frequently misread as playing up or being naughty. Yet generally the only remediation required is for us to learn how to bring our attention to the present moment, instead of allowing our minds to wander off to the unfinished work on our desk, the unpaid accounts, or tomorrow's meeting.
- Be consistent with your communication, your behaviour, and the boundaries and limits you set for your children. It helps them to feel safer and makes life more predictable. They will also respect you more.

The computer department at the school of Nikki's friend's son recently tightened up student access to the Internet since clearly some children had been trying to bypass the system to access undesirable content. He was disgusted, however, when (during his computer lesson) he inadvertently caught a glimpse of the content the computer teacher was perusing on screen – pictures of extremely scantily clad women. How could the teacher be saying one thing and yet doing another?

- Allow your children to experience the consequences of their actions. Do not overprotect them from the mistakes they make. Be especially careful at school. When your children report on issues that took place at school, it is unwise to assume automatically that your children's teachers or friends are wrong and your precious child is right.
- Teach children to respect each other and each other's property by showing them respect too. Bear in mind that respect does not come automatically to Millennial children. They will only give respect when it is earned. They love it when you respect their minds, so ask for their opinions. Be genuinely interested in what they have to say and why they say it.
- The prolific use of cellphones also demands a code of conduct and a good measure of respect. Both adults and children are guilty of ignoring or cutting off people as a result of cellphone use. In addition, both are guilty of texting things they would never say to others in real life. Create a standard house rule: Never text anything that you would not say to a person's face.
- Teach children that relationships bring satisfaction and fulfil emotional needs much more than material possessions. This is a rather tricky issue to navigate when

children are being bought 'things' for doing well in tests and exams, and when a lost cellphone is replaced with a new one within a couple of days.

- Recognise appropriate behaviour as often as possible. Remember that whatever you focus your attention on tends to expand and develop.

> An old Cherokee is teaching his grandson about life:
>
> 'A fight is going on inside me,' he said to the boy. 'It is a terrible fight and it is between two wolves. One is *evil* – he is anger, envy, sorrow, regret, greed, arrogance, self-pity, guilt, resentment, inferiority, lies, false pride, superiority and ego. The other is *good* – he is joy, peace, love, hope, serenity, humility, kindness, benevolence, empathy, generosity, truth, compassion and faith. The same fight is going on inside you – and inside every other person too.'
>
> The grandson thought about this for a moment, and then he asked his grandfather, 'Which wolf will win?' The old Cherokee simply replied, *'The one you feed.'*

- Eat together and play together. By playing games with your children, you demonstrate appropriate winning and losing behaviour, turn taking, playing by the rules and sharing. You also show your children that you enjoy their company and like to spend time with them.
- Work out the love languages[112] of each person in your family and then express love in ways they understand. In Gary Chapman's best-selling book, *The Five Love Languages* (1997), he lists the love languages as words of affirmation, acts of service, physical touch, quality time and gifts. For example, if the primary love language of your first child is words of affirmation, then this child feels loved when you spend time talking with him or her, and affirming him or her with words. But if your second

child's love language is quality time, then he or she really feels loved when you spend quality time with him or her without distraction.

As your children get older, share this information with them so that they understand both themselves and their parents better. By understanding your family's love languages, you will keep your emotional tanks full and be able to respond in ways that are appropriate to each person. This will deepen your relationship by improving the quality of your communication.

- When you talk about your feelings, be sure to label them so that your children understand. A great game to play around the dinner table or while driving in the car is the Sweets and Sours game.

THE SWEETS AND SOURS GAME

This game is ideally played at the dinner table or in the car, when the whole family is together. It enables you to hear about everyone's day and teaches your children how to acknowledge and label feelings – an important step in the journey towards emotional intelligence.

Round 1:
Each person gets a chance to share a 'sour' ('the worst thing that happened in your day'). Mention what it is and how it made you feel. For example: 'By mistake I left my takkies at home so I couldn't play tennis. I was very cross with myself because I really wanted to play.'

Round 2:
Each person gets to share a 'sweet' ('the best thing that happened in your day'). Mention what it is and how it made you feel. For example, 'Robyn came to play with me this afternoon and we had fun. It made me happy.'

During the process, no family member may interrupt another. It is a game about listening and sharing.

Nikki's youngest son was three and a half when her family started playing the game. Nikki thought Matthew would be too young to participate, but was taken by surprise as he actually led the process from the first session, and still does today. Nikki also found her husband's reaction very interesting. At first he would just tell the family what happened and Nikki would have to follow up by asking, 'And how did that make you feel?' Men, in particular, are not used to discussing and labelling their feelings so this is a good exercise for them too!

For younger children (1–5 years)

- Use empathic listening techniques to help children to label their feelings. For example, when you pick up your daughter from school and she is not talking but rather giving off emotional vibes, you can say something along these lines to acknowledge the feeling, which may even open the door to a conversation: 'I can see you are very upset about something', or 'I can tell you are excited. What happened?'

For older children (6–14 years)

- Help your children to work out the difference between a need and a want, and to use money appropriately in fulfilling these needs.
- Teach children about delayed gratification by encouraging them to save up over a period of time to buy something.

When Amy was about to turn seven she asked for an iPod for her birthday. Graeme said that she needed to save up because she was too young for such an expensive item. Amy saved up, worked for money, and requested cash instead of Christmas presents. By her eighth birthday, she had saved nearly R1 000. What is more impressive is that she had worked at it for more than a year. Children of this age can be taught about long-term thinking and setting goals.

- Teach your children to understand another person's point of view. This is best achieved by conversations about how different people view the world. You can use movies and TV shows to start these conversations. After watching a movie, have discussions about key scenes or dramatic or touching moments in the movie. Ask your children what they think the different characters were thinking at the time. Emphasise how and why different characters would have different views of the same event.

Nikki took her children to see the movie *Sponge Bob Square Pants* a few years ago. Matthew had just turned six. It was billed as a suitable movie for children from four upwards. It still stands out in Nikki's mind as highly unsuitable for young children, but it provided a very teachable moment. After the movie, Nikki raised the issue of the despotic king who, as a law unto himself, condemned innocent characters to death without trial. The king was never punished for his injustice and unfair, immoral conduct. Throughout the movie, poor behaviour was neither punished nor rectified. What were children to think and learn? Nikki asked her children what they thought of the king. They immediately said that he was horrible, unfair and ugly. Then she asked them how they thought kings, presidents, prime ministers and leaders should behave. They were quick to tell her that they should be fair, just and, of course, kind. They were incensed that the king had failed to listen to anyone who had tried to tell him he was wrong. Despite feeling that she had watched an animated version of the American War On Terror, Nikki found that this dreadful movie did, in fact, provide a good lesson in emotional intelligence, or the lack thereof.

Relate to others

Daniel Goleman refers to 'social intelligence'[113] and Howard Gardner to 'interpersonal intelligence'[114] in labelling the competencies that determine how we handle relationships with others. Each of these researchers stresses two overarching categories of social competence:

- **Empathy:** This is an awareness of others' feelings, needs and concerns. Empathy requires an understanding of others as well as the ability to sense, anticipate and meet others' needs; the ability to be comfortable with diversity and to leverage it; and a 'political' ability to read a group's emotional currents and power relationship and to respond appropriately.
- **Social skills:** These require an ability to induce desirable responses in others; to persuade others and influence them; to communicate, manage conflict, show leadership, and be a catalyst for change. They also involve the desire to cultivate relationships with and between others; to collaborate and cooperate with them; and to foster group synergies in the pursuit of shared goals.

Many of these skills are developed as children play and live in community with others. If you have more than one child, you need to observe and listen in on their interactions. You may need to intervene to assist them in becoming good friends.

Speak to them about the value of friendship and interactions. Don't just tell them to sort their problems out – they need to learn the skills of negotiation, compromise and discussion. You need to teach your children these skills and to talk about options with them. In addition to these things, there are two further specific areas of expertise that you should work on: communication, and teamwork and collaboration.

Tips for teaching children to relate to others

For all

- Make sure your children socialise with others from an early age.
- Play dates are an important way of helping your children to learn how to relate to others.
- Let your children see you in social situations. It is not always advisable to drop off your child at a friend and to disappear. Sometimes parents need to 'stay and play' too, to show children how to behave in social situations.
- By allowing your children to attend school, you are providing them with an opportunity to relate to others, to socialise and interact.
- Playing sport gives your children an opportunity to relate to others through teamwork or in a competitive situation.
- Eat dinner together as a family.

Communication

There is no doubt that the most successful people in the business world – even today – are those who are able to communicate effectively. This includes public speaking, debating and negotiating abilities, written communication skills and, increasingly, multimedia-based emotive 'edutainment' communications.

The variety of media and on-screen activities available to children today put them at risk of mainly watching and listening rather than talking. Roger Schank (2001) comments: 'Let's assume that you have a reasonably bright child possessing a mind teeming with original thoughts. If, however, your child never learns how to express those thoughts, teachers, prospective employers, and bosses will assume him to be ordinary at best and dumb at worst. Verbal ability, therefore, is what people require to show their intelligence to the world.'

In school, your child is just one of many. This means that, as a parent, you have a great deal more opportunity to develop your child's communication skills than his or her teachers do.

Tips for developing communication skills[115]

For all

- Engage your children in conversation from the day they are born. Talk them clever and model good speech.
- Help your children to verbalise their thinking and reasoning skills by playing word games in the car.
- Eat dinner around a table, face to face, as often as possible. This is where children learn the art of conversation and about listening, taking turns and debate.
- Don't criticise or lecture your children on their verbal mistakes. Correct them as you speak back to them. They will absorb good language usage from you.
- Model good listening skills. When your children talk to you, don't always do other things at the same time. Stay still, make eye contact, and focus on them to let them know that you are really listening.
- If you have more than one child, it is important to spend time alone with each one from time to time so that the more natural communicator doesn't overshadow the less

expressive child.

- Understand your child's learning style and dominance profile to enable you to understand his or her natural communication strengths (see pages 68-72).
- More than anything, show interest in your child's thoughts and ideas. You can also get any child to talk and communicate on subjects that he or she feels passionate about.
- Provide your children with interesting life experiences that they can talk about.
- Watch television or a movie with your children from time to time and chat to them afterwards about the characters, plot, etc.

For younger children (1–5 years)

- Speak to your children as intelligent human beings. Don't talk down to them or use 'motherese'. Talk to them like adults.
- Handle speech impediments with a speech therapist early on. Good, clear speech is a gift.

For older children (6–14 years)

- Play fun word games such as *30 Seconds, Pictionary, Indahoo, Sketch-a-Story* and *Cranium* to exercise verbal skills in an entertaining and humorous way.
- Support your children's speech-making efforts at school. Encourage them to take part in cultural activities such as drama and debating, and to gain confidence and practice through competitions such as ChatterBox and the eisteddfod.

Teamwork and collaboration

We live in a world in which more and more interaction and collaboration is required. Leaders are not those who are technically superior to their peers, but rather those who are able to coordinate, inspire and mobilise their peers to operate as a cohesive unit.

Fact: Nobel prizes in scientific fields have been awarded for over a century now. In the early years, it was typical for individuals to be awarded these prizes. Possibly once or twice in a decade, a team would receive the award. In the last few decades, this trend has been reversed, with individuals only rarely receiving Nobel prizes in medicine, physics, chemistry and even economics. The implication is clear – teamwork is now required for important breakthroughs in science. See the lists of Laureates at www.nobelprize.org.

Tips for developing teamwork and collaboration

For all

- Teach one of your children how to do a task or activity, then ask this child to teach his or her siblings later. Reward all your children when they have achieved this goal successfully.

Recently Nikki has been watching her sons play various on-line computer games together. She has been amazed at the amount of collaboration and teamwork that exists between them, first, to teach Nikki's younger son the tricks of the game and, second, to beat the computer. Ryan and Matthew really help each other out to achieve the best outcome. It's been delightful for Nikki to listen to the mutual encouragement and excitement that emanates from the study. Of course, this is not always the case. At times Nikki's eldest wishes to play individual games without his younger brother around, or simply doesn't feel like assisting him at that particular time. It is then that Nikki has to step in to facilitate the situation.

- The evening meal is a good time for teamwork and collaboration. Children can assist with the preparation of food, from topping and tailing beans to grating cheese. And they can lay the table while you cook. As they get older, they can light candles and pour water into glasses too. By the time you sit down to dinner, everyone can have played his or her part in putting the meal together and preparing the eating space. Then it's back to teamwork to clear the table after dinner, stack and wash dishes or load the dishwasher, and tidy up.
- If you have a dishwasher, then emptying it the next morning also creates an opportunity for teamwork. Even three-year-olds can help. Give them the cutlery to sort into categories of knives, forks and spoons. Then ask them to thread these items on to the hanging cutlery holder or to place them back into the cutlery drawer. Children love being part of a team and being allowed to help. This is an opportunity to convey your belief in their capabilities and to show them that they are a welcome part of the team.
- The same can be done when handling an item or facility that requires regular maintenance, for example the family swimming pool. One person can clear the leaf trap, another can test the water, and someone else can brush the sides of the pool. Then everyone can put the safety net back on the pool together because this just makes it so much quicker and easier.

In certain American Indian traditions, when young warriors participated in competitive sports, the winner of each competition was required to congratulate all those who had competed with him. The reason was that he only did his best because he was pushed to do so by the other competitors. As we encourage our children to become involved in competitive pursuits, this may be a great story to tell. Good sportsmanship is an excellent example to follow.

For younger children (1–5 years)

- Young children love doing chores around the house *with you*. For example, let them wash the car and bicycles with you. Of course, they won't do a great job when they are just toddlers, but enjoy teaching them to do it with you. It won't be too long before they get really good at it. In addition, they are spending quality time with you while you teach them the valuable life skill of looking after possessions.

For older children (6–14 years)

- Almost anyone who works in a corporate environment has been on some kind of team-building activity. These range from the dangerous (such as river-rafting, fire-walking and abseiling) to the strenuous (such as carrying people over an obstacle course, or pushing them through a spider's web of ropes) to the inane (such as building paper airplanes and composing team songs). These activities proved to be fairly corny when you had to do them at youth group and youth camps during your teenage years, and even more corny in the business world. But why not get some use out of them by tackling a variety with your children? They will love these activities, especially if they get to do them with you.
- Encourage your children to play at least one team sport. It's good for them.

Nikki's children recently played in a round robin tennis tournament. Both children played singles and doubles matches. For the first time it became really obvious to them that a big difference exists between the two games. Ryan, the eldest, reckoned it was far more difficult playing doubles because he never knew what his partner was going to do (not being a regular doubles partnership). This made it difficult to develop teamwork and collaboration. Of course, Ryan could recognise how the better the teamwork and collaboration, the greater the chance of winning the match. A good (but frustrating) life lesson, really.

Comfort with diversity

In addition to working in teams, our children will increasingly work in diverse environments. Diversity does not just relate to gender, skin colour, or age. It relates specifically to world views. Media such as TV and movies, social networks, the Internet as well as the global mobility of people ensure that our children interact with others who have very different value sets, religious backgrounds and world views.

We need to raise our children to understand who they are and what they stand for. At the same time, they should accept that not everyone is the same or does things in the same way as they do. In the past, your family friends brought their children up in the same way as you did – they generally had similar values, probably went to the same church, etc. Today this is no longer the case. In fact, you can no longer even rely on your children's Sunday school teacher having the same values as you!

This is one of the 'side effects' of globalisation. Our children have been exposed to a great deal of diversity and are far more accepting of people of different races, colours, nationalities. than we ever were as children – mainly because this exposure was alien to us. The increase in mobile international families has developed a whole subculture of children with a broad life experience at a young age. To these children, we really are living in a global village.

Twenty-first century leaders will become more multi-skilled than their twentieth-century predecessors. Knowledge of languages,

cultures, and a wide range of subjects will be vital to achieve success ... One of the most important characteristics of a multi-skilled leader is the ability to encourage diversity ... The true challenge facing the organizational world is not geographic distance but cultural distance.

(*Management 21C*, edited by Subir Chowdhury, 2000)

Tips for developing comfort with diversity

For all

- Parents must first reflect on their own biases and explore their own feelings about diversity. They need to understand these before they can truly help their children to confront their own. For many this may involve difficult memories of the prejudiced and confusing messages they received about different kinds of people. 'How a child learns to deal with differences depends largely on how parents, caregivers and other important adults deal with differences.'[116]
- Provide your children with as many positive experiences of diversity as possible. Seek out cross-cultural friendships with families from other cultures.
- Encourage your children to learn about different cultures, languages and ethnicities. A well-informed child is more likely to understand and respect other people's values. If you have friends from different cultures or religions, it is highly educational and enriching to be invited to share in some of their rituals.
- Help your children to be proud of their own distinctives – their race, culture, gender, etc. The more they know about *why* your family does what it does, the more they will understand why some other families do not do it in the same way.
- As the cliché goes, there is nothing like travel to broaden your mind. Try to travel to places with different cultures

and deliberately expose yourself and your children to these different cultures.

- Create an environment in which children can see positive images of diverse groups. Comment when you see any stereotypes on TV or in movies. Let children know that it's unfair to label people.
- The media often reports about events and happenings in other countries that may be different to how things are done in your own country. Bring your children's attention to these stories and use them as the basis of discussion. Keep a map of the world handy (either an atlas or a globe) to enable you to point out where in the world this particular story is happening. Context helps children to visualise things.
- As a family, you could sponsor a child from another country through a feeding programme.

> In South Africa and elsewhere around the world, an increasing number of families are adopting children cross-culturally. This should help to create a wonderful new world as mixed families and people of 'mixed race' become increasingly common in the world.
>
> Graeme and his daughters were walking through a shopping centre recently when one of his daughters drew his attention to 'the black man' ahead of them. Graeme was concerned as he felt that he and his wife had tried hard to ensure their children did not notice or mention skin colour when referring to people. He asked his daughter to repeat what she had said, and she explained, 'Look at that black man, next to the green woman'. It turned out that Hannah was referring to the colour of the couple's T-shirts. Often, we impose our issues on our children, rather than seeing the world through their (innocent) eyes.

- Use some of the beautifully illustrated books available in bookshops and libraries about children around the world to teach your children about diversity. These books discuss how children from different countries dress, what they eat, their particular customs and festivals, etc.

- Take your children to eat in different restaurants. It's an easy way to introduce them to diverse cuisine and foreign tastes, some of which they will like and some dislike.

Networking

Networking is simply about connecting with people of similar interests for the purpose of uncovering opportunities, increasing knowledge, and sharing information. More simply, it's getting to know people and building relationships. In the connection economy, *who* you know is critical to success. Trust will become more and more important. One of the easiest ways to develop trust is to network and enjoy the benefits of extended trust relationships.

Technology is hugely assisting the task of networking, with an ever increasing application of social networking. This topic has been discussed earlier in the book, but it is worth repeating that you would be wise to become involved. And assist your children to do the same as they grow older.

Tips for helping your children to network

For all

- Social networking websites are a great start. We have previously mentioned MySpace and Facebook, but there are many others. Be careful about how your children use these websites. In particular, emphasise that they should *never* provide personal contact information *at any time*. But encourage your children to connect with others, to seek out people with similar interests and those who have information that interests them.
- Building friendships is the start of creating a lifelong net-

work of relationships. It is the strength of your relationships in the future that will help you to succeed.

Marketing (Brand You)[117]

This is not about landing a spot on *Oprah*. But it is about realising that you are always in the market! While you may be uncomfortable with some of the preening, self-obsessed children produced by various countries (the biggest culprit, of course, being the US), there is something to be said for a self-confident, reality-based ability to put yourself forward and be noticed.

It's easy to market yourself when you have self-belief, self-confidence and self-esteem, and the certainty that you have valuable or worthwhile skills to offer the world. Having a purpose helps enormously to create passion for who you are and what you do. Undoubtedly, if you want to achieve and draw value from life, you have to go out and get it. Your goals, ambitions and dreams do not just come to you. It is essential, therefore, to have the skills and ability to 'be out there'.

Tips for helping your children to market themselves

We believe it is so important for your children to learn to market themselves that we have dedicated an entire section below to the development of a new type of curriculum vitae (CV) or resumé. We call it a **Talent Profile**, which can be continually updated and used throughout your child's life as a personal marketing tool, starting from the age of eight.

For all

- A key to good marketing is to give out a consistent message, like any strong and memorable brand. Are you modelling this for your children?
- Aim to be a consistent person and avoid having double

standards. Double standards simply confuse your children and make you lose credibility as a parent.

- Help your children to develop their own moral code and encourage them to live up to it.
- Are you doing anything to market yourself personally and professionally? Do you have a Talent Profile, a website, a blogsite, etc?

For older children (6–14 years)

- Help your children to set up a web page and assist them in managing it. It is sensible to start with a social networking system, such as MySpace and Facebook. Ensure that you have suitable Internet security rules in place first.
- Analyse advertising with your children. Watch TV or read magazines with your children, and discuss the advertisements. As you consider the claims of various ads, and debate the messages being conveyed, ask questions such as: 'Do you believe that to be true?'
- Help your children to develop their own Talent Profile. Refer to the details below.

BUILDING A TALENT PROFILE

An unexamined life is not worth living.

(Socrates)

In the Age of Possibility, how we define ourselves is becoming more and more important. Today we need far more than a list of achievements and awards received for school subjects or sporting prowess. Those things are the 'what' – the 'who' is something quite different.

One of a parent's most important roles is to discover the unique genius in each of their children and to help them to express their potential. We need to be highly observant of our children to get to know them as *individuals* – their passions, areas of interest, talents, strengths, weaknesses, preferred learning styles, personalities, temperaments, love languages, and more. In essence, we need to know what makes them tick and what makes them who they are. And, very importantly, we need to remember that they are a work in progress (just as we are) and it would be unwise to box, label and categorise them at too young an age – or at any age, really.

It is not just parents who need to get to know their children. Children need to get to know and to value themselves. As parents, we should kick-start this journey of self-knowledge and self-awareness for our children – a journey that will last them a lifetime.

To pull together all that we have said into something practical and coherent, we suggest that you assist your children in developing a Talent Profile (TP), as mentioned above. This is our 21st-century alternative to the traditional and now outdated CV. Essentially this book is about what you need to understand and do for your children. But, in this section, we strongly suggest that you undertake this exercise for yourself too, in order to become familiar with the process and to start marketing yourself differently. (See pages 287-291 for instructions on developing your own TP.) While Talent Profile may only become important when your children leave school, encouraging the habit of updating their TP and 'keeping it warm' on a regular basis from the age of eight will make your children's development and progress seem real and tangible to them.

Why we need a new type of CV

A curriculum vitae or resumé is essentially a paper trail of your life. Typically it's just a list – unanalysed, and with wooden categories. It's boring and generic. A CV neither reflects the future world of work, nor reflects your passions and desires, or your connection with the company to which you are sending it. A war for talent exists in the workplace, and you and your children need to stand apart from other applicants to be noticed. You need a mechanism to showcase your X-factors, and the Talent Profile is your marketing vehicle.

Some people go to great lengths to be noticed. The story is told of two young advertising design students who sent letters to all the top agencies in the city. Their letters were not traditional applications. Instead, they were personal letters, addressed to the MD and put in floral envelopes. The letters went something like this:

Dear John

I'm not sure if you remember, but 22 years ago we had a night of passion in the back of your old car. Well, that evening passed and we never saw each other again, but it resulted in the twins. Over the years, I have thought of making contact with you many times, but decided not to. Now, however, the boys have qualified and I wondered if you would consider giving them a start in your company – for old time's sake. I enclose a picture – I am sure you can see the likeness, and will consider giving them a start in the family business.

Yours, with loving memories
Mary-Ann

Enclosed was a photo of the two boys – clearly not twins! The company that hired them has the letter framed in its reception area.

This story showcases an innovative and creative approach to getting two young qualified people in the door of an ad agency. It worked because they tailored their application for a creative industry that would appreciate such an original and daring angle. The problem with most CVs is that they ignore the context into which they are being sent.

What exactly is a Talent Profile?

A Talent Profile is a document (and/or website) that provides comprehensive insight into an individual. It attempts to link a person's strengths to specific opportunities that might be available. A TP differs from a CV, in a number of ways:

- It provides a lot more than factual information about a person; it provides insights into the individual's personality, character and various profiles.
- It provides more than just a list of achievements and abilities; it represents an individual's passions and dreams.
- It doesn't just aim to get a person a job; it aims to ensure that the job offered to a person is the type of job he or she really wants to get.
- It is constantly updated; it is a living document.

Help your child to build a Talent Profile from primary school

CVs have always been documents for adults. Talent Profiles, however, are for everyone. Why does a child need a Talent Profile? The answer is because it entails a highly practical and concrete exercise in self-awareness or knowing yourself, as well as a marketing tool to assist your children in times when they need to be noticed.

You can discuss your own TP with your children (in simple

terms for a six-year-old, but fairly adult terms for a 10-year-old) to introduce them to the concept. It could make for an interesting and revealing conversation. Graeme, for example, might say to his daughters, 'I believe I'm a good speaker'. Hannah might then say, 'But you don't talk to us'. This would be a form of peer review, and Graeme may then realise that he has used up all his words on his clients!

We need to help our children become aware of who they are as well as of the track record they are creating from a young age. By doing this, they will develop good self-knowledge long before they enter the workforce, giving them confidence to take advantage of many different opportunities along the way – from leadership positions in school or recreational groups, to involvement in environmental groups, youth exchange programmes, student jobs, and ultimately applications for tertiary studies and full-time employment. In this Age of Possibility, numerous diverse opportunities will constantly emerge. Children will have to learn how to make discerning choices about how to use their time, and which activities to be involved in so that they maintain a balanced life. Prioritising based on their own self-awareness will help to reduce over-scheduling, over-stimulation and general stress, which research tells us many children are experiencing today.

Children can learn a great deal about themselves and their families by developing a Talent Profile. Regular updating of their TP is good training for projecting their vision forward for their lives and giving them hope for the future. (Hopelessness has become pervasive among young people internationally.) It also provides an opportunity for you to encourage and express your confidence in your children – in who they are and what they are capable of. A good self-esteem is matchless in aiding your children to build a successful and satisfying life.

We recommend helping your children to build a Talent Profile from about the age of eight. This exercise will fuel their belief from an early age that they are talented in a unique way by virtue of who they are, and backed up by their life experiences thus far. In a Talent Profile, your child gets the opportunity to be the central hero in his or her own story. Supporting roles are played by family members, friends, teachers and coaches.

Always bear in mind that the Talent Profile exercise is intended to be objective and non-judgemental. It provides:

- a platform for dialogue and conversation
- a means of connecting and engaging with your children about who they are
- an opportunity to discuss choices and responsibilities
- a concrete opportunity to build self-esteem and emotional intelligence
- an opportunity to foster self-awareness
- a forum for fostering resilience.

A Talent Profile will clearly show children their areas of strength and weakness and enable them to set goals for themselves. (These must be realistic.) Perhaps they would like to have a particular new experience to help them in their areas of interest. Your TP discussion should bring this out, making you more aware of your children's 'hot buttons' – ways of connecting with them that will be meaningful to them.

The older your children become, the more you will be able to link their TP to their personal goals for the year. These goals do not need to be 'heavy' – they can even be light-hearted and fun. It may be that your child wants to make more friends during the year, or do a solo rather than a group piece in an annual competition for a change.

It can be very helpful to train your children to assess themselves accurately and to set realistic goals. If your daughter says, 'I'm very good at tennis', you should discuss this with her. Clearly she enjoys the game and would like to continue improving at it. 'You are in the C team now. Are you happy to stay in that team, or do you think there is room for improvement?' And, 'If you want to improve, then what do you think you need to do to make it into the B team?'; 'Is there anything you would like me to do to help you to achieve that goal?'; 'What structures do we need to put in place (coaching time, practise time)?'; 'How will we know if you have been successful?'

Remember to revisit the TP and to update it every six to 12 months or so to keep it real for your children and to allow them to track their progress.

Framework for your child's Talent Profile

When working with young children, remember that the TP is very much a work in progress. The aim is to help them to verbalise where they are at. Outcomes-based education requires children to put together a portfolio of what they consider to be their best work at the end of each year, from the age of nine. The children are also taught to assess themselves at the end of individual and group projects, for example: Did I listen to the opinions of the other people in the group? Did I contribute to the group? Did I find the exercise easy or difficult? In what ways can I improve? The TP extends this assessment process and makes it more personal. Initially it is a private document which, ultimately, can be shaped into a document for more public consumption at a later date.

When your children are in preschool, take note of their natural interests and abilities. Keep personal notes about them somewhere for later use in their TP file. You should encourage your children in these areas. Also gather information about your children, such as their:

- love languages
- temperament
- personality

- brain dominance profile
- learning preference (visual, auditory, kinaesthetic).

This kind of information will help you to understand your children now and help them to understand themselves later. It will be useful for putting together their TP from the age of eight.

Putting together a Talent Profile is a 'togetherness' activity. In other words, be there (be present, not multitasking) to support and acknowledge your child's efforts. Bear in mind that the information provided by your children is a snapshot of how they see themselves at this particular moment. As mentioned previously, you should repeat this process at least every six months or so to update the TP. In this way you will see how the content changes over time as your children become older and move into different developmental phases.

The Mirror Game© for children

Since children learn through play, putting their Talent Profile together needs to be done in a playful and creative manner to ensure that they engage fully in the process. The Mirror Game© makes it easier to elicit information from your children – to tap into their Talent Profile. It's a good idea to spread it out over two or three sessions rather than to do it all at once. You don't want your children to grow tired of their own story!

Encourage your children to do as much of the work as they can themselves. (Obviously an eight-year-old will need much more help than a 12-year-old.) The idea is to try to get your child to own this document. After all, it is a story about your child – he or she is the central character. The instructions that are listed beneath each step should be read out by you to your child.

The children who piloted The Mirror Game© have thoroughly enjoyed the process. In fact, they did not want to stop because it was about them. They have taken great pains to make their 'project about me' look attractive, even though there were no specific instructions to do so. They requested Koki pens and crayons which made the process longer, but the end results were stunning. On the front page they entitled their documents/booklets Matthew's Mirror or Caroline's Mirror, for example.

The Mirror Game© is neither a test nor a deep psychological assessment. It should provide you with valuable information about your child to help you discover more about him or her. And it should be fun – 'Come, let's play the Mirror Game© to find out more about what a hugely special person you are!'

Your children may get stuck from time to time and say something like, 'I don't know what to write down.' You need to be encouraging, without necessarily giving them all the answers. Remember that how you see each of your children and how they see themselves could be different, to a greater or lesser degree. The various steps give them the opportunity to write down how they see themselves, how you see them, how their friends see them, and how their teachers see them. The process is designed to give them an interesting picture of themselves by bringing both internal and external perceptions together in one document. This could lead to some really interesting discussions.

Step 1: My physical mirror (what I look like and how I see myself)

- On a clean page or piece of paper, write the heading: 'My physical mirror'.
- Write down your name and age.
- Draw a rectangle in the middle of the page. Draw a picture of yourself in this 'mirror' – face, body, arms, legs, etc. It can be as creative or as comical as you like.
- Now create a mind map around the mirror, filling

in at least 10 words that describe you physically, for example:
  - tall
  - brown hair
  - blue eyes
  - freckly nose
  - pretty mouth
  - strong
  - dainty fingers
  - smiley eyes

Note to parents:
Try to encourage positive attributes where possible.

Step 2: My emotional mirror

- On a new page or piece of paper, write the heading: 'My emotional mirror'.
- Draw another mirror on this page. (It does not have to be rectangular; it can be circular or oval, for example.)
- Now draw a picture of how you think your heart looks or feels.

Note to parents:
Give your child creative licence here to draw a Valentine's heart or a real biological heart. It doesn't matter what it looks like. Do not judge the picture. You can make comments such as, 'That's a really interesting heart', or 'I love your heart'. There is no right or wrong.

- Now create a mind map around the mirror with 10 or more words that describe how you feel about yourself and your life at the moment, for example:
  - happy
  - sad

- angry
- hurt
- hopeful
- excited
- left out
- friendly
- victimised
- bullied
- worried.

When Nikki's son Matthew was completing this section of The Mirror Game©, he asked if it was possible to be happy and sad at the same time. He had conflicting feelings that day – he was happy because he loves most things in his life, but sad because his beloved teacher had announced she would be leaving at the end of the term to live in another country.

Step 3: My family mirror

- On a clean page or piece of paper, write the heading: 'My family mirror'.
- Draw another mirror on this page. You can choose any shape.
- Now draw a picture of your family, including yourself.
- Create a mind map around the mirror, with five or more words that describe your family, for example:
  - fun
  - loving
  - adventurous
  - boring
  - talkative
  - supportive
  - big/small
  - busy
  - rushed, etc.

- Under your mirror, at the bottom of the page:
  - Write the word Mom, followed by two words that describe her.
  - Write the word Dad, followed by two words that describe him.
  - Write down the name of your brothers and sisters (if you have any) and two words that describe them.

  Note to parents:
  If there is a primary caregiver who spends a lot of time looking after your child in your absence, such as a grandparent or an au pair, then include them in this list.

This is a very interesting section as we rarely ask our children these questions. It will reveal information to you about your family brand, which may or may not be what you expect to hear. Do not show any response if your child says something unexpected or negative. File it away in your head for processing at a later stage or, if appropriate, use it to open up a really interesting conversation with your child once he or she has completed The Mirror Game©. You do not want your child to feel bad for having written down an observation that takes you by surprise. If you have an obvious negative reaction, you will battle to get an honest answer out of your child again. This document should not be a 'parent pleaser', but an honest exercise in self-awareness.

For example, a colleague once asked her 11-year-old twins to describe her in one word. The children said 'rushed'. She was fairly horrified at their perception because it was not how she wanted them to view her. But she saw it as constructive feedback and set about amending how she ran her life in order to alter that perception.

Step 4: My friendship mirror

- On a clean page or piece of paper, write the heading: 'My friendship mirror'.
- Draw another mirror on this page.
- Now draw a picture of yourself with a favourite friend or friends. Label them.
- Down one side of the mirror, write a mind map of all the people you consider to be your friends.
- On the other side of the mirror, write a mind map of some words that describe how you think your friends see you, for example:
    - loyal
    - trustworthy
    - honest
    - kind
    - supportive, etc.

Note to parents:
At this point, you can ask your child: 'Why do you think that your friends say/feel these things?'

- At the bottom of the page, make a list of words that describe what you think makes a good friend.

Note to parents:
Ask your child: 'Do you think you are a good friend to other people? Why?'

Step 5: My school mirror

- On a clean page or piece of paper, write the heading: 'My school mirror'.
- Write down the name of your school.
- Draw another mirror on this page. Inside it draw a picture

of your school or some aspect of your school. It can be anything that comes to mind (the building, a sports field, a big tree, a teacher, the school badge, etc.).

- Now write down five words in a mind map on one side of the mirror that describe your school itself – physically.
- Next write down five words on the other side of the mirror about how you feel about your school – emotionally, for example:
  - happy
  - scared
  - hopeful
  - fun
  - challenging
  - easy.

- Under the mirror write down the following:
  My best subject:

  Note to parents:
  Ask your child why.

  My best teacher:

  Note to parents:
  Ask your child why.

THE 'FIVE WHY' PROCESS

When Nikki's son Ryan was completing this section of The Mirror Game©, he commented that Mrs van Eck was his favourite teacher. Nikki asked Ryan the following five 'why?' questions and found his answers to be quite revealing about what is important to him in the learning situation:

1. **Why is Mrs van Eck your favourite teacher?**
   Because she is on the ball. When something happens in the news, she uses it in the lesson the next day. (A recent example he cited was of a political cartoon from the newspaper about xenophobia, which was used in the English lesson.)
2. **Why is it important for you that your teachers use events in their lessons that are happening right now?**
   Because it makes learning real. It's not just about something that happened long ago, we can relate to it. It means the teachers know what's going on in the world – they are sharp and together.
3. **Why should learning be real?**
   Because then it's more interesting.
4. **Why should lessons be interesting?**
   Because then I pay better attention in class.
5. **Why is paying attention that important?**
   Because then I remember the work more easily and I get better marks in my tests and exams.

The 'Five Why' Process helps you to head down the path towards passion, to reach the core of the issue, and to find what your true value is. You can apply this process to just about anything, and it will help you to align yourself to your highest values. It's a technique often used in management. At the end of the five whys, when the employee has voiced his or her core value, then the manager can ask, 'So how can I help you to do that?'

In the above example with Ryan, Nikki could have gone one step further and asked why it is important to get good marks in tests and exams. This could have opened up a wonderful discussion about Ryan's future. Nikki could have ended the conversation by asking, 'How can I help you to achieve that?'

- On a new page, write two headings:

  Academic goals for the year (beneath this heading, write down what you want to achieve academically).

  Note to parents:
  Discuss what your child needs to do to achieve these goals and what you need to do to help make them a reality. In six to 12 months' time, when your child redoes The Mirror Game©, you will both be able to assess whether or not he or she is on track and why. Ensure these commitments are written down on this page.

  Extramural goals for the year (beneath this heading write down what you want to achieve extramurally).

  Note to parents:
  This is the ideal time to discuss which sports and cultural activities your child would like to do, and how many of these your child should be involved in to allow enough time for work and play. Discuss what your child needs to do to achieve his or her goals, and what you need to do to help make them a reality. Ensure these commitments are written down on this page.

Step 6: Mirror, mirror on the wall ...

This is the final section of The Mirror Game©.

- At the top of a new page, write down the heading 'Mirror, mirror on the wall'.
- Then answer these questions:
  1. What's your favourite colour?
  2. What's your favourite number?
  3. What's your favourite animal?

4. What's your favourite meal/food?
5. What's your favourite chocolate/sweet?
6. What's your favourite holiday and where?
7. Where's your favourite place at home?
8. What's your favourite game?
9. What's your favourite sport?
10. What's your favourite activity with your mum?
11. What's your favourite activity with your dad?
12. What's your favourite activity with your sibling/s?
13. What would you like to do for your birthday this year?
14. What would you like for your birthday?
15. What would you like to be when you grow up?
16. What makes you laugh?
17. What makes you cry?
18. What do you like about yourself?
19. What don't you like about yourself?
20. What are you not so good at?
21. What are you really good at?
22. Is there anything special that you would like to do after school that you are not doing now?
23. Who would you really like to play with/spend more time with at school?
24. Who would you like to help you with your homework (if anyone)?
25. Who in your family would you like to spend more time with than you currently do?
26. Who is your hero (who inspires you, or who do you look up to)?
27. If you could change anything in the world, what would it be?
28. If you could change anything in your life, what would it be?
29. What do your teachers/coaches say about you (how do they describe you)?

30. What do your parents say about you (how do they describe you)?
31. What makes you special (one of a kind, unique)? How would you describe yourself in no more than five words?

Note to parents:
This last question should reveal how your child views himself or herself. In a nutshell, this is your child's personal brand – at this time.

The report card of life

As mentioned previously, Talent Profiles need to be 'kept warm' or constantly updated from the start. Even in primary school, children are required to write letters of motivation if they want to become involved in particular areas of responsibility within the school structure. Ultimately the TP will become your child's ticket to a tertiary educational institution or a job application. More than this future goal, however, it becomes your child's 'report card of life' for the X-factors that school does not test or formally report on.

The idea behind developing a TP is not to create a tool of judgement or assessment as such, but rather to create a document that will help children to get to know themselves and how they operate in the world. It should be a document of which they feel particularly proud, that acknowledges them as human beings and celebrates who they are. Your children should like and appreciate themselves for all their strengths and weaknesses since it is these traits that make them unique.

A TP will also give your children something to look forward to and goals to aim for. Maintaining the current academic average, or improving by just a few per cent, or keeping your place in the team, are all goals. The object of a TP is not to make your children overly competitive or boastful. Rather, it encourages your children to engage in dialogue with themselves. By putting together a concrete record of their life that tells their own story, they build their self-awareness, self-confidence and a large dose of EQ, qualities so essential for a bright future. They are the hero in this story and kids just love that.

Why you should develop a Talent Profile

We suggest you develop a Talent Profile for the following reasons:

- You need to differentiate yourself from others applying for the same job.
- You need to promote your brand (who you are) well beyond just your usual personal information (name, age, language, driver's licence, qualifications, etc).
- You need to match your talent to the job you are applying for (how do you fit, where do you fit, is this a job for you?).
- It shows that you have knowledge of the company (you are interested in it).
- You have really thought about the position on offer and whether you are a match or not. This demonstrates initiative, analytical skills, self-awareness and EQ – right up front.
- It helps to stimulate conversation in an interview, which reduces tension and awkwardness because you actually know the script.
- It will be obvious up front if you are not a fit. You won't get stuck in a bad-fit situation which is often worse than not being offered the job at all.
- It may open doors to other opportunities within the same organisation.

A CV tends to be updated when it is required and not as a matter of course. We suggest that your Talent Profile is quite different. It needs to be kept warm by being updated at least every six months or so (for children), if not monthly (for yourself), so that you are flexible, nimble and ready to move should opportunities arise to change jobs, apply for promotions, pitch for new business, etc.

Keeping your TP constantly updated is a fabulous exercise in self-awareness and an ongoing reminder that you are responsible for your own talent. Whether or not you are employed, self-employed or temporarily unemployed, you remain your own managing director, brand manager, marketing manager, sales manager, human resources manager, etc. The TP allows each of those portfolios to go to work – on you! As Tom Peters states: 'View yourself as the boss of your own show, even if that show happens to be playing just now at Citigroup or General Electric or ExxonMobil. In other words: Distinct or Extinct.'[118]

Creating your own Talent Profile

If you are convinced of, or at least intrigued by, the possibilities of a TP, then follow the steps in the Mirror Process below to create your own. This is an adult version of The Mirror Game© used earlier for your children.

Do this exercise in rough (as a private document) to give you a full picture of yourself as you are today. This will help you either to get to know yourself better, or to package yourself appropriately for the job on offer. Then spend some time editing this information into a presentable document for a prospective employer. Keep it warm by revisiting it and updating it from time to time.

The Mirror Game© for adults

1. **My Personality Mirror** (who I think I am, what I think or believe about myself)

- List your personality traits, for example:
    - introvert/extrovert
    - optimist/pessimist
    - spontaneous/controlled
    - like to follow/like to lead
    - able to influence others
    - problem spotter
    - problem solver
    - fussy
    - headstrong
    - anxious
    - hard to please
    - intolerant
    - sociable
    - funny
    - popular
    - sensitive
    - confident
    - loyal
    - perfectionist
    - consistent
    - diplomatic.

You may have gathered much of this information already through various profiling techniques over the years – from Disc Profiles, Enneagram, Meyers-Briggs, dominance profiling, etc. A good resource is Florence Littauer's book, *Personality Plus* (2005). See Section 2, pages 71 – 72 for details on profiling resources.

2. **My Skills Mirror** (what I am good at)
    - List your strengths, followed by a list of your weaknesses.

3. **My Growth Mirror** (where do I see myself going?)

- Detail your growth opportunities as you see them for yourself:
    - o over the next one to two years
    - o over the next three to five years

4. **My Dream Mirror** (my personal vision)
    - Detail what you believe your purpose is at this point in time.
    - Then detail your vision for yourself in the future.

5. **The 'What I Do' Mirror** (the value I add)
    - This is not a description of your current job and responsibilities. It is more a summary of the value you believe you add to your company or prospective employer, for example a data capturer could redefine her role as 'I'm the underwire bra of the organisation'[119]. In other words, without her there would be no data with which to underpin the organisation's activities!
    - Think creatively about what it is you actually do, e.g. I ensure cash flow, I manage labour resources, I come up with ideas, I'm a hotshot problem solver.

6. **My Personal Best Mirror** (my best work so far)
    - Draw up a list of your best work so far.
    - Then draw up a list of areas in which you think you do your best work.
    - Also list areas of your work that give you the most enjoyment and satisfaction.

7. **My Testimonial Mirror** (what others say about me)
    - Detail what colleagues and employers say about you – the positive and negative.

8. **My Networking Mirror** (who I know – my connections)

- This is more important than it ever was before. List your social networks (virtual) as well as your real-life networks. For some job applications, your networks can determine your worth.
- If you have any social networking websites, include the URL addresses. These would include LinkedIn, Facebook, MySpace, MyGenius, and other similar profiles. Bear in mind that sharp employers will do a Google search for your name anyway. Make sure you do that search first, and see what comes up. Be careful about your digital footprint – it might work against you when applying for jobs. What seems amusing to you and your friends might not be so clever when viewed by a potential boss!

9. **My Work Experience Mirror** (work I have done)
   - Include a portfolio of work experience or projects completed. Be detailed and provide a short list of responsibilities for each position held. Include specific comments from colleagues or superiors if relevant. Give contact details if appropriate.

10. **My Education Mirror** (my education history)
    - List your qualifications and years of study, as well as your academic and curricular responsibilities.

11. **My Biographical Mirror** (my name, address, etc.)
    - This is all the mundane but essential detail about you that needs to be noted – from age, to address, home language, driver's licence, and other details that are important but won't necessarily sell you. If the interviewer is interested, he or she can read the biographical stuff later.

12. **Your Company Mirror** (about the prospective employer)

- What I know about your company.

13. **Your Industry Mirror** (about the industry your prospective employer operates in)
    - What I know about your industry.

14. **The Position Being Offered Mirror** (about the prospective position)
    - Write a paragraph on 'What I believe about the position being offered'.

15. **The 'Do I Fit?' Mirror** (do I fit the job?)
    This is the interesting part of the Mirror Process. At this point, having done some soul-searching and having documented your thoughts, it should now be clear to you whether or not you actually want this job.
    - Detail your reasons for applying for this job/position. Do you believe you would be a good fit with the prospective employer, and why?
    - Link relevant experience that is directly or indirectly connected to the job on offer. You may think you would be a good fit precisely because you have no experience in that area, and therefore would bring a fresh eye and some useful skills into the equation.

This is a superb exercise to have done prior to attending an interview as you will have considered and answered many of the questions you are going to be asked. In fact, you may have given yourself a distinct advantage over other candidates being interviewed for the same job.

Above all, be honest. Smart employers understand that you do not intend to join the company for the rest of your life, so don't make any untruthful promises or statements in this regard. If all you want is three years of experience, then say so. This will establish the correct relationship right from the start.

Taking full responsibility for promoting your own talent is the best example you can give your child. You can now walk your own talk.

CONVERSATIONS, CONNECTIONS, CHOICES

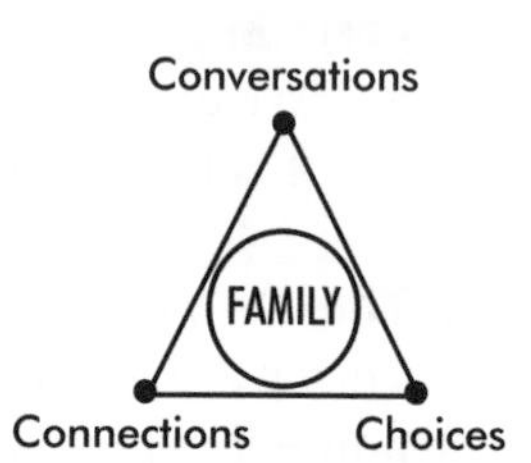

Can you see how developing your child's Talent Profile together gives you the opportunity to develop the three Cs in your parenting framework? A TP will help you to:

- hold interesting and revealing conversations with your children
- discuss important choices with them that help them to discover further who they are and where they are going
- discuss responsibility, accountability and values with your children
- connect and engage with your children about their uniqueness.

This is a wonderfully affirming opportunity. It will also be the start of training your children to develop their own framework for stability in an uncertain future – a conscious connection with themselves. As you build on the three Cs of conversation, choices and connection that make up your parenting framework, so these abilities will become automatic for your children, providing them with a powerful rudder to keep them steady and enabling them to move forwards with confidence in life.

This section has been filled with many practical ideas to help you future-proof your children – from developing X-factors for success to creating your own personal brand. The intention of future-proofing is not to protect your children from the future, but rather to equip them both to survive and to thrive in the world of possibilities that awaits them. It should also give your children the tools to surf the tsunami we discussed earlier, when it comes, as it surely will.

We hope you have realised how much fun the future-proofing process can be. It should now be obvious too how the X-factors are going to be more caught than taught from primary caregivers – generally parents.

The next section of the book extends the personal branding concept. It advocates the idea of developing a family brand as a proactive vehicle for building and strengthening your parenting framework of conversations, connections and choices.

Endnotes

[80] *Coloring Outside the Lines* by Roger Schank, 2001.
[81] From research presented at the annual conference of The National Coalition of Girls' Schools (USA/Canada), 2007.
[82] From the Engines for Education website, accessed 29 July 2007 at www.engines4ed.org.
[83] Meg Fargher was the headmistress of St Mary's School in Waverley, Johannesburg, from 2001 until the end of 2008.
[84] Credit goes to Tom Peters for this phrase, especially in his book *The Brand You 50: Or: Fifty Ways to Transform Yourself from an 'Employee' into a Brand that Shouts Distinction, Commitment, and Passion!*, 1999.
[85] Karl Fisher and Scott McLeod, 'Shift happens' (online video), accessed in June 2007 at www.scottmcleod.org/didyouknow.wmv.
[86] *Extraordinary Minds* by Howard Gardner, 1997.
[87] *Mind Power into the 21st Century: Techniques to Harness the Astounding Powers of Thought* by John Kehoe, 1997.
[88] *Dream Society* by Rolf Jensen, 2001.
[89] This title is from an article by Geoffrey Colvin, 'The Imagination Economy' in *Fortune* magazine, 5 July 2006.
[90] Ibid.
[91] Ibid.
[92] *Resilience: Personal Skills for Effective Learning* by Annie Greeff, 2005.
[93] 'Can you teach resilience?' by Valerie Andrews, 2007.
[94] *Failing Forward: Turning Mistakes into Stepping Stones for Success* by John Maxwell, 2000.

[95] For more on this, read *Don't Eat The Marshmallow . . . Yet! The Secret to Sweet Success in Work and Life* by Joachim de Posada and Ellen Singer, 2005.
[96] From Ash Wednesday to Easter Sunday.
[97] 'Humour complements intelligence' by Alice Cahn, 2007.
[98] Some of these tips were inspired by 'Encouraging your child's sense of humor' by D'Arcy Lyness, 2006.
[99] Some of these tips were inspired by 'How to: The optimistic child: Raise your children to be optimists' by Elizabeth Scott, 2006.
[100] 'Helping your child develop self-esteem', Child Development Institute Report, 2007.
[101] *Seven Times Smarter: 50 Activities, Games, and Projects to Develop the Seven Intelligences of Your Child* by Laurel Schmidt, 2001.
[102] *Parenting with Spirit* by Jane Bartlett, 2004.
[103] Karl Fisher and Scott McLeod, 'Shift happens' (online video), ibid.
[104] From his course notes on 'Emotional Intelligence', 2005.
[105] *Extraordinary Minds: Portraits of 4 Exceptional Individuals and an Examination of Our Own Extraordinariness,* 1998.
[106] Alan Wong, Lifeskillsweb, accessed on 1 May 2007 at www.vtaide.com/lifeskills/index.htm.
[107] Credit for this phrase goes to best-selling business book, *Good to Great: Why Some Companies Make the Leap . . . and Others Don't* by Jim Collins, 2001.
[108] Daniel Goleman, the best-selling author of *Emotional Intelligence: Why it can Matter More than IQ,* 1997, which put emotional intelligence on the map, more recently wrote a book on *Social Intelligence: The New Science of Human Relationships,* 2007.
[109] *Raising Emotionally Intelligent Children* by Leonie Henig, 2002.
[110] 'Helping your child develop self-esteem', accessed on 27 July 2007 at www.childdevelopmentinfo.com/parenting/self_esteem.shtml.
[111] *Social Intelligence: The New Science of Human Relationships,* 2005.
[112] Read *The Five Love Languages* by Gary Chapman, www.fivelovelanguages.com.
[113] *Social Intelligence* by Daniel Goleman, 2005.
[114] *Frames of Mind* by Howard Gardner, 1999.
[115]Here we have used some of Roger Schank's ideas from *Coloring Outside the Lines*, 2001, for inspiration.
[116]*Hate Hurts, How Children Learn and Unlearn Prejudice* by Caryl Stern-LaRosa and Ellen Hofheimer, with the Anti Defamation League, 2000.
[117] 'Brand You' is a concept borrowed from Tom Peters' book, *The Brand You,* 1999.
[118] *Talent* by Tom Peters, 2005.
[119] This example is taken from Helen Nicholson's acclaimed 'Master the art of networking' presentation.

Section 5

Build a family brand – it makes good sense!

You are the storyteller of your own life. You can create your own legend or not.
(Isabel Allende)

We live in a world dominated by brands in one form or another. Today branding encompasses not just products and services, but people too – look at Oprah Winfrey, Richard Branson, and David Beckham, for starters. But even non-celebrities like the rest of us need to develop our personal brand in order to succeed in the working world today (as explained in Section 4). Now take this idea one step further – if we have a family, we also need to develop a family brand in order to assist our children to develop their own identity and moral compass.

The implications for the family of the ideas and arguments that we have presented in this book are clear – the family is now fundamentally the primary value creator for society. We can no longer rely on our government, church or community to create our reality by determining the values, morals and traditions to which our family wishes to subscribe.[120] That was the way the world used to work. The responsibility is now ours and this will increasingly be the case. We are being called to be present, active and conscious parents. It is no longer acceptable to say things like: 'It's wrong for teenagers to take drugs because the government says so.' Or, 'In my church, homosexuality is unacceptable.'

We may choose to belong to various organisations because they support our points of view or values, but we have to take responsibility for our own approach to moral issues and the values our families will live by. Endlessly we see that governments are flawed, religious fundamentalism is dangerous, and that even our friends and children's teachers don't necessarily share the same beliefs and values as we do. We are on our own. The family is our core.

We say this fully aware that families are breaking up and regrouping in ever more interesting configurations on an ongoing basis. However, no matter what your family structure looks like, it is still a *family*, the most important societal unit today. There is little foundation or secure ground on which people can stand today without the family. If you don't have the support, love, care and concern that stems from a family, then you don't have much at all. This statement is supported by the Youth Trax 2006/7 research study, which indicates that youngsters aged between 16 and 24 believe that family is the only place where they can be loved unconditionally for who they are and not because of what they look like or the latest gadgets that they own. Young people are looking for authentic relationships and role models. They believe these can only be found in the family setting.

While all this responsibility sounds rather frightening and lonely, it doesn't need to be. It makes sense to develop or gravitate towards new communities of like-minded people as well as to ensure that your particular religion or belief system does not become fundamentalist. This is our hope for the future, as idealistic as it may sound. As individuals take on more personal responsibility for the world they create around them, we will see churches, business organisations and ultimately governments reflecting this way of being. There will be a significant period of chaos – a few decades at the most – while this takes place. These are the birth pains of a new society.

All periods of transition bring with them moral dilemmas, which are the source of the anxiety we feel much of the time. Little is the same as it was before and very little will be the same again. We are being called to nail our colours to the mast – to create our own personal brand (Brand You), as well as a family brand (Brand Family). We are being called to define precisely who we are and why we do things as we do. This is what the connection economy is all about, and it no longer operates on the basis of top-down command control. Therefore, we can no longer look to external authorities to make decisions for us or to create our solutions.

This is the era in which parents and children alike need to grow, evolve and develop – consciously and constantly. It is an era characterised by change at a speed never before experienced by humankind. Thus, one of the most important traits for people to develop is inner stability. If the environment isn't stable, we need stability within to help us manage ourselves in that environment, and to stop us from major hysteria. Inner stability will be our compass, our due North, and parents must take responsibility for assisting their children to develop this strength.

We believe you can do this by developing your own family brand. Some readers may already have created a strong family brand without knowing it. In that case, you will now understand exactly what you have done.

WHAT IS BRANDING?

Global brands spend vast sums of money researching their markets and communicating with people to buy into their brand proposition. They want a share not just of our wallets (that's marketing and sales) but of our hearts and minds too. Branding is about enticing us to interact with a service or product, to experience it and incorporate it into our lifestyles to make it part of *who* we are..

Global brands are making promises to which we – adults and children alike – are extremely susceptible because:

- we are tired, stressed and time-starved
- we are living in a materialistic, consumer-driven era
- our young children are unable to distinguish between advertising and programme content[121]
- some of our basic human needs are possibly not being fulfilled so anything will do (often things take precedence over relationships).

If we don't package and brand ourselves and our families, we could get lost among other brands which scream out their sales pitch, values, and so forth via billboards, magazines, newspapers and a multitude of technicolour electronic media.

You are the family brand manager

Brands are becoming so familiar to the extent that they are no longer seen as strangers but as friends, companions and partners in life. Brands often promise our children hero status. 'If you have this product/experience, you will be happy, cool, respected, accepted, etc.' This happens almost without us knowing it as our children are bombarded by thousands of marketing messages a week from many different sources, including their friends. That's a multitude of value statements being pumped in their direction! How do we compete?

We need to build bridges to our children so that we can help them to become discerning and media-savvy from a young age. They *can* be discerning if they have a set of values and beliefs against which to judge and measure those streaming in from outside sources. Without such a steady rudder, they will be at the mercy of the messages which they find most attractive and appealing, and that promise to fulfil their human needs and desires (refer back to Section 2 if necessary).

Today, parents need to accept their role as primary values creators. In effect, you have become the family brand manager.

- So what does it mean to be a Smith, a Van Niekerk, or a Mandela?
- How does, or should, it feel to be a member of your family?
- How do your children perceive you?
- How do you want to be perceived by your children?
- What's important to your family?
- What are your values and beliefs?
- What do you stand for?
- When your family is mentioned in conversation, what do people immediately associate with you? What qualities do they mention? Or are you a no-name brand that looks similar to many others?
- What are your family traditions?
- Do you live in black and white or Technicolor?
- Do you know where you are going? Do you have a plan or are you just trundling along?

Brands add value, whether they are commercial brands such as Nike, Levis or Nescafé, or 'people brands' such as

Nelson Mandela, affirms Jeremy Sampson, MD of Interbrand Sampson. He adds that they must add value consistently. Sometimes people become brands very naturally, like South Africa's beloved Madiba. Brands are easily and instantly recognisable by their various signatures or trademarks, such as Madiba with his stylish shirts, his voice, the way he clears his throat, his hairstyle, his dancing and laughter, the kinds of messages he always conveys (compassionate, forgiving, humble, direct, wise), the causes he aligns himself with (children, Aids, nation-building, etc), his integrity and consistency, among many others.

You would recognise Nelson Mandela instantly anywhere and, just from what we have noted above, you would have a clear idea of the values he stands for by the way he communicates, and the causes he supports. Madiba never stands up and says 'I am forgiving'. You just know that he is by virtue of his words, actions and deeds. Madiba models who he is. Parents need to do just the same for their children.

Why create Brand Family?

We see building a family brand as the vehicle for the three aspects of our parenting framework that we have championed throughout this book – conversations, choices and connections (the three Cs), which make up the triangle of conscious commitment. Building a family brand needs to be done consciously and consistently, like any good commercial brand. Consider these various important reasons why you should actively create Brand Family:

- To deliver your message, beliefs and values to your customers (your children) through a combination of communication and experiences
- Because we are all in sales, whether we like it or not; we are continually selling ideas, values and beliefs to

our children, even if this is not conscious but just via osmosis

- To differentiate yourselves from others
- To help your children to create their identity, which is critical between the ages of eight and 18
- To invest in, and build, strong relationships
- To empower children with values and beliefs to make them more discerning
- To beat the marketers at their own game
- To compete with your children's peers as they enter the teenage years.

Brand building is a process

Creating a brand is a continuous process that needs to take place deliberately and consistently over time – by being 'who you are'. Don't get us wrong. We are not advocating that mum and dad head for the family boardroom and put together a clinical business case. It's much more about becoming increasingly aware of the beliefs, values and attitudes you are conveying to your children by being yourselves and deciding whether or not they will be the best preparation for your children in the 21st century. Brands are built over time and are inextricably linked to your own personal development. Rather, we are advocating that it is imperative to understand the big picture for which you are preparing your children and to use it to help you shape your values, beliefs and attitudes. Today we need to take responsibility for how we design our lives.

Children provide us with acid tests for our beliefs and values. 'This is what I believe, but if it happened to my child, then this is how I would feel.' It is easy to adhere to immoveable principles before you have children. You may not agree with abortion until you accidentally fall pregnant with your fourth child. You may be against homosexuality until you have a gay son. Children provide us with reasons to really think about our values and to revisit them in a different context. Children are the reason we need to break away from the remnants of a system that no longer supports families in order to create a new system that, ultimately, is set to be the basis of a new society in the process of being created by pioneering parents.

Since every family is different, each family brand will be unique. However, we would like to suggest three basic pillars on which family brands should be built: values, structure and togetherness (see page 305). These pillars are not prescriptive, but simply provide you with a creative and flexible framework within which you can make your family brand distinctive. They offer all family members a platform to develop Brand You.

We believe this exercise to be imperative, not optional. And we can do it. We have some distinct advantages over marketers:

- We do not have to pre-book media space.
- We can change our strategy and tactics by the day, or by the hour if need be, in order to retain our children's attention, hearts and minds.
- We know exactly how our children operate, so we can tailor our communication and ideas to meet their specific needs. We can personalise our message, which is what kids today seem to want.
- As the context or landscape changes, so we can change our tactics.
- We love our children unconditionally and certainly not because of what they are going to buy.

The question is, are we using our advantage in this noisy, cluttered world – or not?

Creating brand loyalty and a successful brand

Before discussing the framework for a family brand, we

would like to share some of our insights from considering and amending one of the models proposed by international branding guru and futurist Martin Lindstrom, who consults for some of the top global brands today. This model appears in Lindstrom and Seybold's book, *Brandchild*[122]. It is the BrandDynamics™ pyramid, which concerns brand loyalty. 'Brand relationships don't form in a vacuum. You need to create strong attitudinal foundations before people become truly loyal to your brand. We can visualise these foundations as a pyramid. The people who make it to the top of the pyramid hold a strong attitudinal allegiance to the brand – they are 'bonded' to it – and are highly likely to buy it and remain loyal to it over time,' explains Lindstrom.

Figure 5.1 *The BrandDynamics™ pyramid*

Bonding
Advantage
Performance
Relevance
Presence
High attitudinal loyalty
Low

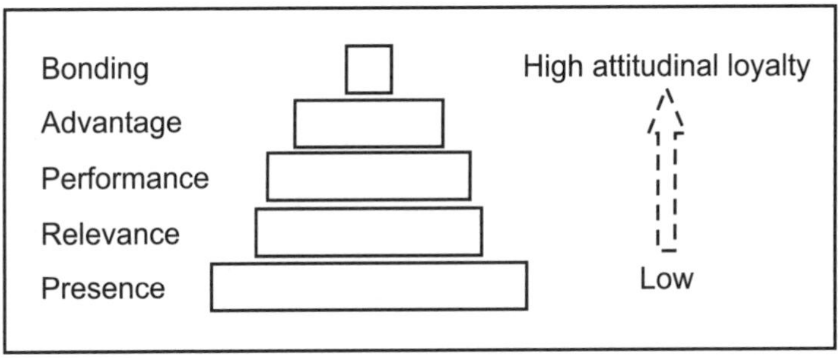

Source: Reproduced with kind permission from *Brandchild: Remarkable Insights into the Minds of Today's Global Kids and their Relationships with Brands by* Martin Lindstrom and Patricia Seybold, 2004

Since we need our children to remain loyal to their values over time, particularly when they are somewhat out of our sphere of influence, such as in the teenage years, we would do well to heed Lindstrom's advice and insight. In fact, we need to start thinking more like marketers when it comes to our own families. Here is our amended model:

Figure 5.2 *The Brand Family model*

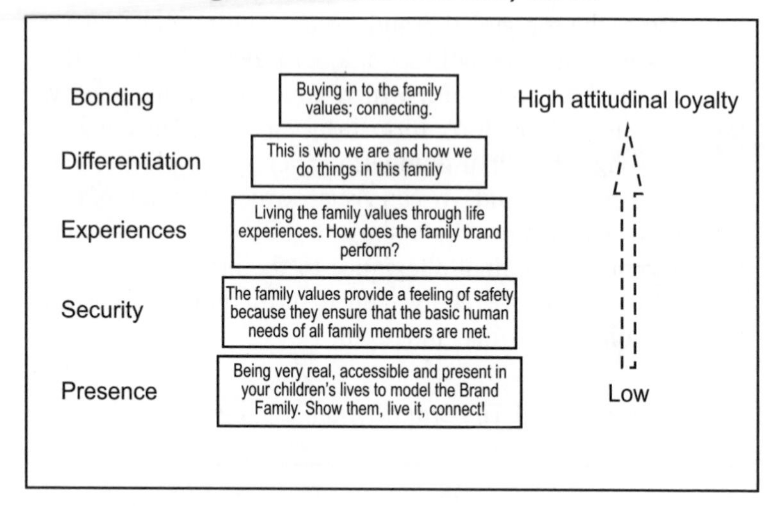

According to Lindstrom (2004), there are six distinct characteristics that make up the most successful brands and toys worldwide. 'What we find is a recipe incorporating the right measures of fear, fantasy, mastery, humour, love and stability.' In applying Lindstrom's work to the development of Brand Family, we would emphasise the following:

- The family needs to provide the answers to the children's fears or uncertainties. It needs to help them to master their fears and overcome them by developing coping skills.
- The family should be a refuge, a place of safety, where the children (and parents) can express their fears without being ridiculed.
- Stability and mastery (to control emotions and learn skills) are the antidotes to fear.
- It's the family who should switch on the lights to scare

away the monsters, bringing understanding. If a child understands what is happening, then he or she no longer has a need to feel scared.

- Humour is a great way to dispel fear, as long as it is not at the child's expense. Laughter can take the sting out of a difficult situation. We need to learn to laugh at ourselves.
- If you play with your children and organise family adventures, you are fulfilling the fantasy and love characteristics of successful kids' brands.

For us, just as rape is the opposite of sex, so child abuse is the opposite of family. Perhaps this is why child abuse incenses people so much, because it destroys what is supposed to be a safe place – family and the home.

The family brand – a personal, real-life experience

The six brand characteristics mentioned above in Lindstrom's sage words – fear, fantasy, mastery, humour, love and stability – all connect, just as the three pillars of Brand Family are interconnected: values, togetherness and structure. The bottom line in any brand-building exercise today, which is vitally important for parents to remember, is that children need experiences in order to absorb the message. In fact, the experience ultimately becomes the message. This is characteristic of Millennials, but it also fits in developmentally with children in the concrete learning phase – they need real-life, tangible, personal experiences for learning to have any meaning for them. Global brands frequently deliver on this promise through viral marketing and grassroots campaigns. So must we.

The next section will help you to provide these experiences for your children, who are the 'show me, don't tell me what you are about' generation. As mentioned earlier, their mantra today is: 'Give me an experience and I'll promise you a relationship'. If you can convey your family brand to your children through a variety of memorable experiences, then you are on the road to having them become co-owners of your family brand by the time they reach primary school. If you can connect strongly with your children, understand their values and needs, and blend them with yours, then the chances are good that they will become co-creators of your family brand with you as they get older. (Remember that personal responsibility is the number-one rule in the Age of Possibility.)

A FRAMEWORK FOR BUILDING BRAND FAMILY

We have emphasised that the three pillars of a strong family brand are values, togetherness and structure. In this section we unpack them, and how they dovetail so well with the three Cs – conversations, choices and connections. Interestingly, they form another triangle for stability in your family, now and into the future. Bear in mind, too, that Section 4 contained numerous ideas for developing the X-factors for success. You will see how these ideas also slot into the Brand Family framework.

Values

All of childhood is preparation for adolescence and beyond. Mothers and fathers are granted a single decade to lay a foundation of values and attitudes by which their children cope with pressures and problems of adulthood.
(James Dobson in *The New Hide & Seek*, 1999)

What is your moral compass? What is your moral centre and

why? These are important questions for 21st-century parents to answer. Values refer to our principles or standards, which are unique to each family. We all have our own blueprint (Brand You) and 'family print' (Brand Family), and both of these are influenced by our values.

Today diversity surrounds us; it is the new status quo. As such, we have to respond to it and make some choices. If your children see you accepting everything and questioning nothing, they will not learn the skill of discernment which is vital to their survival in the future. To learn to be discerning, children need an internalised set of values against which to measure other value offerings in life. If we fail to assist our children to develop values, they may just adopt the values of the most attractive brands on offer. Now that's a scary thought!

It is a fact that many parents today are no longer leaving their children an inheritance because they are living longer and spending their wealth on an exciting retirement and healthcare. However, all children are left a legacy of values. As adults, and particularly as parents, we need to consider the values we have retained from our own upbringing and decide whether these are still applicable to the family we are creating today in the context of the 21st century. We get to choose. Sometimes we add or take away from our values menu, based on personal experiences or what we have seen or heard. Shaping our values and attitudes is a continuous process of learning, unlearning and relearning.

> One of Nikki's friends remembers seeing a movie some time before she got married. The name of the movie has since escaped her, but the phrase 'marinade your children in love' left such an indelible print on her heart and mind that it shaped her attitude towards her children (and other children too, it must be added). It has become the cornerstone of her family's values.

1. **Role modelling**
   - Children do as you *do*, not as you say.
   - They need to see you in action.
   - If children respect you and feel safe, they are more likely to buy in to your values. For Millennials, respect is not a given – we have to earn their respect.

2. **Teachable moments**
   This refers to those moments that just 'happen', which provide a good opportunity for explanation or teaching because your child asks a question, because you reflect what is going on verbally, or by demonstration through your actions or response to a situation. For example:
   - A motorist has broken down. You may stop to help if you feel this would not be a threat to your physical well-being, or you may call the emergency services for assistance. You are demonstrating kindness, helpfulness and compassion.
   - A friend has just had a baby or is ill and you deliver a meal to her home to provide some relief from everyday responsibilities. This shows thoughtfulness, kindness and compassion.
   - You help out in the school library with the covering of books. This shows your support for your child's school and demonstrates helpfulness.
   - You buy the *Homeless Talk* newspaper from the same vendor at the same intersection each week. This demonstrates compassion.
   - You contribute to various charities on a monthly basis as well as give toys to orphanages at the end of each year. This demonstrates generosity, kindness and compassion.
   - You submit your tax return each year. This demon-

strates integrity, honesty and responsibility.
- Your children clean the car with you and wash their bicycles. They learn to value and respect property.

3. **Conversation**
   - Children overhear adult conversations all the time about people and events. You convey your values about things through what they hear. You are often unaware of what they have heard.
   - By answering your children's questions, or helping them to find the answers for themselves, you convey values and attitudes.
   - Become a good listener. We were born with two ears and one tongue, thus we should listen twice as much as we speak. It shows our children that we value their input and what they say.
   - Today children are exposed to many inappropriate things from an early age. Be prepared to have discussions about them. This is an easy way to convey your values, or to develop a family approach to a variety of topics or situations.

4. **Hang around time**
   Hanging around in the vicinity of our children, but not necessarily interacting with them, is time when interaction occurs naturally among family members, usually around the house doing normal family things such as gardening, cooking, tidying up, watching TV, playing or doing homework. Children can often gain your attention in positive ways through the informal banter, by helping each other with tasks, or just by being there. This is time when values are passed on through osmosis.[123]

Bear in mind that you are the role model. Your children will do as you do and not as you say. Choose caregivers well and co-parent consistently with your spouse, ex-spouse, step-parents and caregivers. Inconsistency causes value confusion. Your window of opportunity to form strong relationships and really influence your children's values is shrinking because they are growing up more quickly and entering adolescence earlier. Never give up. Values will make you children safer and more resilient in an ocean of constant change.

Clearly there is going to be no free ride in the future. But there is also no free ride now. You are going to have to make choices to enable your children to develop an efficient moral compass that will make them discerning individuals, capable of standing up for their own values and beliefs in time. And that time approaches sooner than you think. Once your child is pre-pubescent, around nine or 10 years of age, he or she will already be under serious pressure to conform to the peer group – to be cool or be left out. Will your child have a strong set of values to govern or direct those choices? And will he or she have an established, trust-based relationship with you so that the communication lines remain open?

Some moral issues that may face our children one day:

- **Cloning** – When we learn how to clone human beings, will they have a soul? This may sound like a spiritual question, but it isn't. If clones do not have a soul, then they are simply biological robots. They could be sent to war as cannon fodder, or as biotechnical machines. How would the military use them? Would the use of chemicals in war be an issue then? Could clones sue the government if they contracted strange illnesses or developed cancer? Would this be relevant? Some people believe there is no such thing as a soulless person, which is why spiritual and emotional intelligence are so important. What will the implications be of such 'machines' running the world? The ultimate question would be: Are clones real human beings or not?

- **Environmentalism** – The overuse of the planet's resources is a chilling legacy that our children will inherit. We are the first generation of adults who know how we could end the world. From overfishing and deforestation, to pollution and dwindling water supplies – all overshadowed by the spectre of global warming, we know the world is in crisis. We are also the first generation of adults with the wealth, resources, technology and global networks to actually solve these problems. But we need a concerted effort. It is our children who will inherit our mistakes, our inaction, and also our resolve and vision to create a sustainable world to live in. We need to help our children to develop a mindset of sustainability, which includes changing how we live in our homes today.

- **Bioethics** – This is an area riddled with difficult decisions and choices, which could place enormous pressure on the value systems of your children in the future.
    - A good example of bioethics is the stem cell debate. Is it acceptable (or palatable) to fall pregnant in order to abort the foetus to provide stem cells to help your living children effectively fight the diseases they have? Should we interfere with nature? What are the implications of continually bypassing nature?
    - A future mother will have the opportunity to choose to 'house' her baby outside her body in an artificial uterus from halfway through her pregnancy. This

technology exists. What implications does this technology hold for the emotional and developmental aspects of the child, or for mother-child bonding?

- Our children will be able to make choices about the type of child they want. They will be able to alter the gene structure of the embryo by taking out unwanted disease genes such as Alzheimer's. But if they remove that gene, then they must choose what to put in its place. So your grandchild may not get Alzheimer's but he or she may be short, for example. In addition, say you as a potential parent spend $100 000 to remove an unwanted gene (for breast cancer, Alzheimer's, etc) from your in utero daughter because of the family health history, when the time came, would you allow your daughter to marry a person who carries the very gene you had removed?

Togetherness

Do you remember the mantra 'Give me an experience and I will promise you a relationship'? The pillar of togetherness is about creating opportunities for connection and being in each other's company, skin to skin or face to face, sharing the same time, space and place. Because we are so busy, we need to make a conscious choice to be together, whether by having a family adventure away, building a tree house together, playing rough and tumble on the bed, or as simple (and rare today!) as sharing a meal together around a table.

Focused time is when parents and children spend time purposefully together. It can also include everyday, mundane activities such as feeding young children or driving a child to or from an after-school leisure activity. At these times of daily interaction, parents can tune in to their children's needs by empathic listening and by reading the cues and clues that they give about how they are feeling. These are relationship-strengthening times which offer parents a good chance to influence, guide and enjoy their time together.

And, after you have created the togetherness experiences, you can create a family story about them, for example: 'Remember when dad jumped out from behind the bathroom door and mum nearly died of fright!' or 'Remember when the rhino started to charge us in the game reserve and dad couldn't get the car into reverse?' This is the stuff of which memories are made because togetherness stories are so rich in imagery and feelings. Memories create a tapestry that we can claim as our own work of art. And, within this tapestry, family members are the heroes in the very personal stories they have helped to create, giving them a reason to buy in to the family brand.

How to promote togetherness

Children today are surrounded by screens of one form or another, which offer them instant entertainment with a wide variety of choice and flexibility. On-screen media often contain the six characteristics of successful brands – fear, mastery, fantasy, love, stability and humour. However, on-screen media do not meet the togetherness objective that we have in mind for the development of Brand Family. While choosing to play a computer game with your child or to communicate with him or her via SMS or email can be relevant tools to use in the connection equation, in this section we are really referring to togetherness activities that foster face-to-face human contact and connection in a real rather than a virtual way.

In order to compete with the attraction of on-screen media, you will need to take into account the following guidelines to enable you to share time and space with your children:

- Do not place a TV set in a child's bedroom.
- Position the computer linked to the Internet in a public space.
- Be selective about programme content (TV and computer), and choose programmes together.
- Limit on-screen time.
- Play games together.
- Eat together as a family.
- Stay and play instead of drop and run in the early years.
- Create family adventures and holidays together.
- Find reasons to celebrate, honour and acknowledge each other.
- Talk and stay connected.
- Model good listening skills. Don't talk through walls.
- Make eye contact.
- Be interested in your child's world.
- Know your child's love languages.
- Hug and say I love you – often.
- Read bedtime stories (and not the one-minute variety!).
- Spend time together – children want you.

In Section 4 we provided you with many practical ideas for developing the X-factors for success in your children. Many of these can also be used to create 'togetherness' connection experiences. Get creative! By wanting to spend time together, you are conveying many important non-verbal messages to your children that really boost their self-esteem. For example:

- I want to be with *you* right now
- I like being with you
- I'm not going to let anything interrupt our time together or get in the way of our relationship right now
- I don't want to be doing anything else right now
- I believe in you
- I love you.

Structure

You have probably realised that we are rather keen on frameworks and structure. Some of the most successful families we know have developed some form of structure and various family routines that provide a road map for progressing forward. Some of these families are unaware that they have achieved this, but if you consider how their family operates, there is a clear framework that provides security. And, within that framework, there is also freedom, creativity and flexibility.

Natural rhythms and routines

Natural rhythms need to be honoured and respected right from the start, even though we have the ability to override them and to ignore them. From babyhood, children need to learn that there is a time to sleep, a time to wake up, a time to eat, and a time to play or work. They are trained into these routines by their parents. It is a myth that there is no flexibility within routine. In fact, children who have routine are generally easier to take out to places of interest, restaurants, on holidays, etc, as long as they follow their basic routine – more or less. Babies and young children with good routines are easier to 'read' and thus have their needs met appropriately. This is the first step in providing boundaries and in learning frustration tolerance as well as self-management skills.

Providing your children with boundaries through routine is the easiest way of showing them who is in charge, thereby displaying your leadership skills in a very real way. A key component in developing character and personality is discipline. For the first seven years at least, this has to be imposed externally, knowing that young children must develop the ability to let their reasoning influence their behaviour. Children are not born with a built-in morality. They need a sense of right and wrong to be instilled within them.

Thus, the purpose of imposing restrictions on our children – on saying 'no' to them when required – is not to constrain them unnecessarily. Boundaries do not stifle creativity. In fact, limitations are often necessary in order to foster creativity.

Here are some ways to teach our children about natural rhythms and routine:

- Go camping. Wake up with the sunrise and go to sleep just after sunset.
- Listen to the birds, insects and wildlife at different times of the day.
- Gaze at the stars.
- Watch the clouds altering shape and position during the day.
- Work out on which side of the house the sun rises and sets each day.
- Keep pets. Children will learn that pets need regular feeding at specific times of the day, just as humans do. They also need care and attention.
- Allow children to help with household activities from around three years of age. Certain activities usually take place at the same time every day, which teaches them about structure and routine, for example making the beds, laying the table, cooking dinner, putting dirty clothes in the clothes basket, and so on.
- Stick to a routine of cleaning teeth, going to the toilet and reading a story before bedtime.
- Have seasonal celebrations. For instance, go out for a spring picnic at a local park, or hold a last dinner under the stars as summer changes to autumn and the leaves start falling from the trees.

Rituals and celebrations

Certain things make families unique, from the size of the family, to the family values, religion, favourite holiday places, etc. A family is a place in which people can be acknowledged and honoured. It is where members can celebrate their successes and achievements in life and share their failures. Different families do these things differently. Some relate to particular occasions such as Christmas, Eid, Pesach, etc, but all form part of a family's identity – 'the way things are done around here'.

Make a conscious choice to actively use rituals and celebrations to create family memories, to highlight the developmental milestones and to celebrate the rites of passage of your children. Rites of passage, other than religious ones such as bar mitzvahs and christenings, for example, have mostly fallen away in Western society. Research tells us that children are losing hope in the future from a very young age. Some school principals say this is happening from as early as the senior primary phase. 'Why bother? What for? Who cares?' are regular refrains from children in early adolescence. Children are giving up because there is nothing to look forward to any more. Do they really want to lead the stressful lives their parents lead?

We believe that finding ways to celebrate and honour children as they progress from one life stage to another can be of enormous help in validating their worth and uniqueness, and in giving them things to look forward to.

> Both the Codrington and Bush families have created family rituals and consciously celebrate particular occasions. The Codringtons have chosen their children's third birthday as one of these important times. This is the occasion when they give up the dummy. While this can be a traumatic

experience for some children, they have made it a really exciting time because it's a celebration of leaving babyhood behind and becoming a small girl (they have three daughters). A few months before the third birthday, Graeme and Jane start building up to the momentous occasion by dropping hints in general conversation such as 'Little girls don't need dummies, only babies do'. On the morning of the third birthday, the birthday girl takes her dummy and drops it into the dustbin. This went like clockwork for Graeme's first daughter, Amy. At the time of Hannah's third birthday, however, Graeme was going to be away. The Codringtons didn't want a glitch so were going to delay the ritual until Graeme's return. For a week or two before Hannah's birthday, they ignored the issue. But, on the morning of her birthday, Hannah decided to do it by herself, asking her mum if she could throw her dummy away. The use of ritual has helped the Codrington girls to remember the handing over of their dummies as a positive experience.

The Bush family had a ceremonious celebration to acknowledge their children's move into boyhood and conscious living, around their sixth or seventh birthday (depending on the child's maturity). Part of the celebration is to reinforce that the child is surrounded by other loving and supportive adults in addition to their parents, and that they are loved and treasured for their special qualities and character traits (who they are). Being boys, their sons got to choose significant men in their lives with whom to share a special activity.

Ryan's celebration took place in Knysna (his favourite place) when he was six and a half. He chose to go on the Outeniqua *Tjoe Tjoe* and to visit the train museum with his grandpa. Then he went on a boat trip through The Knysna Heads on the John Benn ferry with his dad (an experience deliberately delayed for almost two years to fit in with his celebration). His godfather (an ex-Iron Man) did a mini-triathlon with him (a mini run, cycle and paddle), then Ryan got to build and light his first official braai, and cooked a chicken for dinner. After the meal, all family members who were present took part in a 'wishing well' ceremony by telling Ryan why he was important to them, face to face, and giving him a wish for his boyhood.

Matthew (7) recently had his celebration in the bush. He chose to play his first nine holes of golf with his grandpa, did a mammoth cycle through the game reserve with his dad (the whole family were waiting at the top of the hill to celebrate this feat), and learnt how to build and light a proper campfire with his uncle. Thereafter, the family all sat around the campfire under the stars and conducted their 'wishing well' ceremony for Matthew. The next day, every member of the family – from the youngest (18 months) to the oldest (90) – painted his or her wish for Matthew on to fabric to make prayer flags which blew in the wind for a month, and will be stitched together to form a quilt.

Both celebrations were extremely memorable moments of connection for everyone present and the boys literally 'grew up' overnight emotionally. They received a strong sense of support from loved ones through the celebration, assuring them of a network that exists to catch and carry them on their journey forward.

These examples provide valuable storytelling material that will form part of a child's memories for a lifetime. If no close family members can be present, then invite other significant adults with whom your child has a close affinity. Special rituals and celebrations fulfil many of a child's basic human and developmental needs as well as the six characteristics of a successful brand. They create interest and hope for a child –

and the entire family – because they cast vision forward for the child's life, and express the family's confidence in the child's ability to engage with life and to handle its challenges.

Additional ideas for routines, rituals and celebrations

Here are some more very doable ideas for creating routines, rituals and celebrations:

- Hold seasonal celebrations.
- Eat at the same restaurants en route to the same holiday destination as part of the build-up to getting there.
- Create rituals for special annual occasions – religious or otherwise – that you celebrate. For example, at Christmas time many people decorate their homes. Some families fill exciting Christmas stockings for their children. Some eat their main Christmas meal on Christmas Eve while others have it on Christmas Day. Some families open their Christmas gifts in stages – before going to church, after breakfast, around the tree, etc.

> One family Graeme knows has a tradition at Christmas that every member of the family buys every other member a printers' tray ornament. The ornament sums up their view of that person's year. So the collection of ornaments that each family member receives would act as a succinct summary of what went on in your life that year in a small but meaningful and memorable way. (This would only be applicable from around the age of five.)

- Use candles at dinner time – every day, or once a week.
- Share the Sweets and Sours of the day (see page 253 for the Sweets and Sours game).
- Have lunch at a preferred family restaurant on break-up day each term.

- The birthday person gets to choose a favourite meal for the evening.
- Acquire a hand-painted family celebration plate and use it to celebrate special events or achievements in a family member's life on any particular evening.
- Hold a family meeting on a Sunday evening. Give each family member a chance to ask everyone else to do something for him or her the following week. This is a proactive and encouraging way to deal with discipline issues and to create good habit formation on a weekly basis.
- Keep a drawer or special file for each of your children. It should contain treasured memories. Go through it on a regular basis to make sure it's not just a pile of junk, but consists of meaningful symbols such as programmes from school concerts, certificates, small trinkets, photographs, birthday cards, etc. At the end of every year, sit together and go through the contents of the drawer or file, reminisce with the family, and then decide what to keep or discard for the year gone by.

> Every Sunday after church, a family that Graeme knows would buy some fresh bread and delicious *slap* chips from their local takeaway. Then they would head for the park nearby to eat their chip butties for lunch!

It's really important to have rituals on a weekly, monthly, quarterly and annual basis. Celebrations and rites of passage should occur when appropriate. Don't wait for official reasons to celebrate – be creative and make up some just for fun. Kids love celebrations!

Anyone can build a family brand. You don't need any special qualifications. Even if you feel that your childhood was less than satisfactory or that you don't have a template for doing this, give it a try. The results will be so worthwhile! The things you value in life will be evident in the routines, rituals, celebrations and moments of togetherness that you create. It can be so easy to convey your values to your children and, at the same time, you are letting them know just how much you value them too. Will your family and what it stands for be your children's brand of choice as they grow older?

Remember the two very important frameworks for building your family's brand:

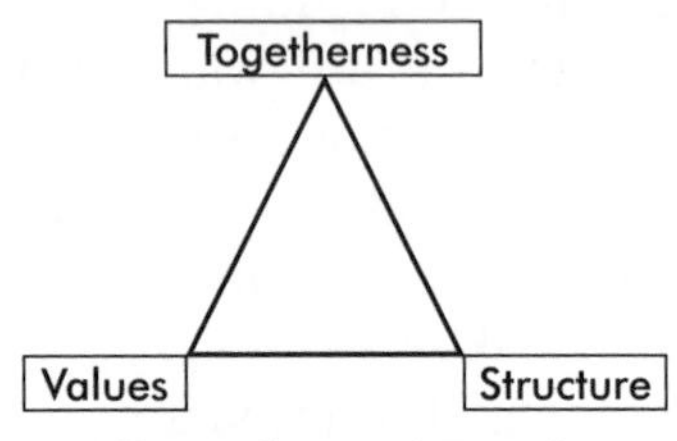

Pillars of Brand Family

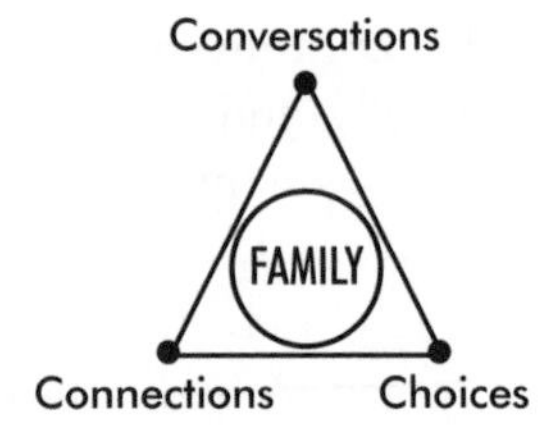

The Triangle of Conscious Commitment

Endnotes

[120] *The Sovereign Individual: Mastering the Transition to the Information Age* by James Dale Davidson and William Rees-Mogg, 1999.
[121] Campaign for a Commercial-free Childhood, www.commercialfreechildhood.org.
[122] *Brandchild: Remarkable Insights into the Minds of Today's Global Kids and their Relationships with Brands* by Martin Lindstrom and Patricia Seybold, 2004.
[123] *Working Parents* by Michael Grose, 1996.

Section 6

A call to action

Ultimately, our children belong to the world. Their destiny is to leave us, to venture out into the world as adults and to create their own lives.

(John Kehoe and Nancy Fischer in *Mind Power for Children*, 2002)

It is wise parents today who build bridges to their children and understand that learning takes place both ways. No longer is parenting about top-down command and control; it's about being the guide alongside your children and co-creating life with them. Children need to view their parents or primary caregivers both as a source of magic and delight, and as a place of safety and security where they know they will be protected and nurtured.

Our children will enter the workforce from 2020 and be in positions of leadership and power from around 2040, when the world will look and operate significantly differently from the world we live in today. Right now they are living in a world of our creation and we are responsible for helping them to navigate it. Our future, however, will quite literally be in their hands. This is why children need parental input and family support.

The number one rule for parents today is to take personal responsibility for all the moves you make in the Age of Possibility. Don't fear it – run to it! In a connected world, the only solution is to build bridges to, and to connect with, your children. And you must lead the connection process, ensuring that you and your children feature as the heroes in your family stories.

When Mother Teresa received her Nobel Peace Prize in 1979, she was asked, 'What can we do to promote world peace?' She replied, 'Go home and love your family.' She couldn't have been more right!

As parents today we have to be wary of operating on our default setting, following the habits and norms we have lived by all our lives. We need to connect to our children consciously and not accidentally. We need to live by design and indeed, by priority, now that we understand the importance of preparing our children for a world that does not yet exist.

This book is a call to parents to act wisely and courageously in the first 10 years of their children's lives (and beyond) to ensure that foundations are laid and connections made before they enter the teenage years and adulthood. Family, and relationships that work, are going to be a cornerstone of what is rapidly being termed the connection economy – driven by technology but dependent on relationships. We are living in a quantum world in which we are all connected or interconnected – part of a greater whole. Remember the TV slogan: 'Because every minute of every day you are a part of everybody'.1[24] So, whether you want to change the world, or just some aspect of your children, the easiest place to start is with yourself. As Mahatma Gandhi said, 'Be the change you want to see in others.'

This is our most important responsibility and challenge: to be, moment by moment, the very best we can be for ourselves because children are watching, becoming what they see. We cannot fail.

(Michael Mendizza in *Magical Parent, Magical Child*, 2003)

We know that this book contains a great deal of information and ideas. Embrace the information overload – it's for the sake of our children and our global future! To recap, here is a reminder of the steps you need to take as parents in the 21st century, echoing the various sections that comprise this book.

THE 10 STEPS TO FUTURE-PROOFING YOUR CHILD

1. Know yourself: – develop your Talent Profile (Section 4).
2. Know your children: – develop your children's Talent Profile (Section 4).
3. Understand your environment: – consider how the world has changed (Section 1) and contemplate the world of the future (Section 3).
4. Know your children's needs: – understand your children's developmental needs now (Section 2).
5. Build your brand: – develop your Talent Profiles (Section 4) and build a family brand (Section 5).
6. Manage your mediums: – through conversations, connections and choices, and by building your family brand (Section 5).
7. Lift your relationship game: – develop the X-factors for success yourself, role-modelling them for your children (Section 4), and build your family brand (Section 5).
8. Future-proof your children: – understand your children's developmental needs (Section 2), develop their X-factors (Section 4), and build a family brand (Section 5).
9. Help your children to become talented: – help your children to develop the X-factors for success and to create a Talent Profile (Section 4).
10. Do not panic and make sure the process is a lot of fun!

Take comfort from the particularly insightful and thought-provoking words of parenting expert Dan Allender:

> **... to be *great* parents, we must allow our children to shape our lives. We must not only guide and shape our children, but we must also go to them as students of life ... Life doesn't unfold in a straight line, and our children aren't computer programs. Parenting is far from a scientific pursuit; it's messy and risky and a huge leap of faith.**
>
> (*How Children Raise Parents* by Dan Allender, 2003)

Parenting is one of the most challenging roles we will ever play in our lives and our biggest personal development adventure. We will only see the real fruits of our labours at the end of a lifetime of investing in conversation, choice and connection. We cannot make an appointment with our children to relate to them. Parenting is a process that takes place over time. The choices we make and the way we plan our time as parents are two important factors that will determine whether or not we invested the precious time spent with our children wisely.

We wish you courage, a sense of adventure and the gift of laughter and tears on your parenting journey. Bear in mind that you, your children and your family are unique, which means that you will always be a pioneer exploring new territory.

> **There's always one moment in childhood when the door opens and lets the future in. [Be the door.]**
>
> (*The Power and the Glory* by Graham Greene, 1940)

The world is as it is. Work with it. Learn from it. Master it. Enjoy the ride. Be the door to your children's future. You are more important than you think.

The world is being flattened. I didn't start it and you can't stop it, except at a great cost to human development and your own future. But we can manage it, for better or for worse. If it is to be for better, not for worse, then you and your generation must not live in fear of either the terrorists or of tomorrow, of either al-Qaeda or of Infosys. You can flourish in this flat world, but it does take the right imagination and the right motivation. While your lives have been powerfully shaped by 9/11, the world needs you to be forever the generation of 11/9 [the falling of the Berlin Wall] – the generation of strategic optimists, the generation with more dreams than memories, the generation that wakes up each morning and not only imagines that things can be better but also acts on that imagination every day.

(Thomas Friedman's message to his children in *The World is Flat*, 2005)

Endnotes

[124] From the children's TV content provider, *Nickelodeon,* see www.nickzols.com.

[125] The information in this section is adapted from Carol Norris's Masters thesis, 'Factors relating to the problem-solving strategies utilized by learning-disabled children', 1991. Some usefull sources on Jean Piaget are: *Child Psychology* by Hetherington and Parke, 1986; *Watching and Wondering* by JG Isaksen, 1986; and *Child Development* by JW Satrock and SR Yussen, 1987.

[126] 'Putting the Mickey back in kiddie research' by J Campbell, 1998.

Appendix 1

Piaget's theory of cognitive development[125]

There are many models of development to choose from, but we are going to look at the basics in the theory of cognitive development, formulated by one of the most famous and influential developmental theorists, Jean Piaget.

Apart from the fact that Piaget had enormous influence in helping the world to understand how children learn and develop, we like his view on learning. He believed that children play an active role in the construction of their knowledge of reality and they do not absorb information passively. Their concept of reality and thought concepts are influenced and modified by their experiences and interaction with the world around them. This means that as children acquire new information (which they do constantly), they are able to interpret it actively and adapt it to fit in with their already existing knowledge of the world (world view).

Piaget suggested that there are four stages of cognitive development through which all children must pass sequentially in order to reach a more mature stage of reasoning. It is important to note here that, although the *order* of the stages is fixed, the *age* at which each stage occurs can vary. In addition, one stage builds on the stage before, so there is a natural timetable.

The sensorimotor stage (0–2 years)

This stage is marked by an infant's ability to organise and coordinate sensations and perceptions with physical movements and actions (hence the term *sensorimotor*). It is the phase of action before thought. It starts out with babies being reflexive beings, merely reacting to their environment, and ends with toddlers who are reflective or acting more intentionally on their environment. This is a pre-language phase during which parents must decode a baby's physical and emotional needs in order to meet them and bond with the baby.

The pre-operational stage (2–7 years)

This stage encompasses the preschool and kindergarten age groups. Piaget regards the major characteristic of this stage to be the development of systems of representation such as language, which he calls the symbolic function. The child's early use of language symbols serves to broaden his or her problem-solving abilities and also allows learning from others' speech. Six fundamental concepts associated with the development of children in this stage should also be noted:

- Children are very *right-brain-focused*. This means that pure imagination, fantasy and magic rule their world and anything is possible.
- Their thinking is *animistic*. They imbue the physical world with human properties, eg, the sun shines because 'it wants to' and a bee stings because it is 'feeling nasty'.
- Children lack the ability to use critical judgement as they are in the *pre-conventional morality* phase. This means that they do not have the ability to discern the intent behind their own actions. They would view their breaking of an entire tray of teacups by accident as a worse crime than their breaking of one cup on purpose.

- Their thinking is *egocentric*. This does not mean that they are selfish – selfishness assumes the knowledge of another person's point of view and a disregard for it. The egocentric child does not know there is another point of view. The child believes the world is organised around him or her, and thus, by necessity, views everything from his or her own perspective.
- Children have no sense of *temporal orientation* – this means they only focus on the here and now, and struggle with temporal references such as flashbacks and flash-forwards in books or films.
- Their thinking is *centrated*, which means they *overcue*. In other words, they tend to focus on only one aspect of an object or a problem at a time. A young boy will focus on the flashing lights on a pair of trainers to the exclusion of any other physical attribute of the shoe (Norris, 1991).

Concrete operations stage (7–11 years)

Certain essential changes take place in children's cognitive processing at this stage. Briefly, these are the following:

- Children's thinking becomes *left-brain-focused* and heralds a shift from fantasy to reality. Father Christmas and the Easter Bunny no longer hold any sway.
- The child obtains *reversible thought*, which enables him to *decentre* and focus on more than a single characteristic of an object or problem simultaneously. For example, a child at this stage will understand that a person on his or her right-hand side could also be on someone else's left, or that a man can be both a father and a son.
- Thought patterns allow for *part-whole inclusion* and the understanding of *hierarchies* and *categorisation*. For example, the child can now understand that a cow is a mammal (subordinate category) but is also an animal

(superordinate category).

- The child develops rudimentary *executive functions*, such as the ability to organise material according to a fairly complex combination of objects. This ushers in the interest in collecting things, for example trading cards, and organising them into categories and hierarchies. It also allows for the absorption of, and fascination with, complex and often minute details and differences in the objects that make up the collection (Norris, 1991).

The concrete operational phase means just that – although children are able to practise reversible thought, they are not able to work on a hypothetical level. This means that they are still *perceptually bound* and can only relate to things they can feel, hear, smell, touch or see with their senses. In research terms, this means that they need *concrete reference points*, for example a page of brightly coloured pictures to represent various concepts.

The formal operations stage (starting at approximately 11–12 years)

The progression into the formal operations stage roughly corresponds with the onset of adolescence. This stage is associated with the further cognitive skills of *abstract thought* and *hypothetical reasoning*.

- *Abstract thought* means that the adolescent is no longer bound by actual and concrete experiences, but can conjure up hypothetical situations and reason with them on a purely verbal basis.
- *Contrary-to-fact reasoning* can be explained by using absurd hypothetical facts for the sake of an argument. In this case, for example, a formal operational child would be able to pretend that coal is white and snow is black.

For the concrete operational child, this premise would make no sense and would be discounted immediately.

- The understanding of *metaphor* allows the comprehension of the subtleties of humour in jokes involving ambiguity. Additionally, the child is now able to understand the abstract meaning of fables and parables.
- *Deductive reasoning* involves the ability to consider alternative hypotheses and work with them in a logical manner by proceeding from the general to the specific (Norris, 1991).
- *Adolescent egocentrism* is a newly coined term to describe a state of self-absorption in which adolescents are capable of viewing the world only from their point of view. It is linked to the notion of *personal fables*, which contends that what happens to adolescents is unique and cannot be understood by anyone else (Campbell, 1998).[126] Personal fables are responsible for the view that negative situations only happen to others, thereby rendering teenagers invincible and invulnerable to problems such as HIV/Aids, drunken driving accidents and drug abuse.

While our children are experiencing these developmental stages, it is important to remain observant in the quest to discover who they are, as well as their preferred way of processing, storing, retrieving and using information. These are the things that make your children unique. They will provide information that will be most useful to you as parents and to your children's teachers and coaches in the future, to help make the learning journey as easy, interesting and rewarding as possible for everyone concerned.

Endnotes

[125] The information in this section is adapted from Carol Norris's Masters thesis, 'Factors relating to the problem-solving strategies utilized by learning-disabled children', 1991. Some usefull sources on Jean Piaget are: *Child Psychology* by Hetherington and Parke, 1986; *Watching and Wondering* by JG Isaksen, 1986; and *Child Development* by JW Satrock and SR Yussen, 1987.
[126] 'Putting the Mickey back in kiddie research' by J Campbell, 1998.

BIBLIOGRAPHY

Acuff, D (1998). *What Kids Buy and Why: The Psychology of Marketing to Kids*. New York: Free Press.

Affleck, C (2005). 'I kid you not'. Paper delivered at the 26th Annual Convention of SAMRA (South African Market Research Association), May.

Allender, D (2003). *How Children Raise Parents*. Colorado: Waterbook Press, Random House.

Andrews, V 'Can you teach resilience?' *WebMD*. Accessed 20 July 2007 at www.webmd.com/balance/features/teach-resilience.

Apteker, R and Ord, J (1999). *Do You Love it in the Mornings?* Johannesburg: DiData.

Association of Graduate Recruiters Research (2003). Wales.

Bartlett, J (2004). *Parenting with Spirit*. London: Rider Books.

Brown, J, Isaacs, D, World Café Community and Wheatley, M J (2005). *The World Café: Shaping Our Futures Through Conversations that Matter*. San Francisco: Berrett Koehler Publishers.

Buckingham, M (2005). *The One Thing You Need to Know*. New York: Free Press.

Buckingham, M, 'StrengthsFinder Profile' at www.strengthsfinder.com.

Buckingham, M and O'Clifton, D (2005). *Now Discover Your Strengths: How to develop your talents and those of the people you manage*. US: Pocket Books.

Bush, N (2003). "What is your child's learning style?'. Smile Family Club Chronicle. September.

Business 2.0. (2004). 'The next delivery?' July.

Cahn, A (2007). 'Humour complements intelligence' in *Family Magazine Group*.

Cairncross, F (2003). *The Company of the Future*. Boston: Harvard Business School Press.

Campaign for a Commercial-free Childhood, www.commercialfreechildhood.org.

Campbell, J (1998). 'Putting the Mickey back in kiddie research'. Paper presented at the Consumer Kids Conference, Sun City.

Campbell, S (2006). 'Denture venturers'. *The Spectator*, 12 August.

Chapman, G (1997). *The Five Love Languages of Children*. Chicago: Northfield Publishing; and at www.fivelovelanguages.com.

Chester, E (2002). *Employing Generation Why*. Lakewood: Chess Press.

Child Development Institute (2007). 'Helping your child develop self-esteem' available at www.childdevelopmentinfo.com/parenting/self_esteem.shtml.

Chilton Pearce, J (1993). *Evolution's End*. San Francisco: Harper Collins.

Chowdhury, S (Ed) (1999). *Management 21C*. New York: *Financial Times*/Prentice Hall.

Chowdhury, S (Ed) (2002). *Organization 21C: Someday All Organizations will Lead this Way*. New York: *Financial Times*/Prentice Hall.

Codrington, G and Fourie, L with Grant-Marshall, S (2002). *Mind Over Money*. Johannesburg: Penguin Books.

Codrington, G and Grant-Marshall, S (2004). *Mind the Gap*. Johannesburg: Penguin Books.

Collins, J (2001). *Good to Great: Why Some Companies Make the Leap ... and Others Don't*. New York: Collins.

Colvin, G (2006). 'The Imagination Economy'. *Fortune*. 5 November.

Cook, J (2005). 'Emotional Intelligence course notes'. Gordon Institute of Business Science, Johannesburg.

Davidson, J and Rees-Mogg, W (1999). *The Sovereign Indiv-*

idual: Mastering the Transition to the Information Age. New York: Touchstone Books.

De Jager, M (2001). *Brain Gym® for All*. Cape Town: Human & Rousseau.

De Jager, M (2006). *Mind Moves®*. Johannesburg: The BG ConneXion.

De Jager, M (2008). 'Brain dominance profiling' at www.theconnexion.co.za.

De Posada, J and Singer, E (2005). *Don't Eat The Marshmallow ... Yet! The Secret to Sweet Success in Work and Life*. New York: Berkley.

Dobson, J (1999). *The New Hide and Seek*. Grand Rapids: Fleming H Revell.

Drucker, P (2000). Quoted in *Business 2.0*. 22 August.

Dryden, G and Vos, J (2005). *The New Learning Revolution*. UK: Network Educational Press.

Einon, D (1998). *Learning Early*. London: Marshall Publishing.

'Engines for Education' website. Accessed 29 July 2007 at www.engines4ed.org.

Farson, R and Keyes, R (2002). *Whoever Makes the Most Mistakes Wins*. New York: Free Press.

Fisher, K and McLeod, S. 'Shift happens' (online video). Accessed June 2007 at www.scottmcleod.org/didyouknow.wmv.

Florence, E (2006). 'Jobs for the future'. *Reader's Digest*, Canada. Accessed 2 July 2007 at www.readersdigest.ca/mag/2000/06/living_job.html.

Florida, R (2005). 'Minds on the move'. *Newsweek*, November.

Forbes magazine. 'Forbes list of jobs in 2020'. Online article, accessed May 2006 at www.forbes.com/2006/05/20/jobsfuturework_cx_hc_06work_0523jobs.html.

Freedman, D H (2006). 'Meet your new executives'. *Inc.* magazine, January.

Friedman, T L (2005). *The World is Flat.* US: Strauss & Giroux.

Friedman, T L (2006). (Updated and expanded 3 Ed) *The World is Flat: A Brief History of the Twenty-first Century.* US: Picador.

Friedman, T L (2006). Interview available at yaleglobal.yale.edu/display.article?id=9044.

Galinsky, E (2000). *Ask the Children Study: The Breakthrough Study That Reveals How to Succeed at Work and Parenting.* US: Quill.

Gardner, H (1998). *Extraordinary Minds: Portraits of 4 Exceptional Individuals and an Examination of Our Own Extraordinariness.* Jackson: Basic Books.

Gardner, H (1999). *Frames of Mind: The Theory of Multiple Intelligences.* Jackson: Basic Books.

Gladwell, M (2002). *The Tipping Point.* US: Little Brown & Company.

Goldhaber, M (1997) 'The attention economy and the Net' IN K Jarett (2003). 'Labour of Love: An Archaeology of Affect as Power in E-Commerce'. *Journal of Sociology* (39).

Goleman, D (1997). *Emotional Intelligence: Why it can Matter More than IQ.* New York: Bantam Dell.

Goleman, D (2006). *Social Intelligence: The New Science of Human Relationships.* New York: Bantam Dell

Gordon, A M and Browne, K W (2003). *Beginnings and Beyond: Foundations in Early Childhood Education* (sixth edition). Kentucky: Delmar Cengage Learning.

Greeff. A (2005). *Resilience.* Volume 1: *Personal Skills for Effective Learning.* UK: Crown House Publishing.

Greeff, A (2005). *Resilience.* Volume 2: *Social Skills for Effective Learning.* UK: Crown House Publishing.

Green, G and Updike, J (2003). *The Power and the Glory.* US: Penguin Classics.

Greenspan, S I (2003). *The Secure Child: Helping Our Children Feel Safe and Confident in a Changing World.* Cambridge:

Da Capo Press.
Grose, M (1996). *Working Parents*. New South Wales: Random House.
Grulke, W (2000). *10 Lessons from the Future: Tomorrow is a Matter of Choice, Make it Yours*. South Africa: @One Communications.
Haas Edersheim, E (2006). *The Definitive Drucker: The final word from the father of modern management.* US: McGraw-Hill Companies.
Handy, C (1996). *Beyond Certainty: The Changing World of Organisations*. London: Arrow Books.
Hannaford, C (1995). *Smart Moves*. US: Great Ocean Publishers.
Henig, L (2002). *Raising Emotionally Intelligent Children*. South Africa: Smile Education.
Hetherington, E M and Parke, R D (1986). *Child Psychology*. New York: McGraw-Hill.
Howe, N and Strauss, W (2000). *Millennials Rising*. New York: Vintage.
Huntington, S (1998). *The Clash of Civilizations: And the Remaking of World Order*. New York: Touchstone Pocket Books.
IBM website:
Isaksen, J G (1986). *Watching and Wondering*. Palo Alto, CA: Mayfield Publishers.
Jackson, D (2001). *Parenting with Panache*. Johannesburg: Wordsmiths Publishing.
Jensen, R (2001). *The Dream Society: How the Coming Shift from Information to Imagination will Transform your Business*. US: McGraw-Hill.
Kaiser Family Foundation (2003). 'Zero to Six: Electronic Media in the Lives of Infants, Toddlers and Preschoolers' available at www.kff.org/entmedia/3378.cfm.
Kehoe, J (1997). *Mind Power into the 21st Century: Techniques to Harness the Astounding Power of Thought*. Vancouver:

Zoetic Inc.
Kehoe, J and Fischer, N (2002). *Mind Power for Children. The Guide for Parents and Teachers.* Vancouver, Canada: Zoetic Inc.
Leaf, C (2005). *Switch On Your Brain.* Cape Town: Tafelberg; www.switchonyourbrain.co.za.
Lindstrom, M and Seybold, P B (2004). *Brand Child: Remarkable Insights into the Minds of Today's Global Kids and their Relationships with Brands.* UK & US: Kogan Page Ltd.
Linn, S (2005). *Consuming Kids: Protecting Our Children from the Onslaught of Marketing & Advertising.* US: Anchor Books.
Littauer, F (2000). *Personality Plus for Parents.* US: Baker Publishing.
Littauer, F (2005). *Personality Plus.* US: Fleming H. Revell.
Littky, D and Grabelle, S (2004). *The Big Picture: Education is Everyone's Business.* Baltimore: Association for Supervision & Curriculum Development.
Lotter, A & Associates. 'Genetic brain organisation profiling' at www.eduprofile.co.za.
Lyness, D (2006). 'Encouraging your child's sense of humor' available at kidshealth.org/parent/growth/learning/child_humor.html.
Maree, D and Ford, M (1995). *Bridging with a Smile.* Johannesburg: Smile Education.
Maxwell, J (2000). *Failing Forward: Turning Mistakes into Stepping Stones for Success.* Nashville: Thomas Nelson Publishers.
Mendizza, M (2003). *Magical Parent, Magical Child.* California: North Atlantic Books.
Menzies, G (2003). *1421: The Year China Discovered the World.* New York: Bantam.
Michaels, E, Handfield-Jones, H and Axelrod, B (2001). *The War for Talent.* Boston: Harvard Business School Press.

Miles Gordon, A and Williams Browne, K (2004). *Beginnings and Beyond: Foundations in Early Childhood Education.* (sixth edition) US: Thomson Delmar Learning.

Monkton, E (2007). *Happiness*. UK: Harper Collins.

Neethling, K. 'The Neethling Brain Instrument®' at www.solutionsfinding.com.

Negroponte, N (1996). *Being Digital*. New York: Vintage.

Nicholson, H (2007). *Networking: The Unwritten Rule of Business You Need to Know*. South Africa.

Nicholson, H and Driver, G (2007). 'He Says – She Says' workshops. South Africa.

Norris, C J (1991). 'Factors related to the problem-solving strategies utilized by learning-disabled children'. Dissertation submitted as fulfilment of the Masters in Psychology degree at the university of Port Elizabeth.

Palmer, H (1988). *The Enneagram: Understanding Yourself and the Others in Your Life*. New York: Harper Collins.

Peters, T (1999). *The Brand You 50 Or: Fifty Ways to Transform Yourself from an 'Employee' into a Brand that Shouts Distinction, Commitment, and Passion!*. New York: Knopf.

Peters, T (2003). *Re-Imagine! Business Excellence in a Disruptive Age.* New York: DK Adult.

Peters, T (2005). *Tom Peters Essentials: Talent*. New York: DK Publishing Inc.

Peters, T (2000). 'What we will do for work'. *Time*. 22 May.

Pieterse, M (2001). *School Readiness through Play*. Cape Town: Metz Press.

Pink, D (2002). *Free Agent Nation: The Future of Working for Yourself.* New York: Warner Business Books.

Pink, D (2006). *A Whole New Mind*. New York: Riverhead.

Prahalad, C K (2006). *The Fortune at the Bottom of the Pyramid: Eradicating Poverty through Profits*. Pennsylvania: Wharton.

Richardson, A (2005). *Toddlersense*. Cape Town: Metz Press.

Riso, D R and Hudson, R (1999). *The Wisdom of the Enneagram:*

The Complete Guide to Psychological and Spiritual Growth for the Nine Personality Types. New York: Bantam.
Robertson, A and Abbey, G (2003). *Managing Talented People*. Santa Monica: Momentum Wcze.
Rushkoff, D (1996). *Playing the Future*. New York: Riverhead.
Santrock, J W and Yussen, S R (1987). *Child Development*. Dubuque, Iowa: WMC Brown.
Schank, R (2001). *Coloring Outside the Lines*. New York: Harper Collins.
Schmidt, L (2001). *Seven Times Smarter: 50 Activities, Games, and Projects to Develop the Seven Intelligences of Your Child.* New York: Three Rivers Press.
Schor, J B (2005). *Born to Buy: The Commercialized Child and the New Consumer Culture*. New York: Schribner.
Scott, E (2006). 'The Optimistic Child: Raise your children to be optimists' available at stress.about.com/.
Scott Peck, M (1978). *The Road Less Travelled.* New York: Simon & Schuster Adult Publishing Group.
Semler, R (2001). *Maverick!* New York: Warner Books.
Semler, R (2004). *The Seven-day Weekend*. US: Portfolio.
Senge, P M, Jaworski, J, Scharmer, C O and Flowers, B S (2005). *Presence: An Exploration of Profound Change in People, Organizations, and Society.* UK: Nicholas Brealey Publishing.
Shaw, R (2003). *The Epidemic: The Rot of American Culture, Absentee Parents and Permissive Parenting, and the Resultant Plague of Joyless, Selfish Children.* New York: Harper Collins.
Sheahan, P (2006). *Generation Y: Thriving and Surviving with Generation Y at Work*. Sydney: Hardey Grant Books.
Simpkins, C (2005). *Change Your Thinking, Change Your Life*. Sandton: CSSC Publications.
Stern-LaRosa, C and Hofheimer, E with the Anti-Defamation League (2000). *Hate Hurts, How Children Learn and*

Unlearn Prejudice. New York: Scholastic Paperbacks.
Stroud, M (1982). *The Gift of a Child*. UK: Lion Hudson.
The Economist (1999). Millennial Special Edition. December.
The World Future Society, 'Forecast 2007'. Accessed 10 July 2007 at www.wfs.org/forecasts.htm.
The Sunday Times (2000). South Africa. 18 February.
Toffler, A (1972). *Future Shock*. London: Pan Books.
Tuggle, C (2007). '10 Hot Jobs for 2007'. *Fast Company*. January
US Department of Labor, Bureau of Labor Statistics. 'Tomorrow's jobs'. Accessed 1 July 2007 at www.bls.gov/oco/oco2003.htm.
Verhaagen, D (2005). *Parenting the Millennial Generation*. Westport, CT, US: Praeger Publishers.
Volf, M and Katerberg, W H (2004). *The Future of Hope: Christian Tradition Amid Modernity and Postmodernity*. Grand Rapids: Wm. B. Eerdmans.
Wacker, W and Taylor, J (1997). *The 500 Year Delta: What Happens After What Comes Next*. New York: Harper Collins.
Wacker, W and Taylor, J (2001). *Visionary's Handbook: Nine Paradoxes that will Shape the Future of your Business*. New York: Harper Collins.
Wong, A.'Lifeskillsweb'. Accessed 1 May 2007 at www.vtaide.com/lifeskills/index.htm.
World Future Society (2007). 'Forecast 2007', available at www.wfs.org/forecasts.htm.
Youth Dynamix BratTrax® (2005/6). *Youth Dynamix 05/06 Research Study*.
Youth Dynamix BratTrax® (2007/8). *Youth Dynamix 07/08 Research Study*.
www.nobelprize.org
www.research.ibm.com/deepblue/.